IRON HEART PUBLISHING

Abu Bilaal Yakub

THE THREE QUESTIONS

IRONHEART
PUBLISHING HOUSE

www.ironheartpublishing.com

ISBN-13: 978-1-9993870-6-8

Published by Iron-Heart Publishing.

www.ironheartpublishing.com

The purpose of this study is purely for an ambition of knowledge and enlightenment.

The contents of this book do not represent a universal view, because a universal view is not absolute and evident. No part of this book is an attempt at predicting or discerning future events or outcomes, nor is there an intent to impose views, doctrines, or ideologies.

We do acknowledge that there may be other intellectual views more accurate and authentic than ours, in which case, we encourage active participation and correspondence through channels enlisted at the end of the book.

Kindly approach this book and its contents with an open mind and an open heart. If a difference of opinion arises, we encourage the reader to do an impartial and objective study so as to present an alternate view by which both the reader and the author can benefit.

In the name of God Almighty, the Most Merciful, the Most
Gracious, whose Divine Majesty perplexes the Hearts and
Minds of many a great people.
In the Hearts of our Beloved Prophets, His Light guides them
to guide us.
In the Hearts of the Enlightened Scholars of Islām, esteemed
as they are, His Light guides the Prophets to guide them.
We are all but slaves and servants to His Greatness.

Like the thirsty in the desert, I yearn for every droplet of
Knowledge, from the Holy Prophet of Allāh Almighty, to
whom I dedicate this book and the Enlightened Scholars of
Islām to whom I dedicate this book.
Lastly…

To my father, Mohammed Shakir Yakub.

May Allāh Almighty shower you all with His Mercy and
Blessings, and a special place in Jannat-ul-Firdaus.
Ameen

When Soul becomes flesh, unto a realm of flesh
When sleep becomes death, unto a realm of essence
Instinctual is made all else, adorned to the pleasure of the blind eye
Henceforth, desire and lust are but the Impostor's pine

Reach not for that scaly hand beneath an apostate skin so cream
For his outer eye sees not what your inner heart can see
Upon his mule he leads the two tribes,
onward their ilk from yonder to abyss
And his rivers deceive of water and fire, his promises are all amiss

Of the Spirit of Life ye must seek only from thy Lord's affair
In solitude Just, Truth, and Pious,
insure thy Faith from vice, beware
And of those bedeviled by Land and Wealth
Currency and Material tribulation dealt
Then remember thee what thy Lord admonished
If you return with your crookedness
He will return with grave recompense

So see ye, hear ye, ponder ye,
lest from this world misguided ye depart
Ye who Believe, from not thy Mind but thy Heart
The Spirit, the Cave, the Journeyman's task
Of these Three do the violators ask
They conceal under their cloaks what the Impostor conceals
And only the Light of your Lord can reveal all what He Wills

INTRODUCTION

PART ONE

THE SPIRIT

PART TWO

THE COMPANIONS

PART THREE

THE GREAT TRAVELER

وَنَزَّلْنَا عَلَيْكَ ٱلْكِتَٰبَ تِبْيَٰنًا لِّكُلِّ شَىْءٍ وَهُدًى وَرَحْمَةً وَبُشْرَىٰ لِلْمُسْلِمِينَ

And We sent down to you this Book, so that it may explain all things, and as a guidance, and a mercy, and glad tidings unto those who have submitted to the Will of Allāh

~Sūrah An-Nahl 16:89~

A
GRIM
TALE

A story, or narrative, is a concise and comprehensive compilation of reports or events, whether fictional or real, presented and articulated in an immersive sequence of written or spoken words, still or moving images, or a combination of all. The word is derived from the Latin verb *'narrare'* meaning 'to tell', further derived from Latin adjective *'gnarus'* which means 'knowing'.

The essence of 'knowing', which contributes to our perception and comprehension of awareness, comes from two streams of 'learning'. From birth, 'knowing' comes from interacting with our physical surroundings brought about by external influential learning. 'Knowing' also comes from internal influences in the form of intuition and instinct, and all these influences are governed by individual intellect, insight, and circumstance.

Both these categories of 'knowing' are states of cerebral existence, physical or metaphysical, bodily or spiritual, and something always exists in the interim of either state of existence to facilitate an avenue of transcendence.

Therefore, a story is but one medium of delivering clusters of information for the sake of 'learning' or 'knowing', whether it is fictional or real. The human mind absorbs the information, computes it and comprehends it, thus converting information into valuable knowledge, and stores this knowledge to memory.

Since knowledge existed before man, and will exist after man, nothing about knowledge is innovated and invented by man. Nothing about knowledge is 'groundbreaking', or 'cutting-edge'. What appears to us in the form of something new and innovative is reformed, enhanced, or augmented information and its medium of delivery. How that information is absorbed and converted into knowledge, and how that knowledge is delivered or passed on. How the story is told, and what the listener gains from it. Whether it is a sense of exhilaration, excitement, and entertainment. Or a sense of moral uplifting, enlightenment, and intellect. Every individual has the basic instinct, the choice, the decisive advantage to interpret any information received and convert it into knowledge in a manner that would either benefit, or destroy.

That choice is yours.

The best of stories, and many will agree, are controversial stories. Conspiracies. They intrigue. They incite. Because such tales are largely considered fictitious with a distinct tinge of truth, and they trigger a deep and inner intuition, caressing the tender and delicate strands of our curiosity. As long as they remain so, they are entertaining and enlivening, maintaining a delicate balance between our cocoon of comfort, and actuality, not because we cannot handle the truth, but because we choose and prefer not to.

Before man could write, before man understood the concept of the pen and ink, stories were, and still are, the most profound mode of communicating ideas. To this day, they remain at the core of delivering knowledge, some shrouded in mystery and fantasy, others informative and educative.

Beyond any allegorical shroud, beyond any cautionary tale, embedded into words and phrases are the footprints of our existence. What happened before, is told today. What happens today, will be told tomorrow. In this flowing river of documenting and narrating, we hand over the knowledge of our ancestors to future generations. We study our past to decode our future.

Why tell you this? Because what we are about to unravel has a reality so harsh, so ruthless, it will tear us from this illusory world we have created for ourselves, and cast us deep into the strident actualities behind enemy lines. They are void of fiction. They are real stories. True narratives. They are a means to deliver knowledge existing before humankind, existing after humankind. So that we can better understand that world yesterday, better contemplate this world today, and better ponder on a world tomorrow.

These tales are not meant to bedeck and embellish a wonderful Utopian future filled with happiness and joy. There is no 'happily-ever-after' to these tales. They are dark, grim, and gruesome for those who choose to remain within their illusory cocoons, but there is enlightenment at the end for those who choose to step out and explore the world for what it truly is. For when the Final Hour manifests itself, each one of us will have to testify to what we did with our Time on Earth, and the Knowledge that was given to us.

Above all, we must concede that every step we take henceforth is for the purposes of study and enlightenment, and we must also acknowledge our limitations as creatures with limitations. What we have been given is but a speck in contrast to what our Creator holds in His hands.

Like the Breath of Life, Knowledge, Wisdom, Intellect and Intuition are also gifts unto mankind.

God Almighty is our Creator and Sustainer. None but He is All-Knowing and All-Wise in all matters across the Heavens and the Earth.

ARABIA

We begin in 6th century Arabia, across the scorching desert sands, in a town called Makkah. An epicenter of trade and economics, a hub for caravans trekking trade routes like the Frankincense Trail, bringing wealth to its native populous, the Arabs, through trade, pilgrimage, and homage.

6th century Makkah, however, was not a time of enduring materialistic benevolence for the Arabs. It was a time of turmoil. The upheaval of a way of life dedicated to paganism and idolatry, not unlike the Romans and even the Egyptians and Babylonians before them. The turbaned and robed populous, shrouded through centuries of misguidance by the devil's whispers, had transcended generations of ignorance in servitude of fabricated deities.

In the heart of the Arabian peninsula, a well-preserved monument stands firm and resolute, first erected by the Prophet Ibrahim (peace and blessings be upon him) nearly four millennia ago, for the worship of the One True God, and by 6th century AD, it was now wrongly subjected to housing lifeless idols, paganistic rituals, and to a woeful extent, witchcraft and sorcery.

Its custody descended his bloodlines through generations, but his teachings and divine message lost to them. They are the ruling tribe of Qur'aysh, and among these pagan Arabs, Allāh Almighty sends his most beloved Messenger, Muhammad, son of Abdullah, son of Abdul-Muttalib, descended from the lineage of Ismā'īl, son of Ibrahim of the Semitic people— descended from Sham, son of Nūh (peace and blessings be upon them all).

Remember this lineage. Its knowledge is vital and crucial to our understanding of the modern world, as will be two other lineages mentioned further along.

Growing up a child to his early adulthood, Muhammad (peace and blessings be upon him) displayed no sign of mistrust, not an ounce of treachery unlike the norm of most of his people. He even earned himself the title of *Al-Amīn,* the Trustworthy. He did not partake in pagan worship, but he did not forsake his people either. So long as he did not interfere, they left him be, trusting him with their wealth and their endeavors. He was not known to lie. He was not known to backbite, nor was he ever known to indulge in the meaningless affairs of the Arabs.

Lo and behold, when he stood before them and, after forty years of earning their trust, preached the Oneness of God, condemning their polytheistic idolatry and paganism, urging them to take the pledge of submission to Allāh, the One and Only.

There is no god but Allāh, and Muhammad is his messenger.

Lo and behold, everything he had accomplished in forty years, including all the titles and praises earned for being trustworthy and truthful, everything belied by the people as soon as he stood to deliver a Divine Message. A message whose core purpose was targeted toward their predominantly established and architected way of life, based on their personal comforts and materialistic ideologies. The Message, in essence, was no different than the Message of every Prophet ever sent to mankind in the entirety of its existence, and every one of them endured contempt from his people.

Every civilization protested against the Divine Message, which preached the Oneness of God, the Divinity of Prophethood, and the Concept of the Hereafter. Because every one of those civilizations had acquired a thirst for godlessness, a rejection to Prophetic miracles, and an unquenchable desire for a materialistic universe.

Like their precursor ancestors, the Qur'aysh were angered and outraged. Most of Makkah felt antagonized and enraged, but more than that, they were all perplexed at the Holy Prophet's determination, persistence, and courage. They tried negotiating with him, pleading with him while they watched, before their very eyes, their own flesh and blood parting from their old ways, and embracing the fold of Islām. They were becoming helpless. They mocked, and whipped, and punished. They bargained and begged. They even tried sorcery, and every attempt was foiled, because he was the Messenger of Allāh, the Most Gracious, the Most Merciful, and Allāh does not forsake His Messengers and true believers.

The Arabs at the time, may have been pagans and godless, but they were not without intellect. They may have lacked in Knowledge, but they were not lacking in ability. It evaded their reason and logic, to disband a love for wealth and money, and embrace a simplistic way of life dedicated to worshiping a God they could not even see or touch.

For all intents and purposes, to their perception, this was detrimental to their endeavors and ambitions. This was a problem, and like any problem, there had to be a solution.

But what to do?

They had tried everything within their reach. The punishments served no purpose. No manner of physical affliction bore any fruition.

Because they were unaware. That faith does not conform to reason and logic. Faith touches the heart, deep within where no manner of affliction can reach it.

They were, however, determined. Among their numerous councils, they had yet another possible route to explore, one that would perhaps yield *something,* if not an absolute solution.

North of Makkah, in a town called Yathrib (now modern-day Madīnah), were three Jewish tribes, descendants of the Children of Israel. They were the Banu Nadir, Banu Qaynuqa, and Banu Qurayza.

Three Israelite tribes who had migrated to Yathrib after the early years of Post-Nicaean Christianity. Three tribes who had settled in the oasis town of Yathrib for a divinely specific purpose. Even when they faced relentless opposition from Yemenite Arabs advancing their conquest across Arabia, prior to the rise of the Qur'aysh, the Jewish tribes remained, steadfast and resolute. Leading them, in religion and governance, were the most revered and renowned Jewish Rabbis of the entirety of Judaism. Not even in Jerusalem could one find these elite Rabbis and Jewish Sages. Where most of their people were scattered across the Semitic Middle-East, these High Priests had strangely chosen to remain in Yathrib.

Why did they remain? *What were you doing there, dear Rabbis, so far from your hearts' desires, so far from the Holy Land?*

19

Muhammad Ibn Ishaq, a renowned Arab-Muslim historian of the 8th century, recounts a conflict between the last Yemenite King of Himyar, Tiban Assad AbuKarib, and the pre-Islāmic residents of Yathrib. Following this conflict, resulting in his son's death, the king swore to raze Yathrib to the ground, to which the Rabbis begged and pleaded;

> 'O King do not do it, for if you persist in your intention something will happen to prevent your carrying it out and we fear that you will incur speedy retribution,' to which they further explained that 'Yathrib was the place to which a prophet of the Qur'aysh would migrate in time to come, and it would be his home and resting place'.

In all previous Scriptures, the coming of a prophet from the lineage of Ismā'īl was divinely foretold. Regardless of the Judaic outlook towards the Prophet Ismā'īl (peace be upon him), the Rabbis still held some adherence to their revealed scriptures. Something, contained in the pages of the Talmud and Zohar, projected immense benefit for the Jewish people, enough to draw them deep into Arab lands, and withstand every hardship despite Jerusalem being their true desire.

Something happened, however, that did not bring fruition to their anticipations. In truth, the Rabbis and their people were waiting for their savior; one whom they thought and believed would *prove* himself to be their promised Messiah, and would carry them on his shoulders to the Promised Land of milk and honey, gold and silver, power and wealth. Even though *they knew,* and despite what the Scriptures truly reveal, a deep and rigorous search of history unveils a dark trend in their methodology and belief system, something that always hinders them from seeing beyond material benefit.

Frustrated and desperate, the Qur'aysh, more coherent in economics and trade, and less in spirituality, decided to consult the Rabbis of Yathrib, whose declaration of a prophet from among the Gentiles was widely known in the land.

They sent a delegation.

Rather than come to Makkah and attest for themselves, the Rabbi's responded by tasking the delegates to carry out the investigation on their behalf. They provided the Qur'aysh with an identifying test;

> 'Ask of him three questions, for only a true Prophet can answer them. If he responds to them accurately, then he is a Prophet. If not, do with him as you please.'

We need to stop here and just think for a moment.

Explore every other scripture in the world today, including the Bible, the Torah, the Zohar, the Talmud, and even the Kabbalah. Nowhere, in any of these texts, is there even a shimmer of evidence that *these three questions* can truly attest to the mark of Prophethood. Further to this notion, there is not a trace in any of these Scriptures to give evidence of *how* the Rabbis knew of these questions or what responses the expected, and if at all they did know, all manner of trace and evidence is conveniently missing from their teachings and scriptures.

Jewish history does not even provide a record of the events of Makkah and Madīnah, even though this was a paramount occurrence which shaped both the lives of the Arabs and Jews. There seems to be no record of Nabi Muhammad, Islām, the interaction with the Rabbis of Madīnah, the three questions, nor the fulfillment of a prophecy so clearly outlined in their scriptures. Furthermore, those Jews who accepted Nabi Muhammad and Islām, similar to those who accepted Nabi Isa, were all excommunicated from Jewish society.

Suspicion rises with every step drawing closer to the End of Times, and it seems more and more apparent that there must have been an ulterior motive behind the Rabbis posing these three questions. In all essence, it evidently appears that they may have also tried to trick the Messenger of Allāh into divulging knowledge beneficial to whatever cabalistic ambitions they had.

These concealed and secretive ploys are the subjects of our investigation.

There are some vile agendas at play in the world today, and almost all of them can be traced back, either to these three questions or the origins of their replies. A holistic analysis attests that the most defining turning points in the last two millennia all came by the decisive stands taken by the Jews as a whole, by rejecting the Good News of Nabi Isa (peace and blessings be upon him), and the Final Message of Nabi Muhammad (peace and blessings be upon him). Both these events have irrefutably and undeniably shaped humanity for what it is today.

All three questions, and their responses, have been well-preserved in the Holy Qur'ān. While most of the world has interpreted the interlinking tales as mere allegories, a select portion of Eschatological Scholarship has evidential reason to believe that these Heavenly Ayāt contain the cipher to unraveling the mysterious transformations engulfing our world today. While absorbing the profound Wisdom and Knowledge of the Holy Qur'ān, we will also attempt to pierce two of the darkest veils set before our eyes, all architected to keep our hearts from taking a righteous path.

The mysterious, yet very real, phenomenon of the Dajjāl, the False Messiah, the Antichrist, the Impostor.

The mysterious nature, origin, and very evident existence of the descendants of *Ya'jūj* and *Ma'jūj*, and their strange alliance with the Dajjāl.

There are numerous methodologies to deciphering and understanding these mysteries, but the most astounding, and accurate way, is by exploring the history of the world as it has unfolded over the last three Millennia, all centered around why the Jewish Rabbis of Yathrib thought they could *trick* the Messenger of Allāh with three questions, and their true intentions, then and now.

Armed with these three questions from the Jewish Rabbis, the Qur'ayshi delegation returned to Makkah and presented them to the Holy Prophet (peace and blessings be upon him).

Question one; Tell us about the *Rū'h*. What is the *Rū'h?*

Question two; Tell us about the Companions of the Cave, for theirs is a wondrous tale. Who were the Companions of the Cave?

Question three; Tell us of the great traveler who journeyed to two ends of the land. Who was this great traveler?

Although there is no documented proof to the order of the questions, we have chosen to address them in the above structure to abide by our methodology of studying the subject of the End Times.

Before we can address these questions and interpret their meanings from the Qur'ān, we must first understand the fundamental building blocks of the Cosmos, for without the proper knowledge, without a proper study and methodology, and without an open mind, deciphering the Divine code of the Holy Qur'ān, and the Prophetic Hadīth, becomes guesswork and meaningless speculation.

TIME
AND
KNOWLEDGE

Perception plays a key role in the scholarship of *any* subject, and the subject of Eschatology is no exception. Sadly though, in the realm of academics, eschatology is given much less a preference largely due to its perplexing nature.

The essence of this branch of *'Ilm* is that it encompasses elements of the past, the present and the future, and is a subject overwhelmingly pertaining not just human and earthly existence, but Cosmological influence as well, thus demanding more from the scholar than just a rational perceptive.

It largely warrants an element of *belief,* and is such that it involves aspects of study which are beyond human comprehension, but just as vital in substance, and these are fundamentals of all existence.

Lacking is every scholarly attempt at decoding the mysterious transformation of the world before understanding the most fundamental building blocks of the Cosmos.

Time and Knowledge.

Philosophical thinking allows us to realize that everything happens for a reason and a purpose. Relying solely on rational thinking, limits our capabilities of deeper understanding as to *why* and *how* history occurred in the manner it did. Why the world is what it is.

Why did the Jewish Rabbis ask those three questions, and *how* have they influenced our lives today?

We realize life becoming ever so difficult, and the quest to seek

23

out answers emerges futile with every attempt. In the end, we are left with speculations and opinions, mere spoonfuls of feigned medicine to sooth the momentary turmoil. But the predicaments persist. The enigmas convolute and bedevil our capacities to persevere. A third give in and give up. A third accept what is and move on, while a third still deliberate the perplexing cipher, and it is this third that eventually realizes that the cipher is not perplexing in the slightest.

The reason we fail in understanding the complexities of modern life is very simple, far simpler than we can imagine. It is because we limit ourselves to rational analysis, rather than profound understanding. We conserve ourselves to a Mechanical passage of Time, rather than marvel at the Divinity of Time. We conserve ourselves to acquiring staggering amounts of Information and we fail to realize Knowledge from any of it.

Because we stop asking *why* for the sake of Knowledge, and accept the Informative theorem as an absolute and evident norm.

This state of existence we find ourselves in is by design, and its architect is none other than the Impostor, the Dajjāl. While skeptics will sooner discard anything to do with the subject, thus conforming to this architectural form of existence, profound thinkers will always strive to seek out an explanation, and that explanation begins with acknowledging that *everything* exists for a reason.

Every aspect of Allāh's creation has a key role to play in the whole of things. Every aspect. Be it as small as an atom, smaller than an atom, as large as a galaxy, much larger than a cluster of galaxies. Anything and everything, between this hardened earth and the Divine Throne of Allāh Almighty, has been put in place for a reason and a purpose.

وَمَا خَلَقْنَا ٱلسَّمَآءَ وَٱلْأَرْضَ وَمَا بَيْنَهُمَا بَٰطِلًا ۚ ذَٰلِكَ ظَنُّ ٱلَّذِينَ كَفَرُوا ۚ فَوَيْلٌ لِّلَّذِينَ كَفَرُوا مِنَ ٱلنَّارِ

And we did not create the Heavens and the Earth and that between them aimlessly. That is the assumption of those who disbelieve, so woe unto those who disbelieve from the fire.

[Sūrah Sād, 38:27]

In its literal declaration, the āyah cannot be disputed with any argument. Everything, between the Heaven and the Earth, has a reason, has a purpose, whether it is to keep things flowing, to keep the enormous machine of the universe running, to regulate the climate on earth and on other planets. Be it the state of governance in the world today, the institutions built by the secular minds, the types of foods we eat, the kind of technology we rely on, *everything.*

This 'everything' encompasses both the tangible and the intangible. It includes the 'Seen in the world of the Seen' and the 'Unseen in the world of the Unseen'. It unravels a broader realm of perception and understanding. It explains the existence of Other Worlds and their impact upon ours. It removes the illusory concept of Mechanical Time and unveils a profound reality of Divine Time.

Every decisive step we take, whether individually or wholesomely, has a consequence, a recurring series of events with consecutive outcomes, some diminishing and others manifesting into greater outcomes. Fate manifests itself as we shape our destinies, because while our destinations are preordained by the Ultimate Creator, the journey is ours to unravel. Nothing, on any level, stage, or point in Time, happens by chance.

Chance is a gambit.

Humans gamble. Jinn gamble.

Almighty Allāh does not gamble.

Once we adopt this mindset, this philosophical way of thinking, we can then take a step further in an attempt to explain things from a perceptive of profound sense as well as rational faculty.

Science explains the rationality of things, because science is a rational faculty. It quantifies our world in a comprehensible manner, enabling the human brain designed to function on logic and rationality. We instinctively tend to acknowledge what conforms to rationality, and discard all else that is irrational.

Faith, however, encourages us to acknowledge even that which cannot be rationalized. In essence, faith does not conform to rationality. It conforms to *sense*, that inner intuitive human 'self' that enables the rational mind to *believe*, regardless of the magnitude of incoherence. Faith conforms to fear and pain, love and affection, sadness and sorrow, insight and intuition, and above all, knowledge and wisdom. Faith goes above and beyond the earthly limitations of science.

Science is a tool for rational analysis.

Faith is the foundation for human sense.

Science is governed by matter and energy.

Faith is governed by *Hilm* (Forbearance), *Hiqmah* (Wisdom), and *Nūr* (Light).

All are governed by Time and Knowledge.

These are the perplexities driving the human urge, the thirst to extend beyond the present. To traverse into the unknown. To delve to the depths of our origins and unlock the mysteries of our existence.

Science defines the origin, the point, the singularity of existence, suspended in a moment of Time, followed by a rapidity of evolution. A process enduring the test Time, quantified for the sake of human perception as billions of years. With what accuracy though? With what evidence? Can man, rooted to this earthly point in Space and Time, reach back to the beginnings and state his theorem with certainty? If so, can man's rational faculty reach beyond and elaborate the origin of that singularity?

Regardless of which faculty man chooses to follow, Science or Religion, man needs to comprehend the two fundamental concepts by which Divine Creation manifests itself. Both concepts are of the Command and Creation of the Exalted Almighty, and their secrets are known only to Him. By extension, both concepts exist beyond a rational faculty.

Time and Knowledge.

In order to understand these attributes, we have to shed our material way of thinking and adopt a more philosophical approach. We need to unlock our inner 'selves', enhance our faculties of Faith in our Creator and seek His inspiration. Follow His doctrine upon a path of Knowledge, Intellect, and Enlightenment.

Knowledge is not acquired by reading off written script. Books and scrolls relay information. The brain deciphers information. Knowledge is not derived from investigation and experimentation, no, those are merely stepping stones. Knowledge is beyond man. Knowledge exists on a plane higher than human comprehension, because Knowledge is a sublime creation of Allāh.

Therefore, Knowledge is Divine, and all that is Divine, is His to give and take away. It constitutes a *part* of all that He has created, and it also serves as the *script* of *all* His creation (*Lauhil-Mahfūdh- Burūj 85:22* and *Abasa 80:13-16*). It is from within and without, a pinnacle of enlightenment and a foundation of faith.

So rather than ask, 'What is Knowledge?' we should be asking, 'How can we understand Knowledge?'

Time is not the clock. It is not the hours, the months, the years and decades and centuries and millennia. No, those are only markers we use to keep track of Time. A tool for measurements.

When speaking of Time, where do we begin?

Where do we conclude?

Do we begin with the beginning?

The beginning of man?

The beginning of Creation? Can we even comprehend the beginning, when we cannot even comprehend this moment?

Time did not arise with the singularity ('bigbang'), because Time is not a point. Time is not a straight line. Time is relative. Time is fluid. Time was existent, and will continue to exist. Time, in essence, is Divine.

So rather than ask, 'What is Time?' we should be asking, 'How can we understand Time?'

The espousal of these two concepts rewards us with a third ability, Wisdom, with which we can better analyze and understand our lives and our purpose.

Imam Ali said, *'Knowledge leads to Wisdom. Accordingly, the educated man is the wise one. Riches diminish by expenditure, while Knowledge is increased by dissemination.'*

It is important to distinguish between a mechanical and earthly concept of Time in order to understand Time as is described in the Holy Qur'ān and Hadīth. Concepts of 'A day like a Year', 'Three hundred years', 'Forty days', 'The Last Day', 'The Final Hour', and various other references become difficult to understand if analyzed in mechanical and quantitative ways.

It is also vital to recognize the interdimensional concept of Time and Existence which explain the reality of the Dajjāl in another world before his emergence, and the 'sleep state' phenomenon of the Companions of the Cave.

In addition to this, it is also very vital to distinguish between Information and Knowledge. While we acknowledge the expanse of information made available to us in the modern age of technology, we must also recognize that simply reading, watching, and listening to everything does not necessarily equip us with an understanding of everything. Effort must be made on every stepping stone to study, discern, comprehend, analyze, ask, question, think and ponder, for the Holy Qur'ān denotes itself as a Book of Knowledge unto those who can Think, Ponder, and Contemplate (*Yūnus 10:24*). An informative perceptive limits our human abilities to our physical senses of sight, sound and speech, but a *Knowledgeable* perceptive expounds our abilities to go beyond.

Entwined with each other, Time and Knowledge lay out the tenacious foundations upon which Epistemology, Theology, Philosophy and Sciences can all be comprehended with authenticity and absoluteness, and together they can all be directed toward our study of Eschatology (*'Ilm ul- ākhiru ul-Zamān*). This will deliver us the reigns by which our beginnings can be understood following which the End of Times can be comprehended with realism rather than mythicism. Herein do we find the correct methodology required to absorb the profound wisdom of the Heavenly Ayāt revealed to us. Herein do we find ourselves with eyes opened and reality unveiled.

The study of the *Rū'h*, as perplexing as the subject is, draws its origins from *Awwal Al-Zamān* (Beginning of Human History), is tied into the very existence of man on earth, life, death, and resurrection all entwined with the conclusion of humanity ushered in with the advent of Nabi Isa, the True Messiah, and the Dajjāl, the False Messiah, and the End of Times.

The study of the Dajjāl arises from the event of the Companions of the Cave, and is tied into Messianic study, interdimensional study, as well as the concept of the *Rū'h*, because the Dajjāl is a human being, rivaling the True Messiah (Nabi Isa), preexisting in another world (dimension), and has an impact on the End Times.

The study of *Ya'jūj* and *Ma'jūj* comes from the event of Dhū'l-Qarnayn, and is also woven into Messianic study, interdimensional study, as well as the concept of the *Rū'h*, because *Ya'jūj* and *Ma'jūj* are human beings, will come to rival Nabi Isa and his followers (us), have impacted on an age before and will impact on the End Times.

All these three aspects consolidate the crux of this book, and are far more complex and multi-layered, webbed into each other with tendrils reaching far and deep into ancient, hidden agendas and doctrines that when uncovered, will shatter our modern perception of reality.

For the moment, we can conclusively say that these three questions were not presented by accident nor as a gambit, and recent events shaping the world today bear enough evidence to point to a vile agenda which can be traced back to these three questions and the ulterior motives behind asking them.

PART ONE

THE SPIRIT

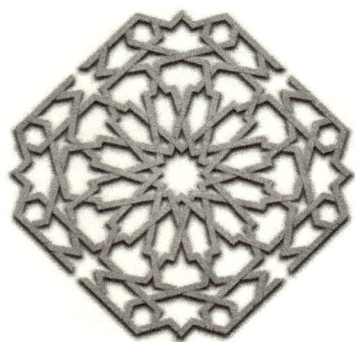

THE
FIRST QUESTION

وَيَسْـَٔلُونَكَ عَنِ ٱلرُّوحِ

And they ask thee about the Rū'h...

The Rabbis were not the first to ask such a question. Every human in history has pondered over the existence of the Spirit of Life, and whether such a phenomenon even exists. How do we realize a part of us we cannot even touch or feel, yet we somehow know is there, if at all it is? How do we quantify its composition, its nature and physical existence? Is the *Rū'h* even real?

It is a complex and difficult question to analyze by itself without an expanse of knowledge, because the Spirit constitutes the pinnacle of our existence, whether we can scientifically prove its reality or not. We have found that the best way is not to address the subject with the goal of explaining the *Rū'h* in rational terms, but rather to understand its relevance, its divinity, and its existence. Furthermore, our goal within the context of this book, is not to study the *Rū'h*, but to study the question asked by the Rabbis.

First and foremost we need to establish a clarity from the chaotic misinterpretations plaguing our knowing for generations. It is with this distinction and clarity that we will better understand the perspective of the questioners.

There is a difference between 'Soul' and 'Spirit', and therefore, a difference between 'Self-awareness' or 'consciousness', and 'Life-force'.

In ancient Hebrew Scriptures, the 'Soul' is translated as *Nefesh*. In Qur'ānic and classical Arabic it is *Nafs*, also meaning 'Soul'. Accordingly, *Ru'ach* is translated from Hebrew as 'Spirit', and in Arabic, *Rū'h*. The similarity between both the languages of the Holy Scriptures is accredited to the fact that both the Arab Muslims and Israelite Jews are descended from one origin, Nabi Ibrahim (peace be upon him).

In Islāmic teachings, both the *Nafs* and *Rū'h* are clearly defined as two separate entities, Divinely interlinked, and the Holy Qur'ān addresses both in their own respects. For example, where the Qur'ān says;

$$كُلُّ نَفْسٍ ذَآئِقَةُ الْمَوْتِ$$

Every Nafs (Soul) shall taste death

[āl-Imrān 3:185]

In contrast to when it says;

$$ثُمَّ سَوَّاهُ وَنَفَخَ فِيهِ مِن رُّوحِهِ$$

Then He (Allāh) fashioned him (man) and breathed into him of His Rū'h

[As-Sajda 32:9]

By definition, the *Rū'h* is the Spirit, the 'Life-force', or the 'Divine Breath of Life' which gives human its humanity, and by extension, all other creation the ability to remain alive. In essence, breath or breathing, is the closest we can attest to being alive. Take away the breath, take away life.

The *Nafs*, on the other hand, is the Soul. It is the entity by which creation can attest to awareness and consciousness. Secular Science defines consciousness as 'Ego' and 'Super-ego', which, in every respect, is a weak analysis. Ego and Super Ego are chiefly attributes of 'behavior', not the essence of Consciousness. The *Nafs* defines our individualities, our existence, our abilities to ponder, reflect, decide, and *feel*. It forms the ethereal link between the Body (*Jism*) and its Life-force (*Rū'h*) by mediating between life and the manifestation of life.

However, when we refer to Judaic teachings, mostly reformed

as per the Kabbalah, the *Rūʾh* and *Nafs* are first considered as a unified entity, the Soul, then parted into three stages. According to the Kabbalah;

~*Nefesh* is the lower part, or 'animal part', of the soul. It is linked to instincts and bodily cravings. This part of the soul is provided at birth. The Gentiles have this Soul.

~*Ruʾach* is the middle soul, the 'intellectual soul'. It contains the moral virtues and the ability to distinguish between good and evil. Only Jews have this Soul.

~*Neshamah* is the higher soul, or 'super-soul'. This separates man from all other life-forms. It is related to enlightenment and allows man to enjoy and benefit from the afterlife. It allows one to have some awareness of the existence and presence of God. Only Jews can attain this level.

This quixotic doctrine completely eradicates the existence of the 'Spirit', and leads to the falsified belief that the composition of man is only body and soul, giving weight to a 'Duality of Existence'. By extension, Secular Science concludes with the inexistence of a soul or spirit, proclaiming the Body and the Conscious as 'Biological existence with Thought and Identity' (meaning, the human conscious is a manifestation of the human brain through intellect, not as an entity by itself).

It, therefore, begins with the questioner. The nature of the questioner. The intent of the questioner.

History has shown that whenever the Children of Israel posed questions to their Prophets, for the most part, they did so in a mischievous, or an ulterior sense. This is not a false propagation or accusation. It is factual by their own history, and even the best among them, those who are true to the worship of Allāh, will affirm what the Qurʾān affirms.

When Nabi Mūsa revealed to them that Allāh Almighty wanted them to slaughter a heifer (*al-Baqarah 2:67-73*), they followed with meaningless questions; *What color should it be? What size should be? How old should it be?*

In similitude, they posed so many meaningless questions and prerequisites to other Prophets of Allāh, such as; *Perform a miracle for us. Prove your validity to us. Speak to your Lord on behalf of us. You and your lord handle the matter for us.*

This repetitive trait of questioning and demanding always led to an unnecessary complication of matters for themselves, as well as making things needlessly difficult for Allāh's Messengers.

Questioning before acceptance, that is, posing an argument

before Faith, or demanding an explanation before Belief, results in a failure of the true test of *Imān*. The entire concept of Belief is structured around *Unconditional Faith* in the Unseen, the Unknown, and the Inexplicable, and it forms the foundation of *any* Religious belief.

While religious disputes can endure aimlessly, questioning for the sake of understanding and acquiring knowledge is not prohibited. Many among the Companions of the Prophets always questioned with the intent of *understanding* Revelation as opposed to questioning for the purpose of validating their own personal thoughts and beliefs.

However, in every single instance of any questioning by the Children of Israel, as mentioned in the Holy Qur'ān, their intents have always proven to be aimless and quite often filled with malfeasance. In posing the question about the *Rū'h*, the circumstance was no different. The response to the question came not in Sūrah al-Kahf, the 18th Chapter of the Holy Qur'ān, as did the responses of the other two questions, but in Sūrah al-Isrā, the previous chapter, also known as Sūrah Bani al-Isrā'īl (Children of Israel).

We, as Muslims, have clearly understood that nothing in all the Seven Heavens and the Earth happens by accidence. Nothing happens by accident in the Holy Qur'ān. There is a Divine Reason and Purpose to be fulfilled, if Allāh Almighty decreed this question and its response to be placed in a separate Sūrah from the other two questions.

$$وَيَسْأَلُونَكَ عَنِ ٱلرُّوحِ ۖ قُلِ ٱلرُّوحُ مِنْ أَمْرِ رَبِّى وَمَآ أُوتِيتُم مِّنَ ٱلْعِلْمِ إِلَّا قَلِيلًا$$

And they ask you (O Muhammad) concerning the Rū'h (the Spirit), say (unto them) 'The Rū'h is from the Command (and Affair) of my Lord and not have you been given of it knowledge but a little'.

[Sūrah al-Isrā 17:85]

Allāh Almighty does not waste words. Every letter, every connotation, every word is fully accounted for. In deliberately repeating the question, there is a Divine element of validation, both to a linguistic, as well as an indoctrinated perspective. They did not ask about the *Soul*. They asked about the *Spirit*. They did not want *to know* about it, they wanted *a clarification* of what they *thought they knew*.

34

From what we have thus read in the Kabbalah, and what the āyah explicitly states, it follows thereof, that their question was not posed from an understanding based on what was Divinely revealed, but from a corrupted concept based off a doctored Rabbinic opinion. Their asking about the *Rū'h* in the āyah above, means that they were asking about the *Ru'ach* as defined by the Kabbalah, hence attempting to trick the Holy Messenger into conforming with their altered and misinterpreted texts.

It is vital to understand their perspective of belief, because it forms the core structure of every ideology propagated against Divine revelation, hence contributing to the foundations upon which they rejected most of Allāh Almighty's Messengers sent to them.

It should be noted that the āyah was revealed in Makkah, *prior* to the Holy Prophet's migration to Madīnah. Chronologically, it is difficult to pin-point the exact date, but many Scholars of Tafsīr have denoted that it was revealed in the last two-to-three years before the Holy Prophet's migration. This point is vital to understand because there is an element of Time passing between their asking, the response revealed, and their countering with an argument. The gap in between attests to a period of validation, that is, the Rabbis validating the Holy Qur'ān's response to what their doctored scriptures held.

Following *Hijra,* the Rabbis did not immediately pose their argument. They waited, they observed, and rather than approach from an intellectual perspective, they asked the question again, to which the Holy Prophet simply recited the already revealed āyah.

This did not sit well with the Rabbis, and with spite and arrogance, they countered with a statement of utmost profanity; *'We have been given immense knowledge. We were given the Torah, and whoever has been given the Torah, then he has indeed been given a wealth of knowledge.'* (Hadīth Al-Bukhārī)

To which Allāh responded by saying;

$$\text{قُل لَّوْ كَانَ ٱلْبَحْرُ مِدَادًا لِّكَلِمَٰتِ رَبِّى لَنَفِدَ ٱلْبَحْرُ قَبْلَ أَن تَنفَدَ}$$

$$\text{كَلِمَٰتُ رَبِّى وَلَوْ جِئْنَا بِمِثْلِهِ مَدَدًا}$$

Say (O Muhammad), 'If the sea were ink for the Words of my Lord, verily the sea would dry up before the words of my Lord were exhausted, even if we brought the likes of it (another sea) as a supplement'.

[Sūrah al-Kahf 18:109]

35

Despite the blanket statement, not only from the Holy Prophet, but from Allāh Almighty directly, their argument did not cease, and they pressed the matter.

'*Who told you this?*' They asked the Holy Prophet.

To that Nabi Muhammad replied, '*Jibrīl brought it to me from Allāh.*'

Which was still not a satisfactory reply for them, and their arrogance knew no bounds when they said;

'*No one has told you that except our enemy.*'

(More on why Judaism considers Jibrīl an enemy is broken down in the following chapters).

And the Qur'ān responded;

$$ قُلْ مَن كَانَ عَدُوًّا لِّجِبْرِيلَ فَإِنَّهُ نَزَّلَهُ عَلَىٰ قَلْبِكَ بِإِذْنِ ٱللَّهِ مُصَدِّقًا لِّمَا بَيْنَ يَدَيْهِ وَهُدًى وَبُشْرَىٰ لِلْمُؤْمِنِينَ $$

Say (O Muhammad), 'Whoever is an enemy of Jibrīl (then know that) indeed he (Jibrīl) has brought it (the Word of Allāh) down upon your heart, by permission of Allāh, confirming what was revealed before it (previous scriptures), and guidance and glad tidings for the Believers'.

[Sūrah al-Baqarah 2:97]

Outlining this conversation, aside from the persisting negligence and outright arrogance of the Rabbis, we also learn that not *all* knowledge concerning the *Rūh* has been kept concealed from our human perception. To a certain degree, something of our spiritual embodiment has been allowed within our comprehension.

Some scholars have affirmed that further pursuing any knowledge concerning the *Rūh* or *Nafs* results in breaking the tenets of the āyah (*al-Isrā 17:85*) and going against the Decree that we *have no knowledge of it but a little.*

However, the concepts of the *Rūh* and *Nafs* have not been kept secret from mankind, only that their expanse is beyond human comprehension much like all that is concealed from our visual perception. The absolute knowledge of the *Rūh* and *Nafs*, their constitution, their composition, their scientific explanations (rational and logical explanations), their exact purpose and nature of existence, all fall under a branch of Knowledge known as *'Ilm ul-Ghaib*, Knowledge of the Unseen. They fall under the categories of the Unseen and Unknown, the Intangible and Unquantifiable.

Some scholars have dismissed the Jewish Rabbinic intent as mere mischief, which was largely one of their behavioral traits and crude attempts at trying to invalidate Nabi Muhammad's Prophethood. Other scholars believe that it was a deflection or a distraction with regards to a deeper intent of asking questions two and three. However, we cannot ignore the fact that not only were they persistent in their asking, but also arrogant and defiant in response to the answer they were given.

It is, therefore, essential to pursue a moderate study of the subject in order to understand all the reasons as to why the question was asked.

The concept of the Rū'h forms the entirety of human existence, and while some uphold it with divine regard, it has been wrongfully given a sinister place in reformed Jewish belief, who are in reality the architects of the modern world.

It, therefore, emphasizes the fact that the first question was not a mere deflection or a just mischievous ploy, but they had also intended on hoodwinking the Messenger of Allāh into disclosing some knowledge tied into *their* belief of the Rū'h and *their* belief of the *Messiah*. They had also intended on testing the Holy Prophet to see whether the religion he preached (Islām) affirmed what the Rabbis had been preaching for centuries, in order for them to accept him as a true prophet. This fact requires no debate, as history has shown that they have taken it upon *themselves* to judge if a prophet is true, not based on the fulfillment of prior prophecies or divine miracles performed, but whether or not the prophet ratified their (the Jewish) belief and way of life.

Studying the subject from the psychological profile of the Jewish Rabbis is relevant because it unravels a common trait that mankind has displayed over history. It is the trait of superiority by birthright. It forms the foundation for prejudice and racial discrimination, but these merely touch the surface. The root cause trickles deeper down, and further back through history to its beginning.

Why the devil *refused* to obey Almighty Allāh's command and prostrate before Adam when Commanded.

The Rabbis were, and still are, convinced that the Jewish soul is different in superiority from the Gentile (non-Jew) soul, and asking this question was from an intent no different than what Iblīs himself believed and still believes.

As we progress through these pages, many similarities in thought and doctrine will arise, and we will begin to see why true Christianity (vastly variant from modern Christianity) is closer to the Heart of Islām, than is reformed and doctored Judaism.

We will do an in-depth analysis of these thoughts and doctrines in the following chapters, because understating the Judaic perspective of such matters is vital in understanding the world today, and in understanding the Dajjāl and the End Times.

Beyond our capabilities, Allāh is All-Knowing and All-Wise.

OF FAITH
AND
RELIGION

Islām lays the foundation of all faith. Islām, and the message of Islām, descended perhaps in different form, context, dialect or terminology with respect to evolutionary Time and the Events that took place during those historical periods and places on earth, but its message of peace and submission to One God has always been the same.

This is the concept of *Tawhīd,* the Oneness of God, Theologically classified by the modern man as monotheism.

As and when it was relevant to the place and people, the same message, and its teachings, descended to address the immediate environs. While the mechanics of worship may have differed in accordance to every historical period, place, and environ, the concept of worship always remained the same. Submission to One God (*Tawhīd*). Believe in the Prophecy of His Messenger (*Nubūwwa*). Know that the End *will* come (*Ākhira*).

Linguistically, the term 'Religion' is a coined description to enable human perception to quantify something that cannot be quantified. In essence, the word simply means 'a particular system of faith and worship'.

In the *Realms of Knowledge* (not information), terminology bears *two* states of existence. That which exists in speech and linguistic, and that which corresponds to an existence in *Essence.* That which is descriptive to the *Rational* faculty of the human brain, and that which bears an essence of understanding to the *Intellectual* faculty of the human mind.

In *essence,* Religion does not constitute a particular belief, outlook or opinion, as has been dastardly classified by the modern secular world. Rather, Religion constitutes a *complete way of life.* It forms the umbrella of a unified system of governance, not only in law and legislation, but in *every aspect* of human existence, including social, civic, domestic, trade, wealth, espousal, lifestyle, ideology, doctrine, and knowledge. It encompasses three levels of human existence, Physical Existence, Conscious Existence, and Spiritual Existence.

The underlining message of every True Religion (that which has been Divinely Ordained), stripped of all eventual corruption and fabricated garb, has always preached the concept of *Tawhīd, Nubūwwa,* and *Ākhira.*

With every religious civilization, history has shown that the defacement and corruption of this concept was always done to suit and adopt a more convenient and easy passage, because in essence, Religion is not 'easy'. Religion requires material sacrifice for the sake of Spirituality, and unconditional Faith in the Unseen and Unknown. The essence of life, as defined by True Religion, is 'Life on earth (*Dunya*) as a test, with the ambition of Spiritual Enlightenment (*Nūr*), purely for the establishment of Life in the Hereafter (*Ākhira*)'.

The Secular Scientific world connotes enlightenment in accordance to academic achievement, steering human intellect away from 'religious myth' and closer to 'scientific fact', and we have deliberately written both these terms in 'quotes', because they are naught but fictitious analogies in the Realms of Knowledge. This secular doctrine appeals strongly to human logic and rationality, but in the Essence of Religion, spirituality does not come from academics. It comes from a heightened elevation of Emotion. From affection. From the belief and desire to be closer to God than the materialistic world. It is from *this* state that higher levels of intellect are opened to the Realms of Knowledge and Enlightenment.

Hence, driven by the devil's whispers, the modern secular world lowers the honor and integrity of Religion by describing it as 'the belief in, and the worship of, a *superhuman* controlling power, especially a *personal* God or gods.'

Superhuman?

Personal?

This indoctrination of *superhuman* has, over time, paved way for the concept that man can become god. In a bid to propagate secularism, the concept of religion has been altered to mean 'belief in a god of your choosing' making it more of an *opinion*, rather than a Divine Decree. The blasphemous indoctrination is that *it does not matter who, or what, Religion or God is, what it can do, or where it comes from. It is just a belief. The existence of God cannot be scientifically proven, so conclusively, God cannot exist. It remains an opinionated belief.*

The conclusion of this entire secular thesis is that Religion is then classified as 'a creation of man' because primitive man, devoid of scientific knowledge, could not explain the creation of the observable universe, and so primitive man merely *imagined* the concept of a divine being in order to help fill in the intellectual gap.

The human mind has been Divinely Designed to ponder and contemplate. We wonder how we came to be. We wonder what our purpose is. We wonder where we are headed. These three fundamental questions of Origin, Present, and Eventuality, are always asked at every point in life, and even though Islām responds to these questions, much of humanity prefers to adhere to its own rational thoughts and opinions. The definitive purpose of life, its existence, and final destination, falls under the umbrella of Faith. As a test of faith, belief in the Oneness of God through submission governs the hierarchies of Faith, beginning with Physical Existence, then Conscious Existence, and finally Spiritual Existence.

These three states of existence manifest themselves in an Actuality of Existence, that is the Body (*Jism*), the Conscious Soul (*Nafs*) and the Spirit of Life (*Rū'h*). The same three states of existence correspond with the hierarchy of Religion, Physical Submission (*Islām*), Conscious Faith (*Imān*), and Spiritual Ascent (*Ihsān*).

The relevance of this study of human existence delineates the foundation of the origin of our being, and further paves the way for understanding the end of our existence. Historically, from the very beginning of our father, Adam (peace and blessings be upon him), every event has laid the decisive stepping stone for its subsequent event, each one with respect to Time. Its relevance to the Three Rabbinic Questions is also a crucial piece of study as it outlines the psychological profile and belief system of the questioners. It lays out the intents and expectations, the reality behind their motives and the transpiring consequences that have unfolded and contributed to the modern world.

Beginning with our history, Adam's creation set the precedence for Iblīs's disobedience. His envy, arrogance, and defiance laid out his blueprint as the sworn enemy of mankind, exiled to earth and condemned to the Hellfire. It should be note here that mankind's destiny and fate was Divinely Decreed to populate the earth, albeit its manifestation took an alternate course. However, Iblīs's destiny and fate on earth was as a result of his own decisive action. Henceforth, every decisive step we take in our lives hangs on a delicate balance between righteousness and his wicked whispers.

Holistically, every other event in human history created a decisive path for every preceding race and nation, but regardless of what transpired, Faith and Religion have always played a key role in governing every step of human existence.

Following the concept of Belief and Worship of One God (*Tawhīd*), with Prophecy (*Nubūwwa*) acting as an intermediary between God and His righteous servants (the Believers), we now have the concept of *Ākhira,* and because of its Unseen and Unknown nature, Allāh Almighty hails our attention through Signs (*Ayāt*).

Among these signs are the Major Signs, definitive and solitary, and Minor Signs, recurring and manifesting. Out of the Major Signs hailing the Final Hour and the Day of Judgment, on a level of Faith and Religion, the advent of the Dajjāl marks the end of human history in every monotheistic religion. It is the convergence of everything that occurred since *Awwal Al-Zamān* (the beginning of history), into *Ākhir Al-Zamān* (the end of history).

The pinnacle of the beginning was marked with a test of Faith on the decisive element (the *Nafs*) of Iblīs. Regardless of his remarkable worship of Allāh Almighty, his submission (*Islām*) was put to the ultimate test of Faith (*Imān*).

وَإِذْ قُلْنَا لِلْمَلَـٰٓئِكَةِ ٱسْجُدُوا۟ لِـَٔادَمَ فَسَجَدُوٓا۟ إِلَّآ إِبْلِيسَ أَبَىٰ وَٱسْتَكْبَرَ وَكَانَ مِنَ ٱلْكَـٰفِرِينَ

And when We said unto the Angels, 'Prostrate yourselves before Adam,' they prostrated, except Iblīs; he demurred through arrogance, and became of the disbelievers.

[*Sūrah al-Baqarah 2:34*]

It is important to note that when the Divine Command was given, it was to *all* who were present, including Iblīs. It is also important to note, that contrary to some assumptions, Iblīs was not, and has never been an Angel. He is a Jinn. (*al-Kahf 18:50*). He is a Jinn with his own *Nafs*. He is a Jinn with intellect and the decisive ability to choose, and he chose his path.

The linguistic definition of *Kufr* is that of 'covering', 'concealing' from a source of denial and rejection. He, the Jinn who had attained such a level of esteem in the Heavens, did but one act of clearly *hearing* his Lord's Command, *understanding* the

Command, but choosing to conceal and cover it through denial and rejection. Hence the Disbeliever. The *Kāfir.*

Let us now analyze his status as a *Kāfir,* a disbeliever, and use his definitive template in identifying those who fall under the same category. The skeleton structure of Belief in *any* monotheistic religion, must abide by Six Tenets, known in Islām as the Six Pillars of *Imān.* These are, Belief in God as One. Belief in the Prophets of God. Belief in the Scriptures of God. Belief in the Angels of God. Belief in God's abilities to Resurrect the Dead, the abilities to give Life and take Life. Belief in God's Supernal Abilities to Ordain and Govern *all* things. The belief in these Six Tenets does not only pertain to one's vocal declaration, rather it denotes a belief from the Heart of the Believer, and in conformity with a Divinely Ordained structure of Belief.

So how did Iblīs's disbelief manifest itself?

He disbelieved in Allāh's power as the Creator of other Creations— mankind, in this case. Because Iblīs placed his faith in himself as a superior being, he failed to believe that Allāh Almighty has the power to Create far superior beings as He Wills.

He disbelieved in Allāh's Prophets, the first being Adam (peace and blessings be upon him). Again, because of his arrogance, Iblīs refused to believe in the Prophethood of Adam who was to be placed unto earth as a *Khalīfah.* Iblīs being a Jinn believed that Earth's *Khilāfah* must belong to him as the King of the Jinn, he being the only one among them to receive a status in Heaven (prior to his permanent exile).

He disbelieved in the Scriptures, the Knowledge given to Adam as the first Prophet to receive Revelation. As a test even unto the Angels, Allāh Almighty bestowed the first of Revelation, Divine Knowledge, unto Adam (peace be upon him). This ability of Adam, as is the ability of humankind, to learn, discern, invent, innovate, ponder, comprehend and advance through varied levels of intellect, filled Iblīs with nothing but envy for humanity.

He manifested his disbelief in the *Malāikah,* the Angels (*al-Baqarah 2:98*), by placing his own superiority over them. Again falling prey to his own arrogance and failing to recognize Allāh's Creation of the Angels. Iblīs proclaimed himself as an 'intellectual' being who worshiped out of choice in comparison to the Angels who worshiped without choice, wrongfully placing himself in a status of superiority. His analogy of the Angels, who had no choice in their belief, is that the Angels, unlike himself, were akin to slavery.

He disbelieved in Life after Death. Iblīs was not created an Immortal being. No creation can boast Immortality before Allāh Almighty. Everything that has a beginning, has an end, save for

Allāh the Eternal, who has no beginning nor end. Therefore, everything that falls under 'a Creation' must have an impending end, including Iblīs. Life existing beyond Death is not a concept easily grasped, nor was it ever grasped by Iblīs who perhaps believed himself immortal, feeding the core ideologies of the secular minds, which believe that immortality *can* be achieved through scientific pursuit. Witness then the relentless agendas of Transhumanism and Posthumanism. The very statement Iblīs whispered into the hearts of Adam and Hawā was;

$$فَوَسْوَسَ إِلَيْهِ ٱلشَّيْطَٰنُ قَالَ يَٰٓـَٔادَمُ هَلْ أَدُلُّكَ عَلَىٰ شَجَرَةِ ٱلْخُلْدِ وَمُلْكٍ لَّا يَبْلَىٰ$$

The Shaytān (Iblīs) whispered to him (Adam), he said, 'O Adam, shall I lead you to the Tree of Immortality and a Kingdom that does not fade away?'

[Sūrah Taha 20:120]

Lastly, he disbelieved in *Al-Qadr*. This is the Divine Decree for *every* single creation and *every* unfolding event, and *every* possible outcome of *every* decisive choice made by *every* one of Allāh's creations, preordained by His Knowledge and in accordance with His Wisdom. It is to believe that everything that happens, good or bad, happens only according to Allāh's Divine Decree, and must be accepted without question or doubt, which is precisely what Iblīs did not do with regards to the creation of humanity.

$$وَإِذْ قَالَ رَبُّكَ لِلْمَلَٰٓئِكَةِ إِنِّى جَاعِلٌ فِى ٱلْأَرْضِ خَلِيفَةً$$

And when your Lord said unto the Angels, 'Verily I shall place a Khalīfah on earth...

[Sūrah al-Baqarah 2:30]

This final tenet plays havoc on weak minds and weak hearts, where most of humanity tends to slip up and adhere to elements of accidental occurrences. A lack of proper understanding of Divine Decree results in confused thoughts and doubts between mankind's 'Ability to Choose', and the false indoctrination of 'Free Will', and this is the most sensitive element of faith which Iblīs enjoys toying with.

The above analysis can be debated and argued from every semantic, linguistic, opinionated, and indoctrinated perspective, regardless of which, the fact of the matter always remains; that a disbelief, a doubt, a rejection, or any misinterpretation of even *one* of the Six Tenets, results in dragging one's soul into the company of disbelievers.

The Six Pillars of *Imān* (Faith) have remained unchanged since the beginning of humanity, and history can attest that every civilization that has discarded these pillars has always followed in the same footholds of Iblīs. The Children of Israel have displayed a common trait in history of always abandoning one, or more, or all of the Pillars of Faith, regardless of their Physical practices of Judaism, and regardless of how many Prophets were sent to remind and guide them.

However, when the *Nafs* (the Soul) repeatedly abandons Faith in pursuit of worldly ambition, material benefit, and earthly dominance, it eventually seals its fate, as Iblīs sealed his own fate.

Here you must understand that Iblīs's "Kufr" was not a Kufr of *rejecting* or *denying* the Existence of God, or even the Oneness of God, and likewise His Angels, Divine Decree, and the HereAfter. Although Messengers, Prophets, and Scriptures had not yet been sent down to the Material Realm at that point in time, there was a Prophet created (Adam), who gave prophecy (showing the Angels what Allah wanted him to show) which then became part of the "*Kitāb*" or ordinance of Allah. Regardless, the Kufr was also not a rejection or denial of their existence.

Rather, this was a Kufr of *disobedience*. A refusal, an unjustifiable defiance. This distinction must be made, and there are two premises from the Qur'ān upon which it is understood.

Foremost, as Allāh says;

$$\text{فَإِذَا سَوَّيْتُهُ وَنَفَخْتُ فِيهِ مِن رُّوحِى فَقَعُواْ لَهُ سَـٰجِدِينَ}$$

And when I have fashioned him and breathed into him of My Spirit, then fall ye to him in Prostration

$$\text{فَسَجَدَ ٱلْمَلَـٰٓئِكَةُ كُلُّهُمْ أَجْمَعُونَ}$$

So they prostrated, the Angels, all of them, all-together

$$\text{إِلَّآ إِبْلِيسَ أَبَىٰٓ أَن يَكُونَ مَعَ ٱلسَّـٰجِدِينَ}$$

Except Iblīs, he refused; he was not with those who prostrated

[*Sūrah Al-Hijr 15:29-31*]

45

Following which, he was then held to account for his refusal or defiance, as Almighty Allāh then asked him directly to explain himself and his actions;

قَالَ يَٰٓإِبْلِيسُ مَا لَكَ أَلَّا تَكُونَ مَعَ ٱلسَّٰجِدِينَ

He (Allāh) said, "O' Iblīs, what is to you, that you were not among those who prostrated?"

[Sūrah Al-Hijr 15:32]

And additionally;

قَالَ يَٰٓإِبْلِيسُ مَا مَنَعَكَ أَن تَسْجُدَ لِمَا خَلَقْتُ بِيَدَىَّ أَسْتَكْبَرْتَ أَمْ كُنتَ مِنَ ٱلْعَالِينَ

He (Allāh) said, "O' Iblīs, what prevented you from prostrating before that which I created by My own hands? Are you arrogant? Or are you of higher rank?"

[Sūrah Sād 38:75]

قَالَ مَا مَنَعَكَ أَلَّا تَسْجُدَ إِذْ أَمَرْتُكَ قَالَ أَنَا خَيْرٌ مِّنْهُ خَلَقْتَنِى مِن نَّارٍ وَخَلَقْتَهُ مِن طِينٍ

He (Allāh) said, "What prevented you that you did not prostrate when I commanded you?" He (Iblīs) said, "I am better than him, you created me from fire, and you created him from clay."

[Sūrah Al-A'rāf 7:12

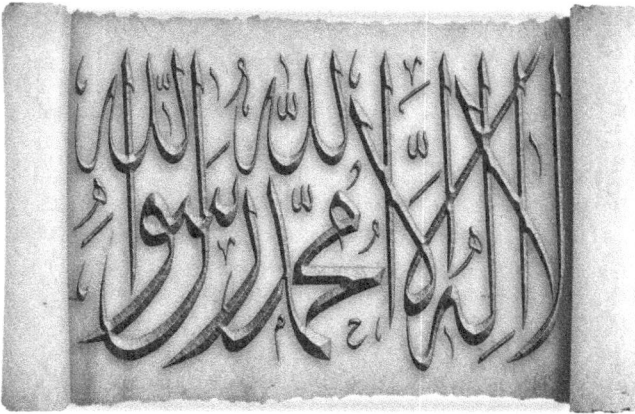

OF FAITH
THE SOUL
AND THE SPIRIT

As described in the previous chapter, inquiring about the *Rū'h* is not unanimous to the Jewish Rabbis, rather it is a question asked by humanity as a whole. What arouses suspicion is the contextual asking, the environ surrounding the question, and the tone and intent of asking.

Foremost, it is vital to understand the existence of the *Rū'h* from a Religious Perspective. By and large, *only* Religion can explain the *Rū'h*, because science, as informative as it is, has proven its capacity to be limited to quantitative analysis.

The mechanics of *Dīn-ul-Islām*, which include the Five Daily Prayers (*Salāt*), Fasting (*Sawm*), Alms (*Zakāt*), and Pilgrimage (*Hajj*), are all mechanical acts of worship performed by the *Jism* (the Human body) and linked to the *Nafs* and *Rū'h*. These Pillars are fulfilled by the physical motions of the body, undergoing the various prescribed rituals in a daily life. When performed in accordance to ordained guidelines, these rituals contribute to the Spiritual well-being of the human 'self', adding to its accountability of righteousness and piety. Disloyalty and unsteadiness in these practices is not tolerable under the umbrella of Islām, and does not grant one a passage to enlightenment. Simply put, one *cannot* be spiritual without being religious. Hence the folly proclamation of atheism, where one claims to be 'spiritual' but not 'religious'.

The divinity of the human body is given by its characteristic as a Creation by a Divine Being. By extension, conscious intentions and acts such as hard-work, marriage, relationships, loyalty, trust, servitude to others, the physical performance of righteous deeds, to mention but a few, all conform to worship under the umbrella of Islām held up by the Five Pillars. They are all *Mechanical* acts of worship performed by the mind and body (*Jism*). The Fifth Pillar of *Shahadah* is not only a Pillar of Islām but also the opening of the Pillars of *Imān,* the Pillars of Faith. Testifying to One God fulfills the Belief in One God which encompasses the entire concept of *Tawhīd* (monotheism). Consecutively, the *Nafs* follows in the process of fulfilling all the Pillars of Faith so as to elevate human existence to a spiritual plane native to the *Rū'h;*

Belief in One God, Allāh Almighty, Belief in His Scriptures, Belief in His Angels, Belief in His Prophets, Belief in the Resurrection, and Belief in His Divine Decree of Predestination (everything happens in accordance to His Will).

Tawhīd forms the foundation of the Belief in One God, His power and Sovereignty. The Possessor of all creation, the Possessor of all souls. In His hands lies the power to Judge with Truth and Justice.

Even though Islām, Christianity, and Judaism all follow the same Abrahamic Religion and despite numerous similarities, there is a very distinctive difference between Islāmic belief, Christianic belief (see the chapter on *The Birth of Christianity*) and Judaic belief, because true Faith in One God does not come from an opinionated definition of monotheism, but rather from a Divinely Decreed definition. While Jewish belief follows in the religion of monotheism, it strongly disagrees with the entire concept, by a hairline of a distinction between righteousness and damnation. To state that the Jewish soul is a Divine piece of God because Jews are 'God's Chosen people' allows them to claim divinity and self-judgment based on their own eschatology (see the following chapter). Further to this, it leads them to follow in the belief that God has a Soul (*Nafs*), whereas the actuality of God is plain and simple, *Unknown,* not because we are lacking in discovery, but that Allāh Almighty has Divinely Decreed it as so. The *Rū'h* (spirit) is of the Command and Affair of Allāh, His breath of Life unto us (*al-Isrā 17:85*), and to classify the *Nafs* and *Rū'h* as God Himself, is to utter blasphemous association to Allāh Almighty. The Holy Qur'ān says;

قُلْ هُوَ ٱللَّهُ أَحَدٌ ۞ ٱللَّهُ ٱلصَّمَدُ ۞ لَمْ يَلِدْ وَلَمْ يُولَدْ ۞ وَلَمْ يَكُن لَّهُ كُفُوًا أَحَدٌ

Say, He Allāh is One. Allāh is the Eternal the Absolute. He does not beget, nor is he begotten. And there is no equal to Him.

[Sūrah Ikhlās 112:1-4]

The first āyah define the Oneness of God by negating 'God as more than one (*Gods*)' or 'God as a composite (*many gods as one*)'. Meaning, He has no multiplicity, particularity, or composite nature. The second āyah attests to the Totality of God as One, by negating 'God as having any deficiency', or 'God having any defect' in addition to negating any form of temporality or spatiality to His existence. Meaning, He is not bound by space and time. The third āyah directly nullifies any concept of God as a result, or the result of God, by negating 'God as a cause or effect', that is, God does not exist as a dependent on anything. The last āyah directly defines God's Oneness by negating a 'likeness or opposite', meaning God does not bear resemblance to, or against, anything imaginable or defined.

Among countless other interpretations and implications, these Ayāt also speak *directly* to the Judaic belief that the soul of the Jew is *not* equal to any form of Divinity, and therefore *not* superior to any other. Before the Almighty Creator, *all* souls bear an equality to His Will. Hence the uniformity of supplicating before Him in daily prayers, where every soul must declare its authority to be as low as the ground, lower if it were possible (*Sujūd*).

This constitutes the First Pillar of Faith, be it in Islām, Christianity, or Judaism. If this Pillar is not fulfilled in accordance to Divine Decree, faith itself has no meaning. Only when *Tawhīd* is fulfilled, can all the other Pillars of Faith be fulfilled.

Belief in the Scriptures does not only relate to the *physical* Books of the Tawrāt, Zabūr, Injīl, and Qur'ān, and all other Scriptures not explicitly mentioned in the Qur'ān, but the Divinity of the Knowledge and Revelation contained in them. No Muslim has the right to condemn other Books and Scriptures without doing a proper study of them. It is also obligatory, by Divine Rule, to preserve the Word of God as it was revealed to man, hence the preservation of the Holy Qur'ān as it has been since it was revealed, as well the utter respect for all other Holy Scriptures.

However, Jewish history, and even Christianic history, has time and again proven to alter and distort the Word of God by writing and rewriting the scriptures by their own hands. These heinous crimes have not remained hidden from humanity as the Qur'ān openly uncovers their vandalism in numerous Ayāt. Distorting the Word of God directly results in a disbelief in His Scriptures. The Qur'ān says;

وَإِنَّ مِنْهُمْ لَفَرِيقًا يَلْوُونَ أَلْسِنَتَهُم بِٱلْكِتَٰبِ لِتَحْسَبُوهُ مِنَ ٱلْكِتَٰبِ وَمَا
هُوَ مِنَ ٱلْكِتَٰبِ وَيَقُولُونَ هُوَ مِنْ عِندِ ٱللَّهِ وَمَا هُوَ مِنْ عِندِ ٱللَّهِ
وَيَقُولُونَ عَلَى ٱللَّهِ ٱلْكَذِبَ وَهُمْ يَعْلَمُونَ

Verily there are among them those who distort the Scripture with their tongue so that you may think it is from the Scripture, but it is not from the Scripture, and they say 'it is from Allāh', but it is not from Allāh, and they speak falsehood about Allāh, knowingly.

[Sūrah āl-Imrān 3:78]

Belief in the Malāikah, the Angels, is the belief not only in their existence but the nobility and divinity of their creation from Divine Light, *Nūr*. Angels are created without the Ability to Choose like Humans or Jinn. Their sole purpose is worship and obedience to Allāh, and have no decisive ability to do otherwise, and Allāh Almighty truly knows best. Even though man has been given a status in contrast to Angels, Angels have also been given a status in contrast to man, and it is through this belief that the Muslim heart praises Allāh's Angels as we praise Allāh's Messengers.

Here arises one of Jewish belief's, and to some extent, even Christianic belief's greatest misunderstanding, which expresses that Satan (Iblīs) was, and still is an Angel, whose 'divinely assigned task is to seduce mankind'.

According to Jewish belief, Satan is also the prosecutor who levels charges in front of the heavenly court against those who succumb to his crafty seductions. In their texts, if the Heavenly court decides that it is time for someone to die, then the Satan is sent down to take his life. In fact, the Talmud states that;

'Satan, the urge to do evil, Lucifer, the Fallen Angel, and the Angel of Death, are all one and the same being. All these titles are simply multiple job descriptions for one angel. An angel fulfilling its divine duty is hardly in conflict with its own Creator.'
(Babylonian Talmud, *Bava Batra* 16a:8)

Further to this blasphemous belief that Iblīs is an 'angel' in addition to associating him with the True Angel of death (*Malak-Al-Mawt*), Jewish belief attests that even Angels can sin, and will be judged on *Yom Kippur* (Jewish Day of Judgment).

There is a notion (Book of Genesis) which regards a doctrine of Nephilim, Angels who descended to earth and succumbed to earthly pleasures, which gives Rabbinic doctrine the audacity to claim that only the Jewish Soul is superior to the Angelic Soul.

> *The Nephilim (Fallen Ones) were on the earth in those days, and also afterward, when the sons of the nobles would come to the daughters of man, and they would bear for them; they are the mighty men, who were of old, the men of renown.*
> *And the Lord saw that the evil of man was great in the earth, and every imagination of his heart was only evil all the time.*
> *And the Lord regretted that He had made man upon the earth, and He became grieved in His heart.*
> *And the Lord said, "I will blot out man, whom I created, from upon the face of the earth, from man to cattle to creeping thing, to the fowl of the heavens, for I regret that I made them."*
> *(Genesis 6:4-7)*

Jewish belief further regards the angelic soul to be lower in purity because of the Angels' inability to decide for themselves, programmed to follow without choice, affiliating them with the likes of slaves. In and of itself, *all* these beliefs are contradictory to each other, and are based off a misinterpretation when Angels were commanded to prostrate before Adam. However, it is vital for the believer's heart to believe that prostration was not made before humanity out of worship, rather prostration was made before Allāh's Creation, Allāh's power, Allāh's knowledge, and Allāh's command, out of respect.

وَإِذْ قُلْنَا لِلْمَلَـٰٓئِكَةِ ٱسْجُدُوا۟ لِءَادَمَ فَسَجَدُوٓا۟ إِلَّآ إِبْلِيسَ كَانَ مِنَ ٱلْجِنِّ فَفَسَقَ عَنْ أَمْرِ رَبِّهِ

And We said unto the Angels, 'Prostrate yourself before Adam', so they prostrated, except Iblīs, he was of the Jinn so he rebelled against his Lord's Command...

[Sūrah al-Kahf 18:50]

Belief in Allāh's Messengers embodies an acknowledgment that Allāh Almighty has created a covenant of Prophets on earth who serve the Sovereignty of Allāh and advocate His Message to humanity. Islāmic belief strongly attaches love, affection, and respect to every Prophet mentioned in the Qur'ān, likewise every other Prophet not mentioned, and in some cases unknown, without a shadow of doubt or disdain. In remarkable contrast, Jewish belief has somehow only ever regarded certain Prophets with respect and adoration if, *and only if,* they brought some material benefit to them in the form of riches, wealth, and dominion, and even then they have continuously made things difficult for their prophets, insulted them, and even killed them. The Qur'ān says;

وَلَقَدْ ءَاتَيْنَا مُوسَى ٱلْكِتَٰبَ وَقَفَّيْنَا مِنْ بَعْدِهِ بِٱلرُّسُلِ ۖ وَءَاتَيْنَا عِيسَى ٱبْنَ مَرْيَمَ ٱلْبَيِّنَٰتِ وَأَيَّدْنَٰهُ بِرُوحِ ٱلْقُدُسِ ۗ أَفَكُلَّمَا جَآءَكُمْ رَسُولٌ بِمَا لَا تَهْوَىٰٓ أَنفُسُكُمُ ٱسْتَكْبَرْتُمْ فَفَرِيقًا كَذَّبْتُمْ وَفَرِيقًا تَقْتُلُونَ

And indeed We sent Mūsa with the Scripture (Tawrāt) and followed him with Messengers, and We gave Isa son of Maryam clear Signs and strengthened him with the Rūʾh al-Qudus (the Holy Spirit). Is it not so whenever a Messenger came to you (Children of Israel) with what you did not desire (a message that abrogated your corrupted way of life), you acted in arrogance, some (of the Messengers) you denied, and some (of the Messengers) you slew (assassinated).

[Sūrah al-Baqarah 2:87]

Belief in Resurrection means believing in a Life of the Hereafter, and it strengthens the foundation of all belief. It, in its knowledgeable entirety, answers all the questions to the meaning and purpose of life. It allows the believer to embrace death, rather than fear it. It kindles love and affection for Allāh and His eternal reward for those who seek it in the Hereafter by striving to succeed in the test of life on earth. The Qur'ān describes resurrection, albeit in an allegorical form (because it eludes human perception), in numerous accounts, such as the event of the Companions of the Cave and the impending resurrection of Nabi Isa in the End Times. See the following chapter concerning the Jewish belief in the Resurrection and the Hereafter.

Of life and death, Allāh Almighty says;

كَيْفَ تَكْفُرُونَ بِٱللَّهِ وَكُنتُمْ أَمْوَٰتًا فَأَحْيَٰكُمْ ۖ ثُمَّ يُمِيتُكُمْ ثُمَّ يُحْيِيكُمْ ثُمَّ إِلَيْهِ تُرْجَعُونَ

How can you disbelieve in Allāh and while you were dead (non-existent) He gave you life (born to earth), then He will cause you to die (end of life on earth), then He will give you life (resurrect you on the Day of Judgment), then to Him will you be returned (in the Hereafter).

[Sūrah al-Baqarah 2:28]

Belief in Divine Decree, or Divine Predestination, is simply the belief that *nothing* happens without Allāh's Command. He controls the Time and every event occurring in respect to Time. Rational thinking cannot address or explain this concept, or any of the above concepts, which is why belief does not come from rationality. The essence of Religion does *not have* to conform to rationality, rather belief comes from *Sense,* and *Sense* is a fruition of Knowledge, not information. Logic dictates that everything that happens must have an explanation and therefore, must have an instigation, but Sense and Belief enlighten us that everything happens for a reason, whether a logical explanation is available or not. Believing in Divine Decree is not blind faith. We may not be able to quantify Divine Decree, but it is a concept very simple to understand.

Every possible decision and occurrence with every possible outcome from every creature and creation, animate or inanimate, is not only Known to Allāh Almighty, it is pre-ordained by Allāh. If it is the manifestation, for example, of a geological activity on earth, the event itself is an eventual creation of the earth, as a result of the creation of the Cosmos.

Understanding this concept requires a deepening understanding of Time and the Cosmos (refer to *The Divinity of Time and Cosmology*), but simply put, it is that Allāh Almighty does not exist in linearity as His Creation does. Allāh Almighty exists in the Past, the Present and the Future, all within any given moment and a mere fraction of His Eternal Existence.

It is His attribute as the All-Knowing and the All-Wise.

Of that which we consider 'inanimate', the Qur'ān says in *Sūrah Al-An'ām 6:59;*

وَعِندَهُۥ مَفَاتِحُ ٱلْغَيْبِ لَا يَعْلَمُهَآ إِلَّا هُوَ ۚ وَيَعْلَمُ مَا فِى ٱلْبَرِّ وَٱلْبَحْرِ ۚ وَمَا تَسْقُطُ مِن وَرَقَةٍ إِلَّا يَعْلَمُهَا وَلَا حَبَّةٍ فِى ظُلُمَٰتِ ٱلْأَرْضِ وَلَا رَطْبٍ وَلَا يَابِسٍ إِلَّا فِى كِتَٰبٍ مُّبِينٍ

And with him are the Keys of the Unseen and no one knows them except He. And He knows what is in the land and the sea. And not a leaf falls without His knowledge, and not a grain in the darkness (or depth) of the earth, nor wet nor dry (fresh or stale, recent or past, new or old), except that it is in clear record (recorded in the Divine Book of Records).

And of that which we regard as 'animate' with reference to our state of existence, the Qur'ān says in *Sūrah Al-Hadīd 57:22*;

$$\text{مَآ أَصَابَ مِن مُّصِيبَةٍ فِى ٱلْأَرْضِ وَلَا فِىٓ أَنفُسِكُمْ إِلَّا فِى كِتَـٰبٍ}$$
$$\text{مِّن قَبْلِ أَن نَّبْرَأَهَآ ۚ إِنَّ ذَٰلِكَ عَلَى ٱللَّهِ يَسِيرٌ}$$

No affliction (disaster, calamity) strikes the earth nor in yourselves, except that it is in a Book (it has been pre-recorded) before We bring it into existence. Indeed, that for Allāh is easy (simple).

However, it is not only Jewish belief, but the belief of many who acclaim that Macro-Cosmological events, as well as Micro-Earthly events, are either spontaneous or randomly afflicted by 'spontaneous events', and only intelligent beings (humans, to be precise) are the unique creatures capable and in control of 'decisive events'. This is the misconception of 'Free will' which deludes humanity into believing it is a superior being. Adopting an ideology of 'Free will' instead of 'Ability to Choose' plunges one's soul into an ocean of Ignorance, Arrogance, Defiance, and Disbelief, akin to the ideology of Iblīs.

$$\text{يَـٰٓأَيُّهَا ٱلَّذِينَ ءَامَنُوٓا۟ ءَامِنُوا۟ بِٱللَّهِ وَرَسُولِهِ وَٱلْكِتَـٰبِ ٱلَّذِى نَزَّلَ عَلَىٰ}$$
$$\text{رَسُولِهِ وَٱلْكِتَـٰبِ ٱلَّذِىٓ أَنزَلَ مِن قَبْلُ ۚ وَمَن يَكْفُرْ بِٱللَّهِ وَمَلَـٰٓئِكَتِهِ}$$
$$\text{وَكُتُبِهِ وَرُسُلِهِ وَٱلْيَوْمِ ٱلْءَاخِرِ فَقَدْ ضَلَّ ضَلَـٰلًۢا بَعِيدًا}$$

O ye who believe, believe in Allāh and His messenger, and the Scripture which He revealed to His messenger, and the Scripture which He revealed aforetime, and whosoever disbelieves in Allāh, and His Angels, and His Scriptures, and His Messengers, and the Last Day, then surely he has lost the way, straying far away.

[*Sūrah An-an-Nisā 4:136*]

Imam Al-Ghazzali in the *Al-Ihyā Ulūm Al-Dīn* expands the finer concepts interlinking all these, and other aspects that conform to the integrality of the human being. Throughout his work, he uses the term 'Heart' in its subliminal sense, as compared to the biological organ, expressing it as the seat of intellectual and emotional embodiment, that which houses the *Nafs* and *Rū'h,* thus giving it a place of honor in the creation of man.

Of the *Nafs*, he writes (we are paraphrasing to concisely condense his words); *It is, by definition, praiseworthy, for it is man's very 'self', his essence and real nature. His identity. It knows God, the Exalted, and knows all other knowable things by its thirst for knowledge.* He identifies the Soul as that which constitutes the actuality and individuality of man. Its attachment to the name of the individual, and its ability to absorb and comprehend knowledge.

Of the *Rū'h*, he writes; *It is the subtle body whose source is in the cavity of the Heart. Overflowing from it of the Light of Life are sense, perception, sight, hearing, and smell, resembling the flood of light from a lamp (An-Nūr 24:35). Life is like the light that falls upon the walls. The Spirit is like the lamp. It is also that subtle tenuous substance in man which knows and perceives. It is the meaning intended by God, the Exalted, in His statement, 'Say the spirit is of my Lord's affair (al-Isrā 17:85)'. It is a marvelous and lordly affair, the real and ultimate nature of which most intellects and peoples' understandings are unable to grasp.*

This uniquely philosophical classification between the *Nafs* and the *Rū'h* underlines the core principles of Faith and Knowledge as aspects of man's ethereal embodiments in contrast to only physical existence and external rationalization. In other words, the Soul and the Spirit are the innermost aspects of man, both of which communicate and co-exist on foundations of Knowledge and Faith. Not 'information as power' and 'perception as belief'.

While it is no man's right to judge another's faith, because faith is a covenant between the individual and his Creator, Islām has clearly defined the Pillars of Faith, and how we should abide by them. It does not necessarily mean that being a Muslim automatically fulfills the Pillars of *Imān*. Fulfillment is an effort on the part of every individual's *Nafs*. Even a non-Muslim can possibly, unknowingly, abide by the Six Pillars of Faith and the inspiration of accepting Islām, as a way of life, is granted to him by Allāh, because faith *is* a covenant between the individual and Allāh Almighty.

The *Disbeliever* is not a person who is unwary of Faith. The disbeliever is he who has *heard* the message and with a very sober and sound mind, *chooses* to reject it. *Chooses* to disobey his Creator. Hence, he *Disbelieves*. It is a rebellious attitude, resulting in doing all that opposes Divine Decree, not just in the mechanical performance of wrongdoing, but an inherent, inbred trait of evil from within (the *Nafs*). As strange as it may seem, the entire concept of being evil is not something we are born with. Rather, it is something we *choose* to follow by submitting to Iblīs and his whispers because he also *chose* to follow the same path.

When we scan our environs, when we witness the atrocity of human upon human, albeit heinous and despicable, the oppressor always seems to have a justification for his deeds, justified deep within a belief system which has shaped and reshaped itself over thousands of years.

Some may regard these incidences to be isolated in nature, where the word 'conspiracy' is defined as 'lunacy', but those who can see beyond the deception are able to realize a systematic adherence to a doctored structure of belief. One that regards the *Rūh* not to be Divine. One that regards the Jewish Soul to be superior to all other beings.

This belief system is not concocted out of thin air. It is not an adrenaline shot of rash ideas. It is carefully introduced, delicately refined and processed, generation after generation, until falsehood successfully cloaks itself as truth, bound to fail eventually. Yet it is blindly accepted, inherent through a streamlined process, until human thought is replaced by artificial logic. It is enacted in every religious homily through the continual alteration and distortion of Divine Scriptures, *within* Divine Scriptures, by an elite few, foolishly and blindly regarded as Saints and Lords (*At-Tawbah 9:31*).

The same elite responsible for the delineation and conception of the modern age.

The same elite who solicited about the *Rūh*.

Now perhaps we can begin to understand the nature of the problem we are dealing with.

The Qur'ān is very clear upon those who lead their faith astray, and is also very clear on what constitutes the foundation of true faith. Having led themselves astray, those who disbelieve cannot blame anyone or anything but themselves for what is surely destined for them. Outrightly discarding the Covenant of Faith, taking a path of Disbelief, as was the path taken by Iblīs, what then has become of the disbeliever's Soul and Spirit?

What is the Rabbinic criterion of the Soul and the Spirit?

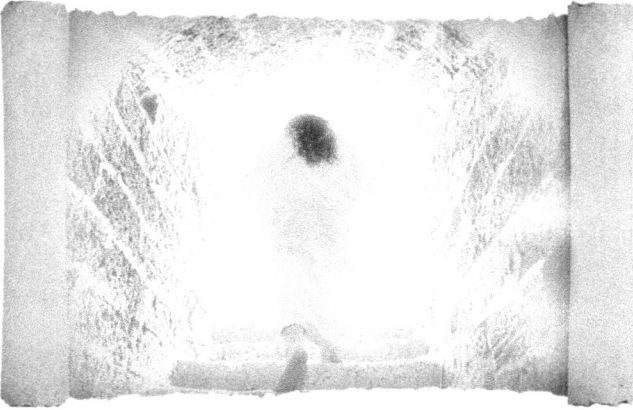

RESURRECTION
AND
REINCARNATION

In light of the deep query as to the destiny of man, where death is absolute, every being asks... what transpires after? Is death the final everything before complete nothingness? Or is there something in its aftermath? And if there is, it being life after death, where does this life take place? In what form? Does the being return to the world of the living, or is there a living other than this?

There are only two concepts regarding the matter, and both have a subtle difference and a subtle similarity between them.

To one is associated the concept of 'Reincarnation,' that the being returns to the same world, a return which when examined, is not forward, but in regression. A 'coming back' to life, so to speak.

To the other is associated the concept of 'Resurrection,' that the being also returns, but not to the same world. To another world in an entirely new continuum.

Both these concepts are tied to a 'return,' and both pertain the body and the soul. The question *we* need to ask then, is not whether *Judaism* upholds a belief in the Soul and the Spirit. When Belief becomes opinionated, people believe what they want to believe. For those who believe in the Soul and Spirit, understand what happens when we die, and for those who do not, surely they are at a loss to find any answers.

No, the question we need to ask is whether *Jews* believe in *Life after Death,* and *Heaven and Hell,* because the very essence of the Soul and the Spirit has everything to do with Life, Death, Paradise, and Hell

The short answer, based on Rabbinic preachings, is 'No'.

Reformed Rabbinic Judaism holds the view that life is life and death is death, meaning, what is alive cannot die and what is dead cannot become alive.

The long answer circumnavigates around the entire concept of Resurrection, and the core of the reason why they rejected Nabi Isa and rejected Nabi Muhammad (peace and blessings be upon them). Both prophets, and all other prophets before them, preached the Oneness of Allāh as well as life into death into the hereafter as a continuum of existence within Allāh's Power. This continuum lessens all value in worldly existence, granting the believer an insight to the profound quest for spiritual enlightenment over the meaningless pursuit of earthly leisure.

First and foremost, Reformed Judaism eradicates the existence of the Spirit and the Soul as two separate entities, fusing both into one, the Soul, regardless of what the scriptures teach or even what linguistics dictate. Thereafter, Reformed Judaism preaches the belief that the Jewish Soul is superior, pure, and exempt from Divine Judgment, because it is a part of 'God's Soul', and therefore *it judges for itself.*

By their belief, Heaven (Hebrew, *Gan Eden*, the Garden of Eden) is only a 'feeling' of pleasure after death, and Hell (*Gehinnom* in Hebrew) is only a 'feeling' of pain after death, both in temporal and transitory forms, so much so that the period of this 'feeling' exists only for a duration of twelve months (in accordance with the Jewish calender), after which the soul reincarnates itself into another 'vessel' or 'body' and life supposedly goes on, but does not end, as that which is 'alive' cannot die.

Truthfully though, whether they choose to accept it or not, this disbelief in Resurrection and Judgment, and this absurd indoctrination comes from a core of fear. Fear of Death. Not out of pain, but out of guilt.

The Holy Qur'ān says;

$$\text{قُلْ يَـٰٓأَيُّهَا ٱلَّذِينَ هَادُوٓاْ إِن زَعَمْتُمْ أَنَّكُمْ أَوْلِيَآءُ لِلَّهِ مِن دُونِ}$$

$$\text{ٱلنَّاسِ فَتَمَنَّوُاْ ٱلْمَوْتَ إِن كُنتُمْ صَـٰدِقِينَ}$$

$$\text{وَلَا يَتَمَنَّوْنَهُۥٓ أَبَدًۢا بِمَا قَدَّمَتْ أَيْدِيهِمْ ۚ وَٱللَّهُ عَلِيمٌۢ بِٱلظَّـٰلِمِينَ}$$

Say (to them) 'O ye who are of the Jews, if you claim to be the Chosen ones of Allāh, from all of mankind, then embrace death if you are truthful (in your claim)'

And nay will they wish for it (death) for what their own hands have sent forth (the crimes they have committed), and Allāh is All-Aware of the evil-doers.

[Sūrah Al-Jumu'ah 62:6-7]

In contrast, both the Muslim and Christian hearts welcome death by welcoming the Hereafter. Stripped of its current and reformed Christian garb (see the chapter *The Birth of Christianity* on how the crux of this reform took place), the concept of Resurrection has always held firm in Christianic faith. The Resurrection of Christ in the End Times forms the structure of Messianic belief, and even in his time, Jesus son of Mary (peace be upon him) did perform miracles in the presence of Rabbinic priests, by which life, death, and resurrection were all made apparent and evident of Allāh's Power.

The Qur'ān says;

وَيُعَلِّمُهُ ٱلْكِتَٰبَ وَٱلْحِكْمَةَ وَٱلتَّوْرَىٰةَ وَٱلْإِنجِيلَ

And He (Allāh) will teach him (Jesus son of Mary) the Scripture, the Wisdom, the Law, and the Gospel.

وَرَسُولًا إِلَىٰ بَنِىٓ إِسْرَٰٓءِيلَ أَنِّى قَدْ جِئْتُكُم بِـَٔايَةٍ مِّن رَّبِّكُمْ أَنِّىٓ أَخْلُقُ لَكُم مِّنَ ٱلطِّينِ كَهَيْـَٔةِ ٱلطَّيْرِ فَأَنفُخُ فِيهِ فَيَكُونُ طَيْرًۢا بِإِذْنِ ٱللَّهِ ۖ وَأُبْرِئُ ٱلْأَكْمَهَ وَٱلْأَبْرَصَ وَأُحْىِ ٱلْمَوْتَىٰ بِإِذْنِ ٱللَّهِ ۖ وَأُنَبِّئُكُم بِمَا تَأْكُلُونَ وَمَا تَدَّخِرُونَ فِى بُيُوتِكُمْ ۚ إِنَّ فِى ذَٰلِكَ لَءَايَةً لَّكُمْ إِن كُنتُم مُّؤْمِنِينَ

And (as) a Messenger to the Children of Israel (say to them), 'Indeed I have come to you with a Sign from your Lord. Lo! I fashion for you from clay like the shape of a bird, then I breathe into it (life) and it becomes a bird, by the permission of Allāh. And I cure the blind and the leper and give life to the dead, by the permission of Allāh. And I inform you of what you eat and what you store in your homes. Indeed, herein is a Sign for you, if you are (true) believers.

[Sūrah āl-Imrān 3:48-49]

The word 'teach' is an unbefitting contextual translation of the word *'Allama'*. Unfortunately, the English language does not bear the capacity to render the deeper meaning, and as a consequence, projected in the mind is a kind of 'teaching' associated with 'classroom teaching.' It must be understood that Almighty Allāh does not 'teach' His Prophets and Messengers in the same manner as an instructor or professor would teach his pupils and students. Nor do the Prophets and Messengers learn in the same conventional manners as the rest of mankind, via sciences or via reading and writing. We say that the Knowledge of the Prophets and Messengers is a Divinely Inspired knowledge which is cast immediately and directly into their Hearts, such that what they know is understood by them purely intuitively.

These miracles performed by Nabi Isa were not just meant to serve as evidence to the Israelites that he was indeed a Prophet, but they were meant to serve as clear Signs of the Oneness of Allāh and the Power of Allāh over life and death.

Islām teaches submission to One God. It teaches the Superiority of One God over all Creation. Before Him, all creation is equal like the teeth of a comb. No one soul is superior to another. Judgment is equal and just for all mankind. Allāh Almighty has the power to resurrect, the power to Judge and the power to decree reward or punishment.

Self-Judgment is not self-reflection. Self-Judgment is selfish, egotistical, and narcissistic, and is formed on the foundation of arrogance and haughtiness. Therefore, blasphemous is the speech that declares the superiority of Soul, whose judgment is not by the Creator, but of itself.

Almighty Allāh is the Ultimate, Wise, and Impartial Judge (*Al-Hakam* and *Al-Hakīm*), His judgment has a predetermined Time and Location, concealed from human knowledge, and it is a Judgment of human responsibility and decision making (between right and wrong) on earth.

The ability given to mankind is not 'Free will' as propagated by Reformed Judaism, or any other doctrine for that matter, rather it is the *'**Ability to Choose** **between good and evil within the defined legislation of Allāh's sovereignty'**.*

In Reformed Judaic belief, however, the concept of resurrection is, for the large part, discarded and distorted to an extent that makes little or no sense whatsoever, rationally, logically, intuitively, or even spiritually by which, despite all, one could not possibly impart even a morsel of respect. Judaism preaches the concepts of reincarnation, an endless cycle until all the commandments constituting Jewish belief are fulfilled. Even though the true concept Resurrection is repeatedly mentioned in most of their scriptures, Rabbinic scholars have always found a way to distort their meanings and interpretations to suit a more 'rational' perspective.

> **We reassert** the doctrine of Judaism that **the soul is immortal,** grounding the belief on the divine nature of human spirit, which forever finds bliss in righteousness and misery in wickedness. **We reject** as ideas not rooted in Judaism, **the beliefs both in bodily resurrection and in Gehenna and Eden** (Hell and Paradise) as abodes for everlasting punishment and reward.
> (1885 Jewish Pittsburgh Reform Platform, Article.7)

They base this belief on the evolving industrial and technological modernization of the world and the newly introduced concept of 'freewill', or 'do what thou will', which strangely enough, also forms the foundation of Luciferian and Satanic cults. Odder still, the concept of Resurrection is recited *every day* in the Jewish daily prayer called the *Amidah,* yet somehow it seems to elude even the most learned of Jewish scholars. In the first part of the prayer, an āyah reads (translated from Hebrew), *You are mighty forever, my Lord; You resurrect the dead; You are powerful to save.*

In the Mishnah Sanhedrin 10, a passage reads;
These have no share in the World to Come; One who says that (the belief of) resurrection of the dead is not from the Torah, one who says that the Torah is not from Heaven, and one who denigrates the Torah.

In Isaiah 26:19;
Your dead men shall live, together with my dead body shall they arise.

So why the blatant rejection? Why the disbelief? Why the distortion of Scriptures? Why the endless and mindless debates when the evidence is so certain and absolute? Is there something missing, or is there an alternative explanation or interpretation?

Alteration and distortion in belief largely occurs when the common man blindly accepts priestly sayings without a proper understanding, and Rabbinic priests and sages have always taken advantage of such ignorance.

They have interpreted every verse which speaks of resurrection to mean that the Day of Judgment *will* certainly occur following the resurrection of humanity, as the Torah speaks, but that Judgment Day and Resurrection only applies to the Gentiles, and not the Jewish people. In other words, only the Gentile souls are subject to Judgment, while the Jewish souls, because of their 'divinity' as the 'Chosen people', are exempted from judgment. This further adds salt to the entire bitter concept of the Jewish soul being purer than the rest of humanity, and even Angels. It follows in the same doctrines of Iblīs when he boasted his self-proclaimed superiority over both Angel and Man by right of birth.

This distortion does not come from an entirely reformed belief system, but rather from select portions which spread out like cancer and eventually become the ruling doctrine. In essence, not every single word in the scriptures is changed or altered, rather a small portion is distorted by which the entire interpretation changes. Plant an evil seed, grow an evil tree, sow an evil fruit, and suffer an evil consequence. Witchcraft and sorcery also follow in the same methods of distorting Holy Scriptures to create blasphemous doctrines by which allegiance is pledged not to Divinity but to demonic rule.

It is the fear of falling into disbelief and evildoing, consequential of such distortion, that Muslim scholars have always held strict discipline when studying the Qur'ān and other Holy Scriptures, because it has been found that by altering even a single punctuation mark or a single vowel, entire Ayāt can end up preaching blasphemy.

Within Judaic scriptures, all Six Pillars of faith have been mentioned and preached in a manner similar to Islāmic scriptures, but in every instance, the Ayāt in Judaic Scriptures and direct Commandments have been altered to bring about a distorted belief system with an inclination to abide by an opinionated and a convenient religious system.

While a small minority of Jews hold on to firm beliefs that can be traced back to the true faiths of Nabi Mūsa and Nabi Ibrahim (peace and blessings be upon them), a large majority have fallen into a way of life pleasing to Iblīs and his ideology. An ideology which confounds the *Nafs* into believing in the here and now, rather than the Hereafter.

Resurrection has been preached in the Torah, Tanakh, Mishnah, and Talmud, but the Rabbis have deliberated and imposed the concocted Kabbalah as the primary spiritual guide of Judaic Scripture. In contrast to all other scriptures, the Kabbalah does not preach resurrection. It preaches the concept of *Gilgul*, which is reincarnation.

This belief in reincarnation states that the Jewish soul, which is purest of all, shall not suffer the punishment of the grave nor the judgment of the afterlife. Instead, the Jewish soul will be revived into another vessel, or body, until it has completed all the *Mitzvahs*, or fulfillment of commandments through good deeds.

The concept of judgment in Kabbalistic belief is paraphrased and surmised as follows;

Upon death, the soul takes a divine path to the heavens. Here the heavenly court provides an account of the soul's life (on earth). Judgment is carried out by the soul itself, and not by a heavenly being. The soul then experiences either pleasure or pain based on its own life in the physical world. Since it has now been 'freed' from the limitations and concealments of the physical state, it can now see 'Godliness'. It can now reflect its own life and experience what it truly was. The soul's experience of the Godliness it brought into the world with its Mitzvahs and positive actions is the exquisite pleasure of Gan-Eden (the 'Garden of Eden'—Paradise). Its experience of the destructiveness it wrought through its lapses and transgressions is the excruciating pain of Gehinnom (Hebrew- 'Purgatory', Arabic Jahannam- 'Abyss of Hell').

This strange and irrational concept continues to impose on the same ideology that the Jewish soul is pure in every aspect. So pure that it is exempt from Judgment in that it achieves godliness to such a degree that it can judge itself, and choose its own punishment or pleasure based on the concept of 'free will'.

Reincarnation comes about after this 'cleansing' process is complete, which according to Jewish belief only lasts twelve months even for the evilest soul. Thereafter, the soul is given rebirth for another chance on earth to complete its path of righteousness under the concept of *Gilgul Neshamot,* the return to earth 'to fill in the gaps of previous lifetimes'.

Jewish belief holds that the entirety of the human race is designated only 6000 years of existence on earth. Towards the end of this period, in Jewish eschatology, is the arrival of the *Moshiach,* the 'divine' ruler who will 'bring all dead souls to life' and will give the Jewish people an eternal rule, on earth, over all mankind. Once humanity as a whole has completed its mission of making the physical world a 'dwelling-place for God', comes the era of universal reward—the 'World to Come' known as *Olam Haba* (also on Earth. Not in Paradise, as the Qur'ān teaches).

According to this belief, the body will be rebuilt as it once was and the soul shall be returned to it in a state of immortality (on earth), meaning 'death will be eradicated forever' with the coming of the *Moshiach.*

In Islāmic faith, the Soul is different from the Spirit, and the fates of both rest in the Hands of God. He decides their Predestination and Judgment. He takes possession of *all* Souls and Spirits. The entire belief structure of spirituality in Judaism is centered on the purity of the Jewish soul and the impurity of every other soul (a focal point on the *Nafs*, not the *Rū'h*), and that the soul is a 'part of God', which further states that the soul is in control of its fate and destiny.

There is an evidential possibility, based on the Judaic belief system, that the intent behind asking about the *Rū'h* was solely to test Nabi Muhammad (peace and blessings be upon him) on whether he would attest or refute this fabricated belief structure. This would explain their retaliation when the response came with a concise and clear-cut statement that *'Ye have no knowledge of it (the Rū'h) but a little'*.

THE SPIRIT
OF
THE MESSIAH

I want to foremost address the use of the term 'Spirit', which has unfortunately become a term associated with *kufr* among Muslims, particularly with certain sects over the past century who have taken it upon themselves to 'purify' the religion to the 'ways of early companions.' This, I believe, is more to their ignorance than it is to any stipulation in the *Sharī'ah*. There is no blasphemy to the term, unless its meanings are rendered as other than what it truly means. Those who have a negative outlook of the term have unfortunately affiliated meanings as they are used in Christian doctrines, particularly with what it means in Christianity as 'the Holy Spirit.' To clarify the matter, as far as Islam is concerned, the Holy Spirit is a truth, but what it means in Christianity is a falsity. To clarify further, the word 'spirit' is a direct and explicit translation in English of the word '*Rū'h*' in Arabic.

In that regard, there are linguistic meanings to words and there are also contextual meanings. When translating, both have to be taken into account. A word cannot be dismissed entirely simply because its use in a particular group means something (contextually), because any particular group does not determine the meanings of words. I felt it necessary to clarify this matter lest a Fatwa be issued against the contents of this book, as you find me using the term 'Spirit' in *all* of my writings. The same applies to the terms 'Holy,' 'Sacred,' and 'Divine,' among several others.

Moving on...

I needn't overemphasize that the concept of the *Rū'h* is complex, unquantifiable, and incomprehensible in and of itself. An inquiry into the nature of the *Rū'h* is futile and pointless for it is not an object that can be studied, measured, and documented. Whatever need be known of it is already known, and anything further than that is pure speculation, which if not regulated will yield incredible fantasies amidst lies and falsehood. This also raises eyebrows as to why the Jews asked about it. What answer were they expecting, and on what criteria would they evaluated the correctness of the response?

Imam Al-Ghazzali iterates the pursuit of the nature or reality of the *Rū'h* in his *Kīmyā' as-Sa'ādat (The Alchemy of Happiness);*

"Knowledge of the Spirit is extremely arduous, since there is no specified path in the Din to its knowledge. Because there is no need in the Din to know it. Because the Din is a struggle, and the sign of knowledge is guidance, Glorified be He has said, 'and those who struggle with Us - We will surely guide them to Our ways... (29:67). And whosoever does not strive on the truth, not is it permissible to seek the reality of the Spirit."

In and of itself, the question asked by the Rabbis is, in fact, a difficult one to address, since aside from their own beliefs, it could also have been referring to the *Divine Rū'h*, or the *Rū'h* breathed into Adam (peace be upon him) when he was created.

It could also have been referring to the *Rū'h Al-Qudus*, identified as the Holy Spirit of Jibrīl (peace be upon him), and strangely so, it can also refer to the *Rū'h* of the Messiah himself, as when Allāh Almighty ordained his birth and breathed into him, through Jibrīl, of his own Spirit, he became *Rū'hullah* and *Kalimatullah (An-an-Nisā 4:171).*

Rabbinic belief holds that the *Soul* was breathed only into the Jewish 'Chosen People', and while other humans do have a soul, theirs is no different than the souls of animals, which constitutes the Jewish belief in their Birth Right of Supremacy over all mankind. It cannot be emphasized enough that Iblīs held the same view of a birthright of supremacy over mankind in his defiance against Allāh's Command.

Prior to the coming of Nabi Muhammad (peace and blessings be upon him) the popular belief held was that Jesus had been *'raised unto Heaven after he was crucified, and he died on the cross, suffering for mankind's sins'.* However, until the Qur'ān revealed it, no one knew that Nabi Isa (peace be upon him) was *not* crucified, nor did he die, he was indeed raised unto the Heavens, and is constantly being strengthened by the *Rū'h Al-Qudus* (Holy Spirit) as the Ayāt describe;

$$\text{إِذْ أَيَّدتُّكَ بِرُوحِ ٱلْقُدُسِ}$$

...I strengthened you (Isa son of Maryam) with the Rū'h Al-Qudus (the Holy Spirit)...

[Sūrah al-Mā'idah 5:110]

$$\text{وَءَاتَيْنَا عِيسَى ٱبْنَ مَرْيَمَ ٱلْبَيِّنَـٰتِ وَأَيَّدْنَـٰهُ بِرُوحِ ٱلْقُدُسِ}$$

...and we gave Isa son of Maryam the clear Signs, and We strengthened him with the Rū'h Al-Qudus (the Holy Spirit)...

[Sūrah al-Baqarah 2:87]

Nor was it known that Allāh Most High had breathed a special *Rū'h* into Maryam (peace and blessing be upon her), by which her son became known as *Rū'hullah* (Allāh's spirit).

$$\text{وَٱلَّتِىٓ أَحْصَنَتْ فَرْجَهَا فَنَفَخْنَا فِيهَا مِن رُّوحِنَا وَجَعَلْنَـٰهَا وَٱبْنَهَآ}$$
$$\text{ءَايَةً لِّلْعَـٰلَمِينَ}$$

And she (Maryam) who guarded her chastity, so We breathed into her of Our Rū'h (spirit) and We made her and her son a Sign for the worlds.

[Sūrah al-Anbiyāh 21:91]

The miraculous birth of Nabi Isa had been disputed for centuries before, and even the honor of blessed Maryam had been cast about until the Qur'ān upheld her in the highest of statuses;

$$\text{وَإِذْ قَالَتِ ٱلْمَلَـٰٓئِكَةُ يَـٰمَرْيَمُ إِنَّ ٱللَّهَ ٱصْطَفَـٰكِ وَطَهَّرَكِ}$$
$$\text{وَٱصْطَفَـٰكِ عَلَىٰ نِسَآءِ ٱلْعَـٰلَمِينَ}$$

And when the Angels said, 'O Maryam, verily Allāh has chosen you and purified you, and He has chosen you above all the women of all the worlds'.

[Sūrah āl-Imrān 3:42]

67

Further to this, the Qur'ān affirmed Nabi Isa's Prophethood and raised *his* status, and the glad tidings he had brought with him, by which he also became *Kalimatullah* (the Word of Allāh - see my book *The One-Eyed Impostor*), which the Jews also rejected;

إِذْ قَالَتِ ٱلْمَلَٰٓئِكَةُ يَٰمَرْيَمُ إِنَّ ٱللَّهَ يُبَشِّرُكِ بِكَلِمَةٍ مِّنْهُ ٱسْمُهُ ٱلْمَسِيحُ عِيسَى ٱبْنُ مَرْيَمَ وَجِيهًا فِى ٱلدُّنْيَا وَٱلْءَاخِرَةِ وَمِنَ ٱلْمُقَرَّبِينَ

The angels said, 'O Maryam, verily Allāh brings you Glad Tidings of His Word; his name will be Al-Masī'h Isa son of Maryam (the Messiah Jesus son of Mary), honored in the world and in the Hereafter, and of those who are closer to Allāh'.

[Sūrah āl-Imrān 3:45]

This has also been illustrated in their scriptures, in the Book of Isaiah as;

Therefore the Lord himself shall give you a Sign; 'Behold, a virgin shall conceive, and bear a son, and shall call his name Immanuel.
Butter and honey shall he eat, that he may know to refuse the evil, and choose the good.
For before the child shall know to refuse the evil, and choose the good, the land that thou abhorrest shall be forsaken of both her kings.'

Isaiah 7:14-16

This passage from Isaiah speaks of several things, which we will examine in the sequence of events as well as affirm each piece with authenticity from the Holy Qurān. The Lord Himself, meaning Allāh would send to the Israelites a *Sign*, *Ayāh* (āl-Imrān 3:49). This Sign was definitive and undeniable, that the Virgin, meaning Maryam (peace be upon her), would give birth to a son, Isa (peace be upon him), and that one of his names or titles would be 'Immanuel.'

The word 'Immanuel' is linguistically two words, *Imman* and *El*, both from Hebrew origin, where *El* means God and *Amman*, which bears the literal Arabic translative of *Ma'ana* معنى (Meaning).

68

It can be, incorrectly so, combined as *Ma'anah-Allāh* (meaning of Allāh), but its correct translation into Arabic is *Kalimatullah* كلمة الله , The Word of Allāh (āl-Imrān 3:45), where, existentially, 'words' are but the meanings of the essences of things, and the 'Prophet' is one who bears the 'Word of God' to deliver it to the people.

Al-Masī'h in Arabic should not be confused with the word *Al-Mamsuah* which means 'anointed', even though the root word *Ma-sa-ha* gives it the same meaning. In its rightful context, *Al-Masī'h* denotes a more divine meaning with a very specific anchor to a very specific individual, the Messiah Nabi Isa (peace be upon him). We cannot fully understand his miraculous actuality without a substantive study, and of course until Nabi Isa (peace be upon him) returns to us, because the concept of *Al-Masī'h* is complex and multi-layered, sublimely and celestially interlinked with the concept of the *Rū'h*, of which we have limited knowledge. Nabi Isa (peace be upon him) is the only descendant of Adam (peace be upon him), who was born without a Father, to a Virgin Mother, and who has experienced such Divine elevation halfway through his life, destined to complete his time and mission on earth at a later date, with a climactic impact. Because this strange concept is tied to the fate of humankind, it is vital to explore it, within Islāmic guidelines, and understand what Islām defines as *Al-Masī'h*. The Qur'ān explains how and why the profound and divine meaning of *Al-Masī'h* is different than its literal linguistic and translative definition.

The difference between *Masī'h* as 'anointed with oil' (from its original Hebrew meaning), and *Al-Masī'h Isa,* is defined by this constant strengthening, or 'being daintily touched' by the Holy Spirit. It elevates Nabi Isa to the status of *Al-Masī'h; he who is touched by the Holy Spirit (Rū'h Al-Qudus).*

Due to a lack of proper understanding and heavy distortion of the Scriptures, Christians ended up combining the Concept of God, Man, and Spirit, all into one as the Trinity, rather than understanding that God is One, Allāh, Jesus is man and His messenger, and the Holy Spirit (*Rū'h Al-Qudus*) is the Divine breath of life by which the Virgin Mary (peace and blessings be upon her) was able to give birth to the Messiah.

Blasphemy occurs when we assume, as the Jews have so often done, that the *Rū'h* is a 'thing', an 'object' of study, or a composition within physical confines, and so we try to explain it as we would explain 'something' using physics, chemistry, and biology. Rather, Almighty Allāh's Divine āyah clearly states that the *Rū'h* is from his Command (*Al-Amr*, the Command by which the process of Creation begins) and therefore not from his Creation (*Al-Khalq*, the process by which Creation manifests itself by His Decree).

$$قُلِ ٱلرُّوحُ مِنْ أَمْرِ رَبِّى$$

...Say, the Rū'h is of the command (Amr) of my Lord ...

[Sūrah al-Isrā 17:85]

The miraculous process by which the *Rū'h* brings about the gift of life in all things living is, in essence, the *Rū'h* partaking in the Divine process of Creation. Creation begins with Allāh's Command and Manifests into Allāh's Creation.

Science may disagree, but it is through this Divine Miracle of Life that human beings receive the flair of *Creativity*, Imagination, Dreams, and Visions. It is through this miracle that mankind has the ability to create things, innovate and invent things. In essence, it is a *gift* unto mankind, not the natural attribute of mankind by which it becomes a superior intellectual race. While mankind does possess the ability to create, Allāh retains His position as the Ultimate Creator of *all* things, including man.

$$فَتَبَارَكَ ٱللَّهُ أَحْسَنُ ٱلْخَالِقِينَ$$

...So Blessed be Allāh, the Best of Creators.

[Sūrah al-Mu'minun 23:14]

The response to the question asked by the Rabbis left them in a state of humiliation, embarrassment, and to a greater degree, utter perplexion. That the Soul is *not* the Spirit, and by definition, the Jewish soul is *not* superior to any other, rather every human has the Divine Breath of Life in them from the *Divine Rū'h*. At no time, in *any* historical Divine Scripture did Allāh Almighty ever make the claim that the *Divine Rū'h* was only breathed into the Jewish 'Chosen People.'

This was not the only reason for rejecting The Qur'ān's response to their question. The Qur'ān further confirmed that Jibrīl (peace be upon him) played a crucial role in the test they had failed, the test of Nabi Isa coming to them as a prophet, a test they failed from the very beginning. To learn that such a miraculous event had occurred, without their knowledge, that an untouched woman had given birth to a child who could speak as an infant, was beyond their comprehension. The test, so uniquely designed by the Ultimate Designer Himself, was that even though he had revealed the coming of a Prophet to them (His *Amr*), he had not

70

disclosed the actual manifestation (His *Khalq*).

The Pharisic Rabbis, at the time, were left gaping with their mouths dry when the truth was revealed to them, and their false divinity was left to dissipate into dust. There rose in their hearts an envy and hatred for Jibrīl, Nabi Isa, Blessed Maryam, and thereafter Nabi Muhammad (Peace and blessings be upon them). Because they all brought clear signs and proofs, as the Qur'ān describes, which exposed their lies and corruptions and whatever other evil deeds they had kept concealed, including violating the Word of Allāh and placing themselves as the 'divine authorities' over the rest of the populous.

Two thousand years of such treachery has endured on the face of the earth, morphing it, chiseling away at its precious beauty, setting the stage for the final act.

Two thousand years of political, social, philosophical, and spiritual upheaval, all because one kind of people could not accept the Word of God because it did not adhere to their personal ideology and dogma.

As the modern age converges into its finality, the world desperately awaits an era when this upheaval will be settled, when the earth will be cleansed, when mankind will taste, for the first time in its history, the divine sweetness of peace on earth. The world awaits its beloved Messiah, the True Messiah. Jesus, son of Mary. Nabi Isa, son of blessed Maryam (peace and blessings be upon them).

In order for Nabi Isa to descend in our time, or in the near future, logic dictates that he must have some knowledge of the state of the world as it has been for the last two thousand years, and its state upon the moment of his descent. He will need to know how his *Ummah* (people) differed from other *Ummah(s)*. He will need a means by which he will battle the Jewish sect who rejected him once, and have spread their corruption on earth, and a means by which he will bring peace between all the nations and peoples of the earth.

The Qur'ān explains how this will be possible;

$$وَإِذْ عَلَّمْتُكَ ٱلْكِتَـٰبَ وَٱلْحِكْمَةَ وَٱلتَّوْرَٰةَ وَٱلْإِنجِيلَ$$

and I taught you the Book (the Scriptures, the Qur'ān), the Wisdom, the Tawrāt (the Law of Allāh), and the Injīl (the Good News)...'

[Sūrah al-al-Mā'idah 5:110]

71

وَيُعَلِّمُهُ ٱلْكِتَـٰبَ وَٱلْحِكْمَةَ وَٱلتَّوْرَٰةَ وَٱلْإِنجِيلَ

And He (Allāh) will teach him (Isa son of Maryam) the Book, the Wisdom, the Tawrāt, and the Injīl.

[Sūrah āl-Imrān 3:48]

The 'Book' here refers to *all* the Holy Scriptures including the Qur'ān, the Tawrāt is the Law of Allāh revealed the Nabi Mūsa, and the Injīl is the Gospel, the Message he, Nabi Isa, was given to deliver to Children of Israel. Because Nabi Isa will descend to a people who are chiefly comprised of two separate *Ummah(s)*, the descendants of Ismā'īl and the descendants of Is'haq, both of whom believe in him by following the Religion of Ibrahim, he will need a means by which to bridge the gap and bring unity between them, which is Wisdom. Regardless of the variances in religious structure, Christians, Muslims, and a select measure of Jews all hold a firm belief in Nabi Isa as the true and forthcoming messiah. Those Jews and Christians, reformed and allied with each other (*al-Mā'idah 5:51*, Refer to *Tyrants of the Modern Age* for more details on this alliance) will have to decide whether they wish to repeat the same grave mistakes of their past. The test upon all of humanity will be to distinguish between the True and the False Messiah

The Qur'ān has directed us to preach Islām by a means of wisdom, and this is how Nabi Isa will preach the Oneness of Allāh and the true Religion of Ibrahim (Islām) to a people who *are not* Muslim, to a people who *are* Muslim and have Islām in their hearts, and also to a people who are Muslim but have *forgone* Islām in their hearts.

The Ayāt above also explain how Nabi Isa will be able to grasp what the current or future state of the world will be, with the aid of Divine Knowledge (not *information*) bestowed upon him with the constant strengthening by the *Rū'h Al-Qudus*, Jibrīl (peace be upon him), who was also responsible for delivering Allāh's Revelation (Knowledge and Wisdom) to other Prophets (may peace and blessings be upon them all).

Having endured thousands of years with the belief that they were the 'chosen people' of the *Divine Rū'h*, and that Prophets only came to them, and that indeed the Messiah will bear the *Divine Rū'h*, why did they reject Nabi Isa, when the signs were brought to them so clear and evident?

Because, aside from signs and miracles, like every other Prophet who faced rejection, Nabi Isa also brought about a complete upheaval of their way of life. A way of life which they had fashioned for themselves, adverse to what has been prescribed by Divinity, fabricated and architected in a way that was, and still is, deceptive and deceitful to the people, misleading them into believing that Rabbinic law was Divine Law. They lived by the doctrines and dogmas of dictating the Way of Life, dominating and controlling the minds and hearts of the people, widely spreading Riba and Usury, wickedness and corruption, and the pure idolatry of money, no different than the age we live in today.

We know that the Dajjāl is one man, but if he were a people, these would be the people.

The questions then posed, are these;

If they rejected Nabi Isa, rejected Nabi Muhammad, and rejected Jibrīl, who represents the *Rū'h Al-Qudus*, why do they still believe that their Messiah is yet to come, and will come from a source of divinity?

By what decree do such acts of atrocity follow and conform to the principles of divinity and purity?

The answers are very simple, and a detailed analysis follows in the next chapter.

In short, they do still hold the belief that their Messiah is from divinity, and possesses a divine soul, but it is a fabricated and opinionated belief. *Fabricated* because it is from the Imposter's scriptures, not the Divine scriptures, and *opinionated* because they uttered it themselves. It is not the Word of God. It is a misinterpretation, and an imposed ideology based off their own corrupted doctrines. The True Messiah is strengthened by the Divine Spirit. The False Messiah, the one they are awaiting and desperately trying so hard to usher in, is not.

Nabi Muhammad (peace and blessings be upon him) prophesied that the False Messiah will claim to be a prophet, and will later claim to be a god, and their belief in the Dajjāl's false divinity is proof that Nabi Muhammad's prophecy is now coming true. In other words, so long as they hold this belief, so long as they continue upon this path, the Dajjāl is succeeding in his mission. He may not yet have emerged in his human form, but his ideologies and doctrines have driven his followers' beliefs for centuries. His foundations have been laid, his infrastructures built. From tall buildings and densely populated cities with complicated lifestyles, to technological virtual worlds designed to entrap our minds and hearts. His time draws to a close when he will make his final appearance and take up the position they have reserved for him.

He has already forwarded his claim to Prophethood. He *will* be accepted when he emerges. He will then lay his claim as God, and Jewish scriptures have already been altered to give evidential support to all his claims.

However, Jewish history has always shown that they are not a people who accept Prophetic declarations without proof. Every Messenger ever sent to them had to prove his validity as per their prerequisites, and the Dajjāl is no exception. As stubborn and stiff-necked as they may be (*Exodus 32:9*) they do bear a certain resilience even to the Dajjāl, but not an impossible one for him to overcome.

Given this, he will have to demonstrate a power, albeit illusory, akin to Prophethood in order to convince the Jews, and the rest of the world, that he is who he claims to be. He will need to prove to the Christians that he is Jesus (down to appearing akin to the imagery of Jesus they have so adored for centuries), and he would have to prove to the Muslims that he is Nabi Isa.

He would have to put on an act worthy of praise, were it not heinous and despicable.

Regardless of the display, the *Mu'min* will easily be able to penetrate the veil and *see* the harbinger of all evil, and so the questions then posed are these;

Who is he to those desperately awaiting him?

What value does he promise them?

How have they become so tangled in his webs?

Why can they not see through his deception?

Why do they revere him so much, despite the thousands of years' worth of Revelation descended upon them?

Who is this False Jewish Messiah?

THE
MOSHIACH

Historically, every Revelation sent to earth arrives in a multitude of levels between the simplest form of understanding, delivering the base structure of the Knowledge conveyed, and a rising level of complexity conveying more Knowledge which even thousands of years later can still be interpreted in accordance to present or future circumstances.

The Holy Qur'ān, for example, contains such levels of complexity, whose Ayāt all along the centuries continually hold true to every generation, and will continue to do so until the End of Time. Similarly, the Tawrāt, Zabūr, and Injīl, even the Scrolls of Ibrahim, although sent to specific people at a specific time, continue to reveal circumstantial Knowledge beneficial to modern times. All these, and so many other Scriptures, contain three levels of Revelation.

Ayāt which impose the Legislation of Allāh, Ayāt which define the Governance of Life (including the sciences of life), and Ayāt which convey relevant Knowledge of the Unseen, which include Knowledge of the Future, or in our case, 'Ilm ul-Ākhir Al-Zamān.

Of this third branch of Revelation, a heavier burden is placed on human intellect to enter a realm of Interpretation and understanding, as opposed to simplified reading and explanation, and within the relevant sub-branches, every Sign (Ayāt) regarding the Dajjāl is vague and obscure, not mentioned by name or description. Not because it eludes comprehension, but because

75

like his arrival and presence, so too is the process of acquiring the knowledge a test upon us.

Rabbinic Scriptures contain numerous passages depicting the True Messiah, all, if interpreted correctly, even on base level of logic and rationality, magnificently describe Isa son of Maryam (peace and blessings be upon him).

It must be noted that when analyzing the following extracts, we must be very cautious not to take them as the absolute truth without proper insight. All research and cross-referencing done with Rabbinic, and even Christianic scriptures, has been done with delicate care and understanding, and every word, phrase, and passage has been carefully and intellectually examined. We have only studied these scriptures for the sake of study, and not for the sake of scrutiny, critique, or antagonism. We have included some of their passages for the sole purposes of readership, and to provide advisable evidence. Past Scriptures have undergone several informative alterations, widely condemned in the Qur'ān, but one thing for certain is that Allāh's Knowledge is Divine and Absolute. Written words can be subjected to alteration, but the Divine Knowledge of the Scriptures can never be altered. From an Islāmic standpoint, all scriptures must be respected and esteemed, for as long as their Knowledgeable contents do not contradict the Qur'ān.

In Sanhedrin 98a, a passage reads;

*It is written, 'There **came with the clouds of Heaven, one like unto a Son of Man**... and there was given to him dominion, glory and a kingdom... his dominion is everlasting.'*
(Book of Daniel c.7 v.13-14)

*And it is written, 'Behold your king will come to you... **lowly and riding upon a donkey,** and upon a colt, the foal of a donkey.'*
(Book of Zechariah c.9 v.9)

*The Rabbinic commentary on both these verses is; **if the Jewish people merit redemption**, the Messiah **will come in a manner with the Clouds of Heaven. If they do not merit redemption**, he will come **lowly and riding upon a donkey**.*

In several Hadīth, the Messenger of Allāh (peace and blessings be upon him) has said that Nabi Isa will descend on the wings of two Angels, and the Dajjāl will arrive on a donkey.

It clearly states from this passage, that the Messiah promised to the Jews was not unconditional, as they had assumed. The condition was a test upon them to accept a path of righteousness and earn redemption from their *Kufr*. Had they done so, had they repented, changed their ways and earned their redemption, the true Messiah would arrive as the Holy Prophet (peace and blessings be upon him) described, on the wings of two Angels, denoted above as the 'clouds of heaven'. Failure to adhere to the condition, their messiah, or false messiah, will now arrive, as described by the Holy Prophet (peace and blessings be upon him), on a donkey, denoted in the passage as 'lowly and riding upon a donkey'.

Another passage in the Sanhedrin describes a conversation between a renowned Rabbi, Yahushua Ben Levi, and the Prophet Elijah (Prophet Ilyas, peace be upon him), who, according to their beliefs, came to him in a vision.

Ben Levi asked Elijah, 'When will the Messiah come?'
Elijah said to him, 'Go ask him.'
Ben Levi asked, 'And where is he sitting?'
*Elijah said to him, '**At the Gates of Rome.**'*
Ben Levi asked him, 'And what is his identifying sign by means of which I can recognize him?'
*Elijah answered, 'He **sits among the poor and who suffer from illnesses**...'*
Ben Levi went to the Messiah and said, 'Shalom, my rabbi, and my teacher.'
The Messiah said to him, 'Shalom.'
Ben Levi said to him, 'When will the Master come?'
*The Messiah said to him, '**Today. Sometime later.**'*
Ben Levi came to Elijah and said, 'The Messiah lied to me, as he said to me; I am coming today, and he did not come.'
*Elijah said to him, 'this is what he said to you; He said that he will come today, **if you will listen to his voice**.'*

There are key identifying markers in this passage which point to Nabi Isa as the true Messiah. The Gates of Rome, at the time, were the arches built at the gates of Jerusalem after the Roman occupation. Therefore, the geographical location of the Messiah, at the time, was Jerusalem.

'He sits among the poor and who suffer from illnesses...' is also another identifier for Nabi Isa, who was known to sit and tend to the poor and ill.

Lastly, the timeline of *'Today. Sometime later'* is depicting Nabi Isa's Messianic mission within his own lifetime, if but, as the response came from Elijah, the people would accept him by *'listening to his voice.'*

It is more than evident from this passage, whether authentic or not, the absolute knowledge of the Messiah's coming was conditional upon the Jews. He would only come to them as the Messiah, if but they listened to him, heeded his Message from God, and took the right path as was decreed. The return to the

Glory Days of Israel (during Nabi Sulaymān's reign) was not *unconditional* out of empathy and sympathy for the Jewish people under Roman rule at the time (see the second-last chapter *The Waves*).

In Micah chapter 5, verse 2 says,

*'Truly, He will leave them until **she who is to bear has borne;** then the rest of his countrymen shall return with the Children of Israel.'*

Their own Rabbis have commented (with obvious alterations) as such; (our comments and interpretations are in brackets)

The Son of David (the Messiah born of the lineage of Nabi Daud) *will not come until the Roman Kingdom will disperse throughout Eretz YIsrael* (the Lands of Israel and Judah which were parted after Nabi Sulaymān's Kingdom fell) *for nine months* (which the Rabbis only denote as a 'period of time', as compared to an actual period of pregnancy) *as is stated, He* (meaning God) *will give them up* (restrain the invading Roman pagans) *until the time when she* (they will never acknowledge it, but the verse is actually speaking about Maryam, peace be upon her) *who is in labor has given birth* (to Nabi Isa) *then the remnants of his brethren* (Nabi Isa and his followers) will return with the children of Israel (and reclaim the Holy Land).

The term Messiah, derived from Judaism, is *Mashiah* (noun) in Hebrew. By its native connotation, the term simply means 'smeared with oil', and olive oil was used for its purity and as medication for its healing properties. *Mashah* (verb) means 'to smear with oil' for medicinal use. Because of it purity (mentioned in several Ayāt of the Holy Qur'ān), olive oil was hence used in ancient Israelite cultures to 'anoint a king, priest, or prophet who came into service of God'. It was a ceremony of respect, dignity, and highest regard for righteous rulers and leaders of the Israelites. As culturally depicted in their history, it goes without saying that the Children of the Twelve Sons of Israel (Nabi Ya'qub) *were* God's chosen, but only when they were righteous. As time has endured over thousands of years, today, it is not a matter of *who* they were, rather it is a matter of *who they have become.*

How an honorable, noble, and almost Divine term has become so corrupted and tainted with abhorrence. They no longer refer to the Savior in its original Hebrew denotation *Ma'asi'iah*, which conforms with the Arabic *Masī'h*, meaning 'he who has been touched by the Divine Spirit' as was the birth of Nabi Isa described in the Qur'ān. The term now used is *Moshiach,* which means 'anointed with authority' by way of 'anointing with oil'. It is less the essence of a Savior, and more the essence of a tyrant. It is less a Spiritual Ritual and more a Ceremonial Act.

According to the various commentaries and interpretations of Rabbinic priests, mentioned in the Kabbalah, Zohar, and Talmud, the *Moshiach* is a patron and a savior of *only* the Jews, who will come at the End of Days and take all the Jews to the Promised Land from where they will rule the world for eternal bliss.

The 1885 Jewish Pittsburgh Platform deliberately altered the true meaning of Messiah from its original context to conform with the modern view, the new age of information, but more so to revert all eyes away from Nabi Isa, by deliberating it as 'anointed by authority', meaning, anointed by Jewish Pharisic authority, if and only if the *Moshiach* arrives with the duly promised eternal glory and *proves* himself to be the savior.

In some cases, the *Moshiach* has also been disregarded as an actual 'person', and more as an 'ideology', 'concept', or 'age', also to conform to the 'modern age of information'. True or not is yet to be seen. However, such belief has also trickled into the hearts of some Muslims and Christians alike (with regards to the Antichrist), that the Dajjāl is a 'concept' or a 'system', but true believers must adhere to Nabi Muhammad's teachings that the Dajjāl is a human being.

The Jews, who are still waiting for their savior, believe that the *Moshiach* will be the one anointed as their rightful king on Temple Mount, on the Throne of the Third Temple, in the end of days. According to the Talmud, all the resources of this planet will be made available to his command and control, and he will oversee everything with his *One Eye*.

Nabi Muhammad (peace and blessings be upon him) said, *'...He (Dajjāl) would then walk through the wasteland and say to it: Bring forth your treasures, and the treasures would come out and collect (themselves) before him like a swarm of bees...'* (Muslim)

The Talmud further says that the *Moshiach* will bring political turmoil to the world, with which he will bring the Jews back to the Holy Land and restore Jerusalem as the world's capital. He will be a political and military leader, and will establish a government in Israel which will be the Governing Body of all the senile Gentiles. He will rebuild the temple court system of Israel and establish Jewish law as the law of the planet, giving the Jews power and dominance over the Gentiles. As of writing this book, these events are currently in enactment, both with attempting to officially recognize Jerusalem as the State Capital of Israel, and to commence the construction of the Third Jewish Temple on Temple Mount.

As stage is being set, an advent which would only cover a matter of a few years, the Dajjāl's physical emergence draws imminently closer.

The Talmud carries on with its description, stating that he will also raise the dead, then he will completely eradicate Old Age and Death, bringing immortality to the Jews and those among the Gentiles who accept him, then he will 'rule as divinity would rule'.

I will reserve my thoughts on this subject for a another publication titled *The One-Eyed Impostor: Messiah and False Messiah,* but to summarize here the entirety of his advent, he will first claim to be a prophet, then he will claim to be a god, and those who follow him will be rewarded and raised to 'godlike' heights, and those who reject him will be punished and condemned to servitude. Here we begin to see the connection between the propagation of the Jewish Soul with a superiority over the Gentile Soul, without even delving into the Jewish misconception of the Spirit.

A Gentile is a non-Jew. According to Talmudic, Zoharic and Kabbalistic teachings, a gentile, or a *Goyim* (Hebrew), is the equivalent of a subhuman or animal. The lowest of the low, from the misled Jewish perspective. Meaning, the Gentile possesses the *Nefesh* soul (refer back to the first chapter), whereas only the Jew possesses the *Ru'ach* and the *Neshama*.

Extracts from the Talmud state;

'All children of the Goyim are animals'

'If you eat with a Goy, it is the same as eating with a dog'

'The Goyim are not humans, they are beasts of servitude'

'You are Adam (man), but Goyim are not called Adam'

Now the true intent behind inquiring about the *Rū'h* is unveiled. It was out of arrogance. To uphold their own superiority by their so-called birth-right. To bring the rest of mankind beneath their feet. To boast their informative alterations and corruption to the *Dīn* of Allāh. It was never for the sake of knowledge or enlightenment. The Torah condemns them;

Know then, it is not because of your righteousness that your Lord God has given you this land (the Holy Land) to possess; For you are a stiffnecked people.

Remember, never forget, how you provoked your Lord God in anger; from the day you left the land of Mizraim (Misr; Egypt) until you reached this place (Jerusalem), you have continued defiant toward the Lord.

(Deuteronomy 9:6-7)

PART TWO

THE COMPANIONS

THE
FIRST TEN

And they ask thee about the Companions of the Cave...

We are now entering the realm of the second question. Who are the Companions of the Cave? What is their account? Why is it relevant, more so, what is the relevance of its documentation in the Holy Qur'ān?

The entire event is recounted in Chapter 18 of the Holy Qur'ān, Sūrah al-Kahf, named after the cave, and its concise narration begins with the 9th āyah in the Sūrah and concludes with the 26th āyah.

Numerous studies and speculations have been made with regards to the Companions of the Cave, also known as the Sleepers of the Cave (although the Qur'ān refers to them as Companions, and not sleepers). Our purpose of study is not to evaluate any speculative validity, nor to investigate the Companions themselves, their origin, nature, or the location of their cave. Our purpose is to understand *why* the Rabbis of Yathrib questioned the Holy Prophet (peace and blessings be upon him). Was there a specific intent? Was it merely a deflection? Or was there an ulterior motive?

Conclusively, our purpose is to determine how the event contributes to *'Ilm ul-Ākhir Al-Zamān*.

We will begin by understanding the entirety of the event as it is told by the Qur'ān, and because we have recognized it as an *actual* event taking place in history, we will explore its origin and environ, and all the relevant historical influences that took place surrounding the event. At the end of the study, we will, *Insha'Allāh,* be able to accurately identify the link between the Companions, the events circumventing this period in history, and how they played a significant role in shaping the modern world.

Like so many Chapters and Ayāt in the Qur'ān, Sūrah al-Kahf was not revealed in its entirety. Most of the Ayāt in the Holy Qur'ān were compiled into their current order at a much later date after the passing of the Holy Prophet (peace and blessings be upon him). However, all the responses to the three questions arrived as wholesome accounts, every āyah in the same order as it is today. The responses to the first two Jewish questions came to Nabi Muhammad while he was still in Makkah, during the last couple of years before *Hijra* to Madīnah. It should be noted that the tale of the Companions (Ayāt 9-26), the poor man and the rich man (Ayāt 32-42), Nabi Mūsa and Al-Khidr (Ayāt 60-82), as well as the rest of the Sūrah, were all revealed in Makkah, while the event of Dhū'l-Qarnayn (Ayāt 83-99), in response to the third question, was revealed in the early years of Madīnah.

It should also be noted that the miraculous journey of *al-Isrā* and *Mi'raj* also took place within the same period as the revelation of this Sūrah.

In essence, there were a number of circumstantial macro and micro-events occurring in and around Makkah and Madīnah, which prompted these key Revelations, sent down to address those events.

Whether or not the journey of *al-Isrā* and *Mi'raj* took place *before* the three questions were presented, is not clear, but there is a possibility that when the Jews questioned about the *Rū'h,* they may have also wanted to trick the Prophet into revealing the exact mechanics of his journey to the Seven Heavens. Although this is a matter of speculation, it can be safe to say that they did not succeed one bit in unraveling that Divine Knowledge, despite them still pestering the Holy Prophet about it well after he had migrated to Madīnah.

The event of the Companions, in and of itself, has everything to do with the element of Divine Time and the Interdimensionality of the *Rū'h,* expounding a fair measure of knowledge pertaining to varied states of human existence beyond what secular science has thus far been able to deduce. The miraculous journey of *al-Isrā* and *Mi'raj* also follows in similar pathways, and both events shed more light on the *Rū'h,* more so on the *Rū'h* of Nabi Isa, his rise to heaven two thousand years ago, and the advent of his return.

Strangely enough, tied into the first question of the *Rūḥ*, the event of the Companions also sheds some light on the Dajjāl himself, his varied state of existence, and his influence upon our dimension of time and space preceding his physical emergence into our physical world.

The word 'Dajjāl' does not appear anywhere in the Qur'ān, yet it was only after the revelation of this event did the Holy Prophet (peace and blessings be upon him) speak more and more on the subject.

By correctly identifying the grave and immense might of this evil being, the Holy Prophet directed our attention to the first ten Ayāt of the Sūrah. It is not only for protection, but also for information and knowledge about the Dajjāl and his vile ideology, his *Fitna* (wickedness), namely because at the time of the Prophet and his followers, there was a scarcity of evidence to fully profile the Dajjāl, in comparison to the mountain of evidence that has thus accumulated over the last fourteen centuries.

Therefore, we are now at an advantage to complete, at least to a certain degree, what the great scholars of Islām at that early stage could not.

Let us understand why the first ten Ayāt of Sūrah al-Kahf are vital, not only in recognizing and comprehending, but also protecting ourselves from the *Fitna* of Dajjāl.

بِسْمِ ٱللَّهِ ٱلرَّحْمَٰنِ ٱلرَّحِيمِ

In the name of Allāh, Most Gracious, Most Merciful

ٱلْحَمْدُ لِلَّهِ ٱلَّذِىٓ أَنزَلَ عَلَىٰ عَبْدِهِ ٱلْكِتَٰبَ وَلَمْ يَجْعَل لَّهُ عِوَجَا

All Praise is to Allāh, who has revealed this scripture (the Qur'ān) to his servant, and has not placed therein any crookedness.

قَيِّمًا لِّيُنذِرَ بَأْسًا شَدِيدًا مِّن لَّدُنْهُ وَيُبَشِّرَ ٱلْمُؤْمِنِينَ ٱلَّذِينَ يَعْمَلُونَ ٱلصَّٰلِحَٰتِ أَنَّ لَهُمْ أَجْرًا حَسَنًا

(He hath made it) Straight (and Clear) in order that He may warn (the godless) of a terrible Punishment from Him, and that He may give Glad Tidings to the Believers who work righteous deeds, that they shall have a goodly Reward (of paradise).

85

مَّٰكِثِينَ فِيهِ أَبَدًا

Wherein they shall remain for ever.

وَيُنذِرَ ٱلَّذِينَ قَالُوا ٱتَّخَذَ ٱللَّهُ وَلَدًا

And to warn those who have said that Allāh has had a son.

مَّا لَهُم بِهِ مِنْ عِلْمٍ وَلَا لِآبَآئِهِمْ ۚ كَبُرَتْ كَلِمَةً تَخْرُجُ مِنْ أَفْوَٰهِهِمْ ۚ إِن يَقُولُونَ إِلَّا كَذِبًا

They have no knowledge of it, nor had their fathers. Grave is the word that comes out of their mouths; they speak not except a lie.

فَلَعَلَّكَ بَٰخِعٌ نَّفْسَكَ عَلَىٰ ءَاثَٰرِهِمْ إِن لَّمْ يُؤْمِنُوا بِهَٰذَا ٱلْحَدِيثِ أَسَفًا

Now, perhaps you (O Prophet) will grieve yourself to death over their denial, if they (continue to) disbelieve in this message.

إِنَّا جَعَلْنَا مَا عَلَى ٱلْأَرْضِ زِينَةً لَّهَا لِنَبْلُوَهُمْ أَيُّهُمْ أَحْسَنُ عَمَلًا

Indeed, We have made that which is on the earth an adornment for it that We may test them (as to) which of them is best in deed.

وَإِنَّا لَجَٰعِلُونَ مَا عَلَيْهَا صَعِيدًا جُرُزًا ٨ وَإِنَّا لَجَٰعِلُونَ مَا عَلَيْهَا صَعِيدًا جُرُزًا

And indeed We will certainly reduce whatever is on it to barren ground.

وَإِنَّا لَجَٰعِلُونَ مَا عَلَيْهَا صَعِيدًا جُرُزًا

Do you think that the Companions of the Cave and the Inscription were a wonder among Our Signs?

$$\text{إِذْ أَوَى ٱلْفِتْيَةُ إِلَى ٱلْكَهْفِ فَقَالُوا۟ رَبَّنَآ ءَاتِنَا مِن لَّدُنكَ رَحْمَةً}$$

$$\text{وَهَيِّئْ لَنَا مِنْ أَمْرِنَا رَشَدًا}$$

When the young men fled into the cave, they said, 'Our Lord! Bestow on us from your mercy and facilitate for us from our affair the right way'.

[Sūrah al-Kahf 18:1-10]

It is crucial to study these Ayāt before studying the event of the Companions of the Cave in determining its link with the Dajjāl, as Nabi Muhammad (peace and blessings be upon him) strongly cautioned us to abide by this particular Sūrah for protection against the Impostor.

A more comprehensive analysis of the above Ayāt in relation to the Dajjāl has been made in another book titled, *The One-Eyed Impostor*, but we will explore these Ayāt here with respect to analyzing the second question.

The first ten Ayāt begin with a remarkable statement and declaration, and also as a response to the Israelite declaration that only *they* have been given knowledge and scripture which is divine. By first bequeathing praise unto Himself for having sent down the Revelation of the Qur'ān unto Nabi Muhammad, Allāh Almighty is clarifying not only to the Muslims, but to the Jews who, for centuries, believed that Divine Knowledge and Prophets were the sole properties of the Children of Israel. The emotional drama behind these Ayāt is not arrogance, but an open challenge to those who have altered the Religion and its texts and beliefs. By doing so, they challenged the Lord of Worlds, and Allāh Almighty is throwing the challenge back.

These Ayāt also indicate something else, that the advent of the Dajjāl is tied not only to Muslims, but to the entirety of humankind. The Ayāt follow one another in sequence of the various transgressors and their transgressions, they reveal the kind of people most appealing to the Dajjāl, and the kind of people who are working to usher in his wickedness in the modern age.

The corruption of Knowledge with subjective and opinionated information; the use of the word *I'waj* (āyah 1). The reward of abiding by the true Scriptures and their Knowledge (Ayāt 2-3). The concepts of *Shirk* and association, not only the Duality or Trinity, but also with associating objects or concepts before the worship of Allāh (Ayāt 4-5). The believer's heart grieving when he sees, not just the godless, but even his own people following in the footsteps of the Dajjāl (āyah 6). The materialization of the earth and all its ornaments as a test upon our *Nafs*, and the eventual eradication of it all (Ayāt 7-8).

And finally, following the materialization, thus begins the event of the Companions of the Cave (Ayāt 9-10), indicating their link to the modern age of *Fitan*.

The event of the Companions highlights several key components by which they can almost entirely be mapped to the modern age. Their minority under oppression by a majority which is godless and tyrannical. Their having to follow rules, laws, and doctrines which are either absurd in nature, or directly in opposition to what religion outlines. The growing and evolving trends of society. Complexity of governmental hierarchies and bureaucracies. The worship of other deities, lifeless concepts, secular systems, personalities and icons. And Money.

Most importantly, there is a core element of superiority and supremacy of race and ethnicity.

Once again, our study redirects us to the Children of Israel. The Israelites are descended from the lineage of Ya'qub (peace be upon him) son of Is'haq, and every Prophet they accepted between him and Isa (peace be upon him) was of the lineage of Is'haq. Every other prophet of Gentile descent was rejected by them. Strangely though, the Jews were prepared to accept an Arab prophet (descended from Ismā'īl) if and only if he proved himself as per their prerequisites, but were never quite prepared to uphold Nabi Muhammad with the status of a Jewish Soul.

Allāh Almighty clarifies their fruitless claims by upholding the best of divine scriptures (the Holy Qur'ān) and the best of Prophets (Nabi Muhammad) to a status of highest honor, and clarifies, that although the Israelites had webbed their fingers into previous scriptures, He would not allow their crookedness (*I'waj* in the āyah) to come anywhere near the Qur'ān. This āyah, among many other similar Ayāt, bears strength and hope for the true believer when he struggles to penetrate the reality of the Dajjālic illusion in order to hold dear to his heart, absolute knowledge.

The explicit warning in the second āyah comes not to a specific sect or religion against another. Muslims (who abide by the Qur'ān), Christians (who profess the father and the son), Jews (who have distorted previous scriptures and are the questioners in context), and the godless, the pagan, the atheist, and the *Mushrik* (those who associate other than or more than one god besides Allāh Almighty), are all being addressed collectively under the entirety of humanity. The distinction between those who will earn His favor, or wrath, is the distinction between a believer and disbeliever in His Divinity. There is a grave and eternal punishment for the disbelievers and wrongdoers, and a divine and eternal reward for the believers and the righteous.

It is important to understand the difference between *Believer* and Muslim as a difference between *Imān* and *Islām,* in order to understand the Dajjāl and his mission. One must always remember that a defining characteristic of the Dajjāl is the word *Kāfir* on his forehead, *disbeliever* (refer to *The One-Eyed Impostor* for more details).

The implication of a uniform address to humanity is that the Dajjāl's ambition is to infect *everyone,* including his own followers, and his most powerful weapon is to shift and imprison our perception and belief in the tangibility of our existence, hence the importance of āyah 8.

The definition of Materialism is the *'tendency to consider material possessions and physical comfort as more important than spiritual values,'* and a more philosophical definition is *'the doctrine that nothing exists except matter and its movements and modifications.'*

Our material world, the tangibility of our environ, exists for the purpose of testing our spiritual selves. The enlightened believer acknowledges the material universe as a gift from his Creator, and he praises and gives thanks to Allāh Almighty for bringing him the tools to survive, the bounty to enjoy, and the comfort to ease his time on earth. The tempted disbeliever does not thank nor praise. He does not acknowledge a Divine power, and so he upholds himself as the sower and harvester of the material world, and is ever in pursuit of more and more.

The word *Kāfir* on the Dajjāl's forehead signifies his placement as the leader of the disbelievers, and he uses temptation to increase value in the material universe and lessen the benefit of spirituality. In that way, he is the devil's ultimate advocate, and the devil does not come to us in red-skin and horns, but disguised as our heart's deepest desires.

From the depth of each and every āyah, we uncover more and more of what to expect as and from the Impostor. Herein lies the Knowledge meant to empower us.

Something unique and interesting unveils before us. The Holy Prophet (peace and blessings be upon him) told us, *'If anyone learns by heart the first ten Ayāt of the Sūrah Al-al-Kahf, he will be protected from the Dajjāl.'*

'Learn by heart', while many would argue, does not just mean 'memorize'. Refer back to Al-Ghazzali's definition of the Heart and its correlation with Knowledge and Intellect (chapter 3). The implication made by the Holy Prophet (peace and blessings be upon him), is to 'study, discern, ponder, contemplate, and understand'. While reciting the Qur'ān, as a whole, does bring about an elevation of serenity and protection, learning and understanding its knowledge brings about enlightenment— *Nūr*. It is with this *Nūr* that the believer is able to penetrate and see through the dark veil of the Dajjāl, and this *Nūr* of Knowledge offers a protection unlike any other in our age of information, an age architected by the Dajjāl.

Knowledge is not a subjective study. It is much broader than our perception. It constitutes sense and understanding, not just logic and awareness. In order to search for the Knowledge of how to identify and protect ourselves from the Dajjāl, we have to understand how he came to be. How his initial ideology preceded his advent which is currently preceding his emergence.

History provides the evidence.

THE
COMPANIONS

There are many theories regarding the time and place, along with which there are also many speculations. Some bear plausibility, others farfetched.

The dominant, in my view, is one that places the timeline of the Companions in and around the infantile formation of Christianity. This is given by the description of early Christianity in Ayāt 4 and 5, as well as the word *Ar-Raqim* in āyah 9, and the fact that the entire event has been documented in Christian History, albeit variant from the Qur'ānic account. Because this is an event that occurred on a historical timeline, there is a dire need to explore events surrounding and influencing the occurrence of the Companions.

In other words, we are investigating the holistic circumstances which prompted the Companions to exile themselves into solitude. If this investigation is possible and fruitful, then we will have taken an immense leap closer to understanding why the Rabbis of Yathrib posed the question. More importantly, we will be one step closer to understanding how those events have shaped the world today.

Aside from the Christian version termed as the Sleepers of Ephesus, there are two Islāmic Scholarly theories, among several speculative theories, which attempt to explain the Companions of the Cave. It is important to understand and study both theories in their own respect, but it is far more imperative to distinguish the accuracies of both theories. This is because both theories have differing timelines, which if not correctly studied, with the proper methodology, can result in vastly differing outcomes and conclusions, detrimental to penetrating the End Times.

One theory speaks of a time shortly before the birth of Nabi Isa (peace be upon him) of a Jewish sect known as the Essenes who isolated themselves in the caves of Qumran, where the 1946-1956 Dead Sea Scrolls were discovered. Based on the word *'Ar-Raqim'* in āyah 9, meaning 'Inscription' some have assumed these Essene to be the Companions of the Cave, and that their 'sleep' is only represented here as a symbolic 'isolation' from the rest of the world.

This theory is, however, very weak and irrational, as the Qur'ān extensively describes the actual sleep in great detail and many other scholars who refute this theory state that the 'Inscriptions' are not necessarily the Dead Sea Scrolls, but rather 'Scriptures' as in the Holy Scriptures of the Tawrāt, Zabūr, and Injīl which the Companions took with them for guidance.

In his *Message Of The Holy Qur'ān,* Muhammad Assad renders the expression *Ar-Raqim* occurring in the āyah as 'Scriptures', lending stronger evidence to the Holy Scriptures over the Dead Sea Scrolls. As recorded by Ibn Jarir Al-Tabari (9th-century), some of the earliest authorities – and particularly AbdAllāh Ibn Abbas (7th-century) – regarded the expression as synonymous with the word *'Marqam'* (something that is written) and hence with the word *'Kitaab',* meaning 'Scripture'; and Ibn Zakariya Al-Razi (9th-century) adds, 'All rhetoricians and Arabic philologists assert that *Ar-Raqim* signifies the same as *Al-Kitaab'.*

The theory that Dead Sea Scrolls were *Ar-Raqim*, and of relevance to the Companions of the Cave, is weak because the scrolls themselves were discovered in a cluster of several caves, rather than the 'one cave' as described in the Qur'ān. In addition, neither of the caves, nor the surrounding areas, have any archaeological ruins of a temple as described in āyah 21 (see the next chapter). Archaeological findings have also conclusively reported that the caves of Qumran were only used to *store* the scrolls, and were not 'dwellings'. Most of the scrolls were inscribed in the residential town of Qumran. Further evidence to refute this theory includes the contents of the scrolls themselves which contain texts heavily contradicting the Holy Qur'ān. The scrolls also describe the characters and personalities of the Essenes as contradictory to the Qur'ān's description of the Companions (described as young and faithful). The Essenes were, in fact, chiefly comprised of an older generation, and were a radical and extremist sect of the Jewish Temple whose isolation came not as inspiration from God, but rather from the fact that they were sectarian Jewish authoritative figures who were exiled from Jerusalem by the rest of the Rabbinic authority.

Another theory draws the account from the known Sleepers of Ephesus (a town in modern Turkey), and historians place their timeline midway through the 3rd century. Evidence to this theory conforms with the Qur'ān's description of a dog in their midst, an oppressive and tyrannical state of rule, a singular cave, as well as the construction of a place of worship after they were discovered.

Renowned Classical Scholars such as Ibn Khaathir and Al-Tabari, as well as Al-Razi, along with several other notable contemporary scholars such as Muhammad Assad, Dr. Fadhlur-Rahman Ansari, Dr. al-Isrār Ahmed, Sheikh Ahmed Deedat, and my teacher, Sheikh Imran Hosein, among so many others, have all researched and concluded that the Companions of the Cave were not only of Hebrew descent, but may have also lived in the surrounding areas of Ephesus, Turkey (Anatolia at the time of Roman rule, before it became Byzantium). Again, only Allāh knows best who they were, where they were and how long they slept.

Since the Holy Qur'ān uses the word 'Companions' instead of 'sleepers' as is widely used by Christian narratives, while exploring this event we must be careful to distinguish the fine line between the Christianic account and the Islāmic account, while adhering to the fact that even the Christianic account may contain a moderate measure of accuracy which we can only validate using the Qur'ān. Due to their esteemed regard in both Islām and Christianity, there is almost no doubt that they were true believers of Nabi Isa and the Oneness of Allāh, therefore they are well within the fold of Islām, but we also know that they were not of Arab nor Roman descent, rather they were of Hebrew descent. They were of the Banu Israel, hence the importance of their asking. Considering their ideology of superiority, the Jewish Rabbis would otherwise *not* have bothered with their tale, had they been of any other descent.

Keeping this distinction in mind is very vital when we relate with our Christian and Jewish brothers and sisters, in that there were, and are, many among both sects, even today, who still do hold a belief as true and firm as the Companions of the Cave.

The greatest disputes, among the scholars who research this event, have been the nature of the companions, their names and ages, their numbers and the duration of their sleep. In response to these speculations, the Holy Qur'ān says;

سَيَقُولُونَ ثَلَثَةٌ رَّابِعُهُمْ كَلْبُهُمْ وَيَقُولُونَ خَمْسَةٌ سَادِسُهُمْ كَلْبُهُمْ رَجْمًا بِالْغَيْبِ ۖ وَيَقُولُونَ سَبْعَةٌ وَثَامِنُهُمْ كَلْبُهُمْ ۚ قُل رَّبِّي أَعْلَمُ بِعِدَّتِهِم مَّا يَعْلَمُهُمْ إِلَّا قَلِيلٌ ۗ فَلَا تُمَارِ فِيهِمْ إِلَّا مِرَآءً ظَٰهِرًا وَلَا تَسْتَفْتِ فِيهِم مِّنْهُمْ أَحَدًا

93

They will say three, the forth their dog, and they will say four, the fifth their dog, speculating the Unseen. And they will say seven, the eighth their dog. Say (tell them - those who speculate), my Lord knows best their number, none but a few know (few who have been given that knowledge). So do not argue about them except apparency (with truth), and do not ask of them (the companion) from anyone among them (the speculators)

[Sūrah al-Kahf 18:22]

And in response to how long they slept, the Qur'ān says;

وَلَبِثُوا۟ فِى كَهْفِهِمْ ثَلَٰثَ مِا۟ئَةٍ سِنِينَ وَٱزْدَادُوا۟ تِسْعًا

قُلِ ٱللَّهُ أَعْلَمُ بِمَا لَبِثُوا۟ لَهُۥ غَيْبُ ٱلسَّمَٰوَٰتِ وَٱلْأَرْضِ أَبْصِرْ بِهِۦ وَأَسْمِعْ مَا

لَهُم مِّن دُونِهِۦ مِن وَلِىٍّ وَلَا يُشْرِكُ فِى حُكْمِهِۦ أَحَدًا

And they had remained for three hundred years add nine.
Say, 'Allāh knows best how long they remained. For Him is the Unseen of the Heavens and the Earth. How clearly He sees and hears (everything). Not for them (besides Allāh) is any protector, and He shares not His commands with anyone.

[Sūrah al-Kahf 18:25-26]

As with any Islāmic Science, we must base the entirety our study to be in conformity, validity, and in accordance with the Holy Qur'ān. If Allāh Almighty has not revealed the affair, whether explicitly, symbolically, allegorically, or through implication, speculating over their numbers, their names, the duration of their sleep, or any other minute detail is of no relevance to us. What is of greater relevance to us here, is the Passage of Time. Because everything occurring in our lives, does so with respect to Time, and the Timeline of the Companions is vital to our understanding history as it has shaped the outcome of humanity.

We have so far determined that prior to them making their retreat, Christianity had not yet formed as 'Christianity'. It was a scattering and a split between those who believed in Nabi Isa (who were further subdivided into numerous other sects), and those who did not. This was known as the Schism of Judaism, preceding the official indoctrination of Christianity as a formal religion of the State (of the Roman Empire).

Indeed, many of the Christians who later came to accept Islām and Nabi Muhammad as the Messenger of God, were among those who clung to the same beliefs prior to the formation of Christianity (see the next chapter on the formation of Christianity).

Therefore, these particular youths were the few righteous descendants of Banu Israel. They were not Roman. They were not Christian. They were the kind of Banu Israel who shall, *Insha-Allāh*, earn Paradise on their own merits.

Let us explore their tale as it has been rightfully told by the Holy Qur'ān in Chapter 18, Sūrah al-Kahf;

فَضَرَبْنَا عَلَىٰٓ ءَاذَانِهِمْ فِى ٱلْكَهْفِ سِنِينَ عَدَدًا

So We cast (a veil) over their ears (their hearing) in the cave for a great number of years. [11]

Scholars have understood the 'Veil over the ears' as a kind of sleep where the eyes remain open. Let us first understand the definition of 'sleep' in the context of the event.

While the actuality of this kind of sleep remains solely in the Knowledge of Allāh Almighty, we can, to some extent, attempt to understand with what little we know in order to relate with what the Ayāt are speaking of. Scientifically, during normal human sleep (an eight-hour cycle), the stage of sleep where the eyes remain open, or partially open, is chiefly characterized during a REM sleep cycle, or Rapid Eye Movement. A deeper state of sleep also exists, which is not sleep as much as it is a comatose state known as a Vegetative State, during which the eyes can remain open, but all vital senses are unresponsive. By and large, sleep is categorized as a 'state of existence' very much like 'conscious and unconscious states of existence'.

In Islāmic Spiritual Sciences, sleep is characterized akin to death (unconscious state), where the *Rūh* departs, temporarily, from the *Jism* (body). Sūrah Al-An'ām 6:60, and Sūrah Az-Zumar 39:42 explain the process where the Spirit leaves the body by night (when asleep) and returns for those whom death has not yet been ordained.

In order to understand the varied transitional states the Companions underwent, it is advisable not regard the process as 'sleep', but rather as a 'State of Existence'.

ثُمَّ بَعَثْنَٰهُمْ لِنَعْلَمَ أَىُّ ٱلْحِزْبَيْنِ أَحْصَىٰ لِمَا لَبِثُوٓاْ أَمَدًا

Then We raised them (resurrected them) that We may make evident which of the two (groups between them) could best tell the length of their stay. [12]

95

The 'Raising' described here is not so much the phase of awareness, as is the process of the *Rūh* and *Nafs* returning to the body to revive it from 'unconscious' to 'conscious'. The Arabic word used, *Ba'atha*, means 'to raise' and also means 'to send', as in the Souls and Spirits were 'sent back to the earthly realm'. This word, paired with the root word *Labatha*, meaning 'to stay' or 'to remain', describes *'remaining in a particular state of existence', after which their Souls and Spirits were returned to their bodies, 'raising' them from a state of 'unconscious' to 'conscious',* or in essence, *a resurrection.*

'Awakening' in the sense of becoming aware would then follow *after* the resurrection, where awakening would be the conscious integration of *Nafs* and *Jism*, or 'Mind' with 'Brain and Body'. This awakening, from the long duration of Time, was a test upon them to determine the length of Time, the 'Passage of Time' endured, and we can now appreciate the emphasis of understanding Time in its Divinity and its importance in *'Ilm ul-Ākhir Al-Zamān.*

نَّحْنُ نَقُصُّ عَلَيْكَ نَبَأَهُم بِٱلْحَقِّ إِنَّهُمْ فِتْيَةٌ ءَامَنُواْ بِرَبِّهِمْ وَزِدْنَٰهُمْ هُدًى

We narrate to you (O Muhammad) their tale with truth! Indeed they were youths who believed in their Lord, and We increased them in guidance. [13]

Time endures, and its endurance causes events to become historical, and history is as defined, a story from the past. Truth tends to become elongated, fact becomes fiction, fiction becomes legend, and legend becomes myth. Not all truth is lost to history, but how then can we discern the truth from the tales of the past?

As we have analyzed in the previous chapter, the tale of the Companions was not unknown to the people of the land, but like any tale, story or narrative, speculations and alterations are inevitable, because information is subjective, while knowledge is absolute. The Knowledge of the Holy Qur'ān, as revealed to us by Allāh Almighty, is the absolute truth, and the āyah here gives testimony that the only true narration of this tale, or anything for that matter, can only be found in the Holy Qur'ān.

وَرَبَطْنَا عَلَىٰ قُلُوبِهِمْ إِذْ قَامُواْ فَقَالُواْ رَبُّنَا رَبُّ ٱلسَّمَٰوَٰتِ وَٱلْأَرْضِ لَن نَّدْعُوَاْ
مِن دُونِهِۦٓ إِلَٰهًا ۖ لَّقَدْ قُلْنَآ إِذًا شَطَطًا

And We made firm their hearts when they stood up (in prayer) and said (declared), 'Our Lord is the Lord of the Heavens and the Earth. Never will we invoke besides Him any other god, for if we did, we would have uttered in blasphemy. [14]

Paired with the āyah above (the Companions described as *Mu'min* in contrast to *Muslim)*, the firmness of the heart when standing in prayer, in and of itself, is at the very foundations of *Imān.*

The testimony of the first Pillar of Islām, the *Shahadah* (bear witness), is a part of the structure of the *Kalimah,* which means *'a declaration, given word,* or *testify',* by which one is held accountable in Allāh's Court. In essence, the declaration is made to Allāh as the *One and Only God worthy of worship,* and it is made in numerous forms, regardless of the structure of words.

The declaration is made by the *Heart ('made firm their hearts'* in the āyah above) of the *Believer* (previous āyah), regardless of language or dialect, although in Islām it is imperative to testify the Oneness of Allāh in Arabic, and it is required sound it out so it is *heard,* clearly and concisely, as a testimony, even if one were alone. The variances of the *Kalimah* can be found in the Hadīth and numerous Ayāt in the Qur'ān such as the entire Sūrah Ikhlaas, and even the āyah above. The words used by the Companions (as the āyah describes) may differ in structure and dialect (of that time), but in essence, they concisely define the declaration of One God, rooted into their Hearts by way of belief and faith (*Imān*).

هَـٰٓؤُلَآءِ قَوۡمُنَا ٱتَّخَذُوا۟ مِن دُونِهِۦٓ ءَالِهَةً ۖ لَّوۡلَا يَأۡتُونَ عَلَيۡهِم بِسُلۡطَـٰنِۭ بَيِّنٍ ۖ فَمَنۡ أَظۡلَمُ مِمَّنِ ٱفۡتَرَىٰ عَلَى ٱللَّهِ كَذِبًا

These our people have taken besides Him (Allāh) other gods. Why do they not approach with clear authority (produce a clear proof of them)? And who can do more wrong than the one who fabricates lies against Allāh?' [15]

In addition to the numerous speculations of the origin of Nabi Isa (next chapter), the speculations of his divinity, and the introduction of the Duality and Trinity, there was also the immensity of paganism and polytheism among Romans, Celts, Greek, and Egyptians, widespread throughout the land. As attested by the youth, neither of these forms of worship had any backing evidence to claim the divinity of their gods, whereas Allāh's Divinity is always evident in the entirety of His Creation as Signs of His Supremacy (*Ayāt*). The origins of Jupiter, Zeus, Odin, and Osiris, might seem illogical and mythical to our modern age, suitable for adaptation into mainstreams of entertainment, but in pre-historic ages, they were strong beliefs among pagans and polytheists.

In actuality, these figures may have truly existed in flesh and figure, not as gods or divine beings, but as humans. Humans who made some impact on society, good or bad. Human, who were later revered as their deeds became widespread in their lands, and just as Iblīs always hopes to corrupt, his whispers would have corrupted the hearts of the people, coercing them into believing that such individuals were gods, when in fact they would have been human.

Herein, the concept of association does not only include gods, deities, or idols, but *anything* placed before the worship of Allāh.

وَإِذِ ٱعْتَزَلْتُمُوهُمْ وَمَا يَعْبُدُونَ إِلَّا ٱللَّهَ فَأْوُۥٓا إِلَى ٱلْكَهْفِ يَنشُرْ لَكُمْ رَبُّكُم مِّن رَّحْمَتِهِۦ وَيُهَيِّئْ لَكُم مِّنْ أَمْرِكُم مِّرْفَقًا

And when you withdraw from them (the tyrants and disbelievers) and what they worship beside Allāh, retreat to the cave, your Lord will spread His mercy for you and will provide for you from your affair with ease. [16]

This is the manifestation of āyah 13, '*and We increased them in guidance*'. While disputes and speculations still endure over the subject, guidance from Allāh Almighty enters the Heart of the believer in the form of inspiration. When we find ourselves on the brink of destruction, on the very edge of our limits, and we turn to our Creator with utmost humility and submission, we open our Hearts and ask for his Mercy (love and affection). Often, when we realize how narrowly we have evaded an impending threat or something detrimental to our lives, we relate to Allāh's inspiration on us (while the secular mind says 'luck'), but seldom do we stop to ponder the relation between *Imān* and *Inspiration*. Thoughts, ideas, notions, intuition, insight, and revelation, are all forms of Guidance from Allāh.

When the Heart seeks and submits to His Divinity, the Heart is Guided by His Mercy.

ARISEN
AS THEY WERE

The human brain, as a three-dimensional object in a three-dimensional world, acquires information in such a way as to enable the mind to perceive and acknowledge the existence of other relative objects in dual-dimensionality. To recognize that there is that which can be seen, and there is that which remains unseen and unknown. Hence the idea that there are always two sides to everything. In some instances, more than two. In actuality, while human existence is limited to a three-dimensional world, human perception *can* possibly transcend multi-dimensionality in terms of *knowing* and *understanding* that which lay beyond the sensorial plane. Scientific rationality cannot quantify or provide evidence of such transcendences, but *spiritually,* all that is unseen can be acknowledged as existent.

Evidence is given by the existence of Adam (peace be upon him), in a world above, and in this world below. Evidence is given by Nabi Muhammad (peace and blessings be upon him) and his miraculous journey of *al-Isrā* and *Mi'raj* through Time and the Seven Heavens. Evidence is also given by Nabi Isa (peace be upon him) and his transcendence to the Heavens above. While these can be categorized as Prophetic miracles and effectual only to the Prophets and not to 'normal' humans, there are incidences documented within the Qur'ān that such transcendental possibilities can occur to whomsoever Allāh Almighty chooses, such as the Companions of the Cave.

The various implications of these accounts in the Qur'ān show that humans do have the capability to exist in other worlds, in dimensions *beyond* earthy confines, and in dimensions *within* earthly confines. It is advisable to refer to *The Divinity of Time and Cosmology* for a deeper study and understanding of inter-dimensionality, but we will highlight a summary for the purposes of understanding the tale of the Companions.

Al-Kawn-ul-Ghaib, meaning the Realm, or World of the Unseen, does not only apply to the Unseen world of the Jinn, but all worlds unseen by human visual perception. As per Allāh's Command, varying from whomsoever He chooses, some of his creatures can perceive others and other worlds, while some of His creatures have a 'veil drawn over their eyes' or 'drawn over their ears', or senses as a whole. For example, Jinn can see Man, but Man cannot see Jinn, and some animals may have the ability to perceive Jinn.

The World of the Unseen can relate to 'a place or point in Time and Physical Space in the observable universe', but can also relate to 'a State of Existence in Time and Spiritual Space across the entirety of the Cosmos', or both. Aspects such as the Knowledge of the Future, Other Worlds, Life after Death, and States of Existence, all fall under the umbrella of *Al-Ghaib*, Unseen and Unknown, at least to human perception.

While we may not be able to categorically rationalize what lies beyond our Sensory Perception, investigating for the sake of knowledge is not beyond reach. The Holy Qur'ān has been sent down to all of mankind as a Book which explains *all* things (*an-Nahl 16:89*) to those who *think* (*Yūnus 10:24*). It is, therefore, important to recognize knowledge beyond what we have *rationalized* for thousands of years, study what the Qur'ān has to teach with an open mind and an open heart, and comprehend states of existence beyond human perception in order to fully appreciate and understand the tale of the Companions of the Cave.

Why?

Because our beloved Messenger of Allāh (peace and blessings be upon him) strongly emphasized it by revealing the unique link between Sūrah al-Kahf and the Dajjāl.

There is a strong and evidential connection between the first ten Ayāt of Sūrah al-Kahf and the tale of the Companions, which begins with the 9th and 10th Ayāt. There is also a connection between the tale of the Companions and the second question asked by the Rabbis of Yathrib. The Jews *rejected* the *True* Messiah, and so the implication is that they have *accepted* the *false* messiah, the impostor described by the Holy Prophet, and all other Prophets before him (peace and blessings be upon them) as the Dajjāl.

Therefore, without a shadow of a doubt, if we are seeking an explanation of our current state of existence, we must consult the Qur'ān, and if we are seeking an explanation of the Dajjāl, we must understand the tale of the Companions of the Cave.

Aside from acquiring the beneficial moral and ethical values from the tale, a surface analysis reveals very little as far as the subject of the Dajjāl is concerned. This is because, in actuality, his existence prior to his physical and biological emergence, is not definitive. It is *interdimensional.*

There are, categorically, two main markers which explain the advent of the Companions, not as sleep, but as 'a state of existence in both *Time* and *Space*'. In the relative Ayāt, Allāh Almighty has *not* used the word 'sleep'. He has described the process as 'placing a veil over them' for a period of Time, then 'raised them' (not 'awaken'), and then asked them 'how long have you *remained*' in that 'state'?

By using the word 'remained' (*Labithu*), Allāh Almighty does not explicitly describe it as 'sleep', but to allow human perception to comprehend this 'state of existence', He says in āyah 18, *'And you would **think** (human perception) them awake, though they were asleep'.* This can also be interpreted as *'You would perceive them to be existent and present, though they were inexistent and absent form our physical dimension'*, meaning they were absent in their individuality (*Nafs*), though their biological selves (*Jism*) were well within observable range.

The youths understood it as 'sleep', as was their human perception. By literal definition, they lay down and shut their eyes, just as all living beings do every night.

In the context of the study, āyah 259 of Sūrah al-Baqarah also describes a similar event of a man who was caused to 'sleep' for a hundred years, after which he was 'raised' (*Ba'atha*). In this āyah, the 'sleep' is described as 'caused to die', but again, the question posed to him is 'how long have you *remained*' in that state?

To understand the concept of 'sleep' in these Ayāt, we must abandon our linear and mundane perception of normal sleep. We must consider 'sleep' as a *state of existence* within our three-dimensional world, as well as in worlds of higher or lower dimensions. Of the kinds of 'sleep' we *do* know, comprehend, and quantify, is our daily eight-hour 'sleep', which is different from a half-hour 'nap', which is different from short-term 'unconsciousness', different from long-term 'unconsciousness', different from a 'Comatose State', different from 'Vegetative State', and different from 'death', which in and of itself is also a form of 'sleep'.

In each of these different states of 'sleep', the mind, the organs, the external body, the *Nafs,* and the *Rū'h,* all exist in various different respective states, and simultaneously in different dimensions. Even within these different 'sleeps', there are different cycles and micro-states of existence.

Therefore, we can acknowledge that the 'sleep' experienced by the youths is of a kind undiscovered by human intellect, and therefore truly puzzling and perplexing to our human perception.

Simplicity is in our ability to explain and understand things, and our Creator understands us better than we understand ourselves. Therefore, to simplify a complex subject, our understanding of the tale of the Companions has been projected in its simplest form; *sleep*.

However, simplicity is not to our limitation. We are a complex creation, and our perception does possess the ability to venture into complex studies. The complexity of the event arises with their endurance in their 'states of existence'. For their biological bodies to exist for such a lengthy period of time, without nourishment, without food and water, without even a sign of age on them, is truly perplexing.

Perplexing only if we do not brave a quest into simplifying its complexity, and our Creator, who knows us better than we know ourselves, has provided us with the tools necessary. Time, Knowledge, and Wisdom.

We will attempt to deconstruct the event from its complexity, and reconstruct it in order to put into perceptive the reasoning behind *why* this event has been preserved in the Qur'ān for hundreds of years, and *how* it relates to the End Times.

وَتَرَى ٱلشَّمْسَ إِذَا طَلَعَت تَّزَٰوَرُ عَن كَهْفِهِمْ ذَاتَ ٱلْيَمِينِ وَإِذَا غَرَبَت
تَّقْرِضُهُمْ ذَاتَ ٱلشِّمَالِ وَهُمْ فِى فَجْوَةٍ مِّنْهُ ۚ ذَٰلِكَ مِنْ ءَايَٰتِ ٱللَّهِ ۗ مَن يَهْدِ
ٱللَّهُ فَهُوَ ٱلْمُهْتَدِ ۖ وَمَن يُضْلِلْ فَلَن تَجِدَ لَهُۥ وَلِيًّا مُّرْشِدًا

And (had you been present) you would have seen the sun when it rose inclining away from their cave to the right and when it set passing away from them to the left and while they lay in the open space thereof. That was from the signs of Allāh. Whoever Allāh guides is (truly) guided. But he whom He leaves astray, never will you find for him a protecting guide.

[*Sūrah al-Kahf 18:17*]

The āyah does not reveal the exact location of the cave, although, by the positioning of the sun's movement, rising on the right and setting on the left, we can deduce that the cave's opening faced north, and Allāh Almighty knows best. The exact geographical location of the cave is irrelevant. Information relative to the study is the astronomical anomalies occurring within this particular dimension of their existence. This āyah cannot be interpreted without pairing it with the corresponding āyah;

وَتَحْسَبُهُمْ أَيْقَاظًا وَهُمْ رُقُودٌ ۚ وَنُقَلِّبُهُمْ ذَاتَ ٱلْيَمِينِ وَذَاتَ ٱلشِّمَالِ ۖ وَكَلْبُهُم بَٰسِطٌ ذِرَاعَيْهِ بِٱلْوَصِيدِ ۚ لَوِ ٱطَّلَعْتَ عَلَيْهِمْ لَوَلَّيْتَ مِنْهُمْ فِرَارًا وَلَمُلِئْتَ مِنْهُمْ رُعْبًا

And (had you been present) you would think them awake while they were asleep. And We turned them over, to the right and the left, and while their dog stretched its forelegs at the entrance. Had you seen them, you would have turned in flight, and surely you would have been filled with terror.

[*Sūrah al-Kahf* 18:18]

Abiding by the methodology of 'two sides to everything', we have identified the Companions to have existed in 'two' dimensions (two states of existence); both within earthly dimensions. Refer to *The Divinity of Time and Cosmology* to understand Outer-dimensionality between Earth and Above, and Inter-dimensionality within the confines of Earth.

Scientifically, both Time and Space are relative (see Einstein's Theory of Relativity), and the Qur'ān has described the relativity of Time and Space in various Ayāt. Relativity means that Time and Space are not stationary and linear as perceived; rather they differ in quantity and vector, subject to the observer. The observers, in this case, are the Companions of the Cave, observing from two different points in both Space and Time. *Biological* (Physical) and *Spiritual* (Metaphysical).

Firstly, they existed in our *biological* dimension where we could *see* them with our *physical* sight, wherein they existed for the *lengthy* period (of 300 years - and Allāh Almighty knows best), and wherein their *biological* bodies were affected by the rising and setting sun in *our* dimension.

Here, the rising and setting of the sun in āyah 17 can be understood as the source of nourishment for their biological bodies. The turning of their bodies, in conformity to the sunlight (*phototropism*) entering the cave twice a day, would have prevented ulcers and bed sores. Prevented the sedimentation of their biological organs. Prevented their bones and joints from seizure, their vessels from clotting. Allāh in His Glory and Mercy gave their bodies a characteristic which science *cannot rationalize*. Allāh being all Powerful, the Sustainer and Provider, nourished their *biological* bodies with as minimal a nourishment as sunlight. He avowed to guide and sustain them in their affair, and He fulfilled His vow. *Then which of the signs of your Lord will ye deny? (Sūrah Rahman).*

103

Now we can analyze their existence on the 'other side'. The other dimension. Since we cannot *perceive* this dimension with our physical senses, we cannot quantify and describe its composition. However, based on the Ayāt above, we *can* understand and acknowledge its existence. When the Ayāt say *'had you seen them'*, the implication is, 'we *would* have seen them' if we had been present in *Time* and *Location,* or in that *Time* and *Space.*

The following analogy requires a broader perspective and understanding, far removed from the rationality of secular science.

The literal description of the rising and setting of the sun, in the āyah above, does not conform to our *physical* dimension, in the sense that within the physical composition of our planetary system, the sun's position is fixed, with the earth's orbit being its relative. Sunlight, therefore, is compliant with the earth's spherical motion. If one were to face north, the sun would rise from the right, which would be east, and would set on the left, which would be west, hence *arising from one horizon*, and *sinking into the other horizon,* like a pendulum attached to a spinning wheel. However, here the āyah describes the motion of the sun in a strange manner, *inclining away* from the cave to the right, and *passing away* to the left. The interpretation here, and Allāh Almighty truly knows best, is visually describing an alternate dimension with an alternate set of Astrophysical Laws, wherein their non-biological 'selves' existed for a *short* period of Time (half a day, as per their perception), and wherein their *spiritual* selves were unaffected by the Passage of Time (memories, thoughts, rational analysis, and perception).

An excellent analogy to interpret this āyah in terms of describing inter-dimensional intersection, is to imagine two archery bows. Refer to my *The Divinity Of Time And Cosmology* for an detailed analysis.

If we place the bows side by side, one tip extending into another, the bows become *linear* (Sequential Time). One portion begins and ends, followed another portion. This can be understood as the *Unidirectional* Passage of Time (always moving forward) such as when describing the ages of human existence on earth. If we place the bows in adjoining arches, both tips touching together to form a 'circular' shape, it becomes a *loop* (Cyclical Time). This can be used to describe the Passage of Time on earth such as when describing a Cyclical occurrence, like the Four Seasons. However, if we *invert* the bows so that their tips point *away* from each other and only the curves touch together at their apexes, we form an *intersection* (Dimensional Time), described here allegorically as when the sun rose and set in an incline *away* from the cave.

The implication is that the essence of their existence, irrespective of their biological bodies, followed one Timeline (in the physical dimension), intersected at a particular point (when a veil was drawn over their hearing), and continued in an alternate Timeline (in another dimension). Both dimensions continued to run independent of each other, one abiding by the physical Passage of Time (our dimension where 300 years passed) and the other abiding by its own Passage of Time (where the fluidity of Time evolved differently).

Interpreting the complexity of their existence (the temporal duality of existence between two dimensions) bears great significance when trying to identify the parallel link between their existence and the Dajjāl's existence, as well as their existence with relation to our existence in the modern world. This temporal duality, physical and metaphysical, biological and spiritual, form of existence creates the evidential possibility that within the planetary confines of the Earth, there exist dimensions other than human, Jinn, and *Malāikah*.

The additional dimension of the Dajjāl.

This allows for a more rational interpretation of the Hadīth of Nabi Muhammad (peace and blessings be upon him) with his recount of Tamim ud-Dari's encounter with the *Jassasa* and the Dajjāl on an island. (Refer to the book *The One-Eyed Impostor*). It provides us with the profound insight of identifying and understanding the manner in which, even though the Impostor has not biologically entered into our realm, his existence among us is evident through his influential ideology through which the structure of society and civilization is being morphed, shaped, and prepared for his personalized accommodation.

The perception of 'sleep' therefore occurred in *our* dimension of Space and Time, and for the sake of our comprehension, the Holy Qur'ān describes their advent in the most simplistic of terms. Sleep.

وَكَذَٰلِكَ بَعَثْنَٰهُمْ لِيَتَسَآءَلُوا۟ بَيْنَهُمْ ۚ قَالَ قَآئِلٌ مِّنْهُمْ كَمْ لَبِثْتُمْ ۖ قَالُوا۟ لَبِثْنَا يَوْمًا أَوْ بَعْضَ يَوْمٍ ۚ قَالُوا۟ رَبُّكُمْ أَعْلَمُ بِمَا لَبِثْتُمْ فَٱبْعَثُوٓا۟ أَحَدَكُم بِوَرِقِكُمْ هَٰذِهِۦٓ إِلَى ٱلْمَدِينَةِ فَلْيَنظُرْ أَيُّهَآ أَزْكَىٰ طَعَامًا فَلْيَأْتِكُم بِرِزْقٍ مِّنْهُ وَلْيَتَلَطَّفْ وَلَا يُشْعِرَنَّ بِكُمْ أَحَدًا

إِنَّهُمْ إِن يَظْهَرُوا۟ عَلَيْكُمْ يَرْجُمُوكُمْ أَوْ يُعِيدُوكُمْ فِى مِلَّتِهِمْ وَلَن تُفْلِحُوٓا۟ إِذًا أَبَدًا

Likewise, We raised them (from one state to another), that they may ask one another. Said a speaker among them, 'How long have you remained (in this state)? They said (in response), 'We have remained (in this state) a day or part of a day.' They (then) said (in conclusion), 'Your Lord knows best how long you have remained, so send one of you with this silver coin of yours (your money) to the city and let him see which is the purest of food, and let him bring for you provision from it, and let him be cautious, and let no one be aware of you.

Indeed, if they come to know of you (if you are discovered), they will stone you (persecute you) or return you to their woeful ways, and never will you ever succeed.'

[Sūrah al-Kahf 18:19-20]

As we approach the dramatic conclusion to their tale, among numerous other morals, two key lessons are to be drawn by the modern observer, us.

The concepts of Time and the Divinity of Resurrection.

The existence of Realms beyond the Earth and the Observable Universe. The Heavens and the Cosmos.

Allāh Almighty unveils before us the fluidity of Time, independent of our existence, and our linear perception of it. Understanding Time in its actuality enables us to appreciate our lives with regards to *Ākhira* (The End). It also gives us the insight, and deepenning realization, that we are but a breath of life away from death, and our most prized, most valuable currency, is our Time. Our purpose, hence, is how we spend it.

Within the event of the Companions, and several other events mentioned in the Holy Qur'ān, lies the evidence of Resurrection. Dust to dust defines our physical and biological beginnings and ends, but the essence of our creation, when appreciated from the Powers of the Almighty Creator, far supersede our mundane perception. In other words, there is more to life than birth and death. Its purpose may not be unveiled in its entirety, but it construes the spirit of Faith in Our Creator.

The Companions were chosen by Allāh Almighty as a Sign unto the rest of humanity, and the entire process defines the process of Life, Death, and Resurrection.

Following resurrection is the process of 'awakening', the consious revival from a previous 'State of Inexistence' to a Biological 'State of Re-Existence'. Here the entire test is finalized, and the results are presented for full accountability and judgment.

Upon their revival, the reintegration of *Nafs* and *Jism* (Mind and Brain), the Companions' first thoughts were to rationalize their perceptions, and they based their analysis on a few simple matters akin to sensory perception. Their clothes were unchanged. Their bodies unchanged. Their thoughts and memories unchanged.

Unwary of what had truly transpired, one among them ventured into town with a *Silver Coin*.

Thus were they discovered;

وَكَذَٰلِكَ أَعْثَرْنَا عَلَيْهِمْ لِيَعْلَمُوٓا۟ أَنَّ وَعْدَ ٱللَّهِ حَقٌّ وَأَنَّ ٱلسَّاعَةَ لَا رَيْبَ فِيهَآ

إِذْ يَتَنَٰزَعُونَ بَيْنَهُمْ أَمْرَهُمْ ۖ فَقَالُوا۟ ٱبْنُوا۟ عَلَيْهِم بُنْيَٰنًا ۖ رَّبُّهُمْ أَعْلَمُ بِهِمْ ۚ قَالَ

ٱلَّذِينَ غَلَبُوا۟ عَلَىٰٓ أَمْرِهِمْ لَنَتَّخِذَنَّ عَلَيْهِم مَّسْجِدًا

And likewise did We cause them to be discovered (by their silver coin), that they (the people) would know that the promise of Allāh is True and that of the Hour is doubtless. When the people disputed among themselves (about the affair of the Companions), they said 'Build over them a structure (in commemoration), their Lord knoweth best concerning them'. Said those who prevailed (in the matter), 'Verily we shall build over them (over the cave where the Companions then died) a place of worship'.

[Sūrah al-Kahf 18:21]

The Silver Coin (āyah 19), depicting Money, regardless of its form today in contrast to yesterday, or to the Companions, is one of the greatest betrayals to our *Nafs* (self-consciousness), and this is largely because of its Materialistic value to materialistic acquisitions beyond necessity, in a region within the *Nafs* which plays host to desire and temptation. It is the region where the *want* is stronger than the *need,* and the value of money becomes worthless currency.

The symbolic implication of the Silver Coin in the āyah, the *reason* why it has been stated, and Allāh Almighty truly knows best, is to bring our attention to benefit of Fair Trade with intrinsic value (the exchange of Silver for food, silver having intrinsic value), as well as the detrimental effects of allowing money to become the governing factor of life, where it ends up being naught but a betrayal. The greater the wealth, the greater the betrayal.

Argumentatively, money construes a key element of survival in the modern age, and the lesson taught here by the Holy Qur'ān is not to regard it as evil incarnate, but tainted with evil properties. If allowed, these evil properties can overcome the benefits of having money as a medium of fair exchange, and the defining factors often tend to be vague and obscure, especially in the modern age and its complexity of Monetary Economics.

What the Holy Qur'ān, and Islām is teaching us, is not to regard money as a defining factor of life, but as a necessity, and to leave it within those bounds of necessity without attachments, emotional or otherwise. Within its moderate boundaries, the *Nafs* will always learn to maintain a balance between the material necessity and spiritual desire, but for as long as money draws desire over necessity, money takes the corporeal form of idolatry, and its worship is attested by the fact that man would rather spend his precious Time in pursuits of money, over spiritual attainment.

Everything that happened in the event of the Companions, repetitively occurs in our world today. They may differ in literal design, but the same key trends recapitulate over and over again. Albeit more complex in design, the base structures are similar in every way. Our modern democratic governments tighten the noose around our necks ever so steadily. Endless taxes and absurd legislations. Our religious leaders cast us out if we speak but a word in contradiction to their opinionated understanding. Within our communities, our own people are ever fabricating their own versions of religion to better suit their own conveniences. Money is the driving force behind *every* ambition, from the age of schooling, to the age of retirement. From the most learned academics to the most influential religious clerics.

The warning comes as thus, *they will stone you*, and then it says, *or they will turn you back to their ways*. Directly translated as, *they will oppress you and persecute you with ideology and punishment, and they will push you to the cusp of changing your ways to suit them.*

In this modern age, they are pushing onto us western ideology, pressing upon us with terroristic ideologies, imposing terminologies such as Radicalist, Extremist, Islāmist, Terrorist, Fundamentalist, *this*-ist and *that*-ist, coercing us ever so closer to *compromising* our own Faith and Religion into something called Moderate Islām or Liberal Islām.

Be wary of this deception, for it is the biggest of all threats on the Muslim Soul.

This is the final, and gravest of warnings given to us by the Divine Knowledge of the Qur'ān from the event of the Companions. Be cautious. Be wary. Do not let them discover you. Do not allow yourself to fall into their ways, for rather you suffer a persecution on your body, than eternal waste on your soul.

Unfortunately for us, in our age, we tend think the adverse. Physical pain is more daunting than eternal punishment. We fear *their* whips, more than we love our *Creator*. We love *their* material bounty, more than we aspire for *His* eternal reward.

Who are *they?* And who is their *leader?*

THE
SCHISM OF
JUDAISM

Within the first ten Ayāt of Sūrah al-Kahf, we learn of 'those who associated Allāh with a son' or in essence, those who embarked on the worship of 'God and a Son of God' (may Allāh protect us from such blasphemy). Ayāt 5 and 6 speak of the key concept of 'association', which is *shirk*, but more so, they explicitly speak of a 'father-son' concept, and although only *one* religious sect is widely known to propagate this concept, in and of itself, it is not a concept unknown through humanity.

Odin and *Thor* (Norse), *Kratos* and *Zeus* (Greek), *Ra* and *Osiris* (Egyptian), *Saturn* and *Jupiter* (Roman), *Lugh* and *Cu-Chulainn* (Celtic), *Enlil* and *Utu* (Sumerian), all among countless more. Almost all of these concepts, traditions, and cultures were, in some form or the other, adopted into Post-Nicean Christianity throughout the centuries, resulting in the various modern western celebrations of Easter, Christmas, Valentines, and Halloween.

The relevance of studying the origins of Christianity is vital because of its links with Messianic study and the formation of the modern world, and also of its resemblance to Judaism, and even more to Islām. It is also important to distinguish between modern Catholic Christianity and modern Orthodox Christianity, and the rift which took place in the 11th-century. Although this is not within the context of our study here, it holds a vital place in *'Ilm ul-Ākhir Al-Zamān,* especially when interpreting the Holy Prophet's AHadīth about an End Times - Muslim Alliance with *Rum*. In order to give the subject its due attention, *Insha'Allāh,* we will extend a separate study entitled *An Ally In Byzantium.*

Both Muslims and Jews, in their own context, have widely regarded Christianity to be a fabricated religion, but what is it truly? Theological evidence shows a strange bond, stronger and more affectionate, between Islām and true Christianity, regardless of a contrast in practice, and more evidence shows a hatred between Judaism and Christianity, regardless of both religions following an Abrahamic origin.

Many would tend to argue, perhaps out of a lack of knowing, that no such enmity truly exists, at least not in the west. On the surface, the arguments are valid insofar as the root definition of the word 'alliance'. Religion is not an 'alliance', meaning religion, no matter its origin, does not have gray areas. However similar it may be to another religion of the same origin, the two cannot blend unless one envelops the other, through hostility or otherwise. It goes without saying, that it does not necessary endorse enmity, for to be human is to exist in nation, race, ethnicity, and faith. Peace is a prevailing factor, and a natural incline.

An 'alliance', however... now *that* is an entirely different relationship altogether, especially when religious doctrine is involved. For as long as Muslims and Christians hold affection for Jesus son of Mary, there need not be an 'alliance' required. Friendship between both *Ummah(s)* is unspoken, regardless of semantic practices. It requires no elaboration, so long as the bond is mutual and respectful. However, were Muslims to condemn Jesus as he had been condemned by the Pharisic Sanhedrin, *any* alliance formed thereafter is void of affection and mutual respect, and therefore, this modern 'alliance' between Judaism and Christianity is purely political, and politics under religion cannot prosper if Religious doctrines are oceans apart. This is because both communities are sectarian of the same origin, and bridging them together is like repairing a broken vase cleft in two. The seam will never be whole, unless divinely repaired, one of the reasons, among many, for Nabi Isa's return to mankind.

The question then posed, is this;

If divine intervention has not yet occurred, meaning the intervening mediator, Nabi Isa, has not yet returned, how can this alliance authentically exist, and if it even does, how does it bear validity and fruition?

The answer is, it *cannot* bear any essential significance, save for material benefit. It is an alliance built for political purposes.

Hence the need to globally create a rift between religion and politics for the sake of giving the alliance its validity. This modern alliance, born of secularism, exists to mask the two halves of the same vase, Judaism and Christianity, and it is known as the Neo-Judeo-Christian alliance (refer to the book *Tyrants of the Modern Age)*. We have been strongly warned against this alliance (*al-Mā'idah 5:51*), and yet, sadly, a large populous of our Muslim brothers and sisters are their pledging unbound loyalty to it by adhering to secular ideologies by way of 'moderating' and 'liberating' Islām.

Miraculously, through the event of the Companions of the Cave, the Holy Qur'ān brings our attention to the unfolding of a remarkable moment in history, a moment which defined and set in stone the parting of ancient Judaism and the birth of Christianity from its loins.

The tale of the Companions is widely known and revered in both Islāmic and Christianic accounts, but strangely left out of Judaic script, and a deeper study of history raises great suspicion over the matter.

The questions then posed, are these;

Why would the Rabbis of Yathrib inquire about the Companions of the Cave, when nowhere in their scriptures, or their historical accounts, is there even mention of this remarkable and significant occurrence?

Aside from them being of Hebrew descent, the Companions were among those who accepted Jesus son of Mary as their Prophet and guiding Light. Why then would a Jewish sect, who disbelieved in Jesus, need to know about the Companions?

The event is very real and authentic, not just a parable. It occurred historically in a tangible place at a tangible Time. A Time when Christianity was taking its infantile steps.

With increasingly heavy resistance from the Roman Empire, and the excruciating arrogance and defiance of the Jews, the early followers of Nabi Isa (peace be upon him) were mostly among the youth, the poor and destitute folk of Roman-Judea. They were of *Hebrew* descent. They were *Israelites*.

Contrary to popular misconceptions, the religion of Nabi Isa was *not* Christianity. The early followers of Nabi Isa were *not* Christians. The entire structural faith of Nabi Isa was following in the religious system of Mosaic Faith (Nabi Mūsa). Regardless of the mechanics of worship, the structure of religion, formed around the Six Tenets of Faith, is the same structure of religion that we Muslims follow. The terminologies, semantics, and exact mechanics may differ, but the Pillars of Islām and *Imān* are the same for Muslims today as they were for Nabi Isa (Jesus), as they were for Nabi Mūsa (Moses), and Nabi Ibrahim (Abraham). God Almighty proclaimed all His Prophets, including the above mentioned, to be pious and elevated among humanity. However, elevation does not make one God, and this falsification is hosted by the devil, riled by the opinions of opinionated scholars, regardless of their scholarly integrity (*Maryam 19:37*). Sectarianism, hence,

111

is the result of an opinion-driven rift sown from the seeds of doubt and confusion.

So when and *how* did the rift take place?

After the Jews, incited and influenced by their Pharisic Rabbis, subjected Nabi Isa (peace be upon him) to cruelty and persecution, many of his followers were forced into hiding, clinging dearly to the teachings of the Gospel (Injīl) and the preachings of their Prophet. Adhering to their Faith was like holding on to hot coals under a tyrannical Roman rule whose pagan, polytheistic belief not only included ancient Roman religions based on planetary and precursor worship, but also a strange adaptation of ancient Egyptian, Greek, Babylonian, Nordic and Celtic polytheism. Notice the replication of the 'father-son' concept. Idolatry and planetary worship were as a result of deepening and darkening roots in witchcraft and sorcery, heavily influenced by Egyptian as well as ancient Babylonian culture, which astonishingly still constitutes the foundations of modern paganism in the form of Atheism, Scientology, and Alienism, which in reality all narrows down to Satanism.

The belief that Nabi Isa (*Yeshu* or *Yeshua* in Hebrew) was a man and a Messenger of Allāh (*Yhwh*, in Hebrew), and his resurrection will come, still held true to many hearts, but under heavy Roman oppression, especially after the complete siege of Jerusalem and the destruction of the Second Temple, the believers of Nabi Isa were forced to part and scatter to escape persecution. During this phase of utter confusion incited by the Pharisic Rabbis themselves, the faithful few held on to a single and universal belief in Nabi Isa and the Injīl. However, parted by the vastness of the empire and an overwhelming Roman rule, the scattered faithful eventually became unsynchronized in religious practice. Some fled into Assyria, Persia and Arabia, and further into Hind (Indian peninsula), Himyar (Yemen), Abyssinia (Ethiopia) and Egypt (recounted as *Misr* in the Qur'ān as it had been since ancient times), while others spread out into Anatolia (Turkey) and further into Roman Europe.

Aside from the surrounding areas of Anatolia, Assyria, Egypt, and Abyssinia, Israelites who believed in Nabi Isa adhered to *Mosaic* teachings, and still do to this day, facing heavy oppression from reformed Judaism, a reform that has been ongoing for centuries, and constitutes a remarkably larger majority of modern Jews.

At this juncture of the 2nd Century, the believers who fled to Egypt and Abyssinia, were beginning to doubt and question Nabi Isa and his Prophethood, innovating a belief system entwined with the ancient Egyptian pagan belief of *Ra* (the sun-god), *Uzuris* (Osiris), and *Hurus* (Horus), in order to ease the transition of converting pagan Egyptians and Abyssinians. Here, we begin to see the consequences of Moderating and Liberating a Religion for the sake of compromising with a secular and godless environ, and perhaps modern Muslims will realize the consequences of their actions and take heed. The process of altering the religion was so slow, subtle and deliberate, over the two centuries or so, it was hardly noticeable among the people.

The Holy Qur'ān truthfully reveals to us the process of Nabi Isa's birth, depicting Allāh Almighty as the All-Powerful Bestower of Life, He who declared 'Be' and Nabi Isa was born (*āl-Imrān 3:47*). Then we see Jibrīl (peace be upon him) who appears to Maryam when she was in isolation (*Maryam 19:17*). The word used in the āyah is deliberated as *Rū'hana*, 'Our Spirit', which is understood as the Spirit of Jibrīl, also known as *Rū'h Al-Qudus,* the Holy Spirit. Thereafter follows the birth of Nabi Isa to a Virgin Mother (*Maryam 19:20*), and this miraculous birth and Life comes from no other a source but Divine. Hence the Spirit of Life breathed into the Womb of Maryam, and was born the Messiah Jesus (*Maryam 19:21-22*).

The entire event does not negate God Almighty, the Holy Spirit, and the Messiah, rather it negates them as one and negates the elevation of the latter two to the status of God. The debate has endured for centuries, between Islāmic and Christianic Scholars, neither backing down from a clear-cut argument, and with all due respect to Christian Scholars, Jesus did not proclaim himself to be God, nor did he proclaim the Holy Spirit to be God, rather, as the Holy Qur'ān describes the essence of what can only be identified as a 'trinity', God Almighty alone is worthy of worship. The Holy Spirit is the Angel Gabriel, and Jesus Christ was a man and a Messenger of God.

Regardless of the obvious, distortions endured, and at the core of the debate was a dispute in the divinity of Christ. The word Christ is *Crist* from Old-English, *Christus* from Latin, *Khristos* from Helenistic Greek, and a derivative of Greek *Khriein* (Annointed) and Hebrew *Ma'asi'iah* (Savior). As we deduced from the chapter The Soul of the Messiah, there is indeed an element of Divinity to Nabi Isa which gives him the more unique titles of *Al-Masī'h, Rū'hullah* and *Kalimatullah*. Regardless of all these, he is still human, albeit a human elevated by God Almighty Himself.

The distortion emerges when the common man regards his fellow man as divine based on the miracles performed.

This distorted version, of what has now become the Christianic Trinity, was heavily disputed by the faithful in the western Roman Empire who were, on the other side of the spectrum, struggling to convert pagan European Romans to the way of Christ. Within Roman Judea, Nabi Isa's disciples were struggling to maintain their faith amidst an outbreak of war between the Israelites and the Romans, which resulted in complete Roman domination and the exile of hundreds of thousands of Israelites. In truth, this was not coincidental nor oppressive, as the Jews have so often propagated in history. They had brought it upon themselves, an event that has been accounted and clarified in the Qur'ān (see the following chapters).

Known better as the 'Religion of the Gentiles', the advent of Pre-Christianity thus began at the turn of the 2nd century, on the baked plains of Asia Minor, modern-day Turkic region. Today, it can be difficult to imagine Christianity without the New Testament, or to imagine Christianity without the term 'Christianity', but at *that* time, it was all but a 'religion without name' since it was originally meant to be *Mosaic, Isaaic,* and *Abrahimic,* based on Nabi Isa's Prophetic lineage from the family of Is'haq.

It should also be noted that Nabi Sulaymān's Kingdom had split between Israel in the north and Judea in the south, with the ruling Sanhedrin and Pharisic Rabbis chiefly dominating Judea in the south. It is from this dominance that Judea was recognized over Israel, as the face of Abrahamic Faith. Hence the terms *Judaic, Judaism,* and *Jewish.* 'Jew' is a derivative from Middle-English and Old-French, *Juiu,* via Latin and Greek *Ioudaios,* via Aramaic and Hebrew *Yehudi,* from *Yehudah,* which is Judah.

The subsequent religious conflicts, internally and externally arising, were hence based on this underlining matter— Was the religion of Nabi Isa, still Judaic?

Among countless more, the questions then posed, were these;

Since the Sanhedrin and the Pharisic Rabbis had classified Judaism as an exclusive religion to Isaaic Bloodlines (through the lineage of Ya'kub and his twelve sons), was there room for conversion? Could a Gentile become Jew? Were the Judean followers of Nabi Isa, Jews or outcasts? If so, who were they now? What religion did they truly follow? Did they still merit a place in the lands of Judah and Israel? As had been promised to those who followed the religion of Abraham, Jacob, Isaac, Moses, David, and Solomon (peace be upon them all). Jesus was descended from the same bloodline, and if the Jews had rejected him, did he still, by Divine Law, inherit the lands and rights of his forefathers?

This posed a major issue. On one end of the spectrum was a Semitic descent rejecting a Messenger from its own lineage. On the other end was a widespread pagan empire who wished to have nothing to do with this religion nor its people. The faithful few sought to spread the Good News of Jesus (the Gospel - *Injīl*) as far wide as possible. Rejection from their own people, forced them to look to the Roman pagans. However, the task was simpler said than done.

Pagan Rome was wrought with what is termed in Islām as a *Jahiliyah* (Ignorant) way of life, and ignorance, by all accounts, is bliss. This 'bliss' revolved around the concept of 'do what thou will', or 'free will', and the pagans were more than comfortable in their ignorant way of life. At core of Roman paganism was Phallic worship, a devilish belief drawn from ancient Egypt and Babylonia, a practice still rooted in modernized Western Cultures. Hence the significance of structures such as the Washington Monument and the Vatican Obelisk among the Sphinx, Pyramids, and the Eye of Horus. Refer to *The Abyss of the New World* for more details.

Religion requires sacrifice, more a sacrifice of inner-self, temptation, and a battle against the devilish urge to 'do what thou will'. Religion means following, not just a doctrine, but a way of life governed by Divine Law, not the law of man. It means sacrificing materialism for spirituality under the Law of Allāh Almighty.

This was not a sacrifice the Romans were prepared to make on any account, at least not wholeheartedly.

As a result, there arose a doctrine following in the ideologies of Paul, regarded as the 'Father of the Church'. He laid the initial foundations, and proposed that for the Gospel to be spread to the Anglo-Roman people, certain Judaic principles had to be abandoned, namely, circumcision. In truth, as crude and ludicrous as it may sound, the fate of Western Society hung primarily on this concept, because the teachings of Jesus were formed on the foundations of Mosaic Teachings (Nabi Mūsa, Daud, and Sulaymān - peace be upon them), laws which required circumcision for a non-Jew to convert to Judaism. This had never before posed an issue, since the Jews always assumed that they were an exclusive faith, the 'chosen people of God', and so it was never really an option for a Gentile to take the Religion of Abraham. Rites such as circumcision were a part of the religious system, performed at birth, as it is today even for Muslims and it constitutes a key principle of cleanliness and purity within religion.

In truth, however, this ideology of the 'chosen people' was never preached nor advocated by Nabi Ibrahim, nor *any* subsequent Prophet including Nabi Daud, Sulaymān, Zakariya, Yahya or Isa (peace and blessings be upon them). It was purely a fabrication of the Pharisic Rabbis (originating with their slavery in Babylonia) who preached the 'holy bloodline of Isaac', thus resulting in the racial discrimination between Jews and Gentiles, a prejudicial and racial ideology still being propagated today through supremacy and superiority (*Tyrants of the Modern Age*).

Paul, who is considered a church father by Catholic Christians, denoted circumcision, among many other requirements of joining this new faith, as crude and rationally impractical (note the colossal difference between *Belief* and *Rationality*), calling for drastic reforms in order to make it *easier* for those willing to convert. His arguments before the other religious leaders stated that, since the Jews had openly denounced the message of Nabi Isa, there was no reason hence to abide by the Mosaic Laws. New religious laws could be formed on the guidelines of the Gospels 'as narrated' by the various disciples.

In essence, when analyzed correctly, it seemed no different than an attempt to invent and introduce a convenient religion as had always been with the predominant Jewish Rabbis. Paul, among various other church fathers, professed that for faith to really grow and become an unstoppable force, the political and military might of the Roman Empire would have to be embraced into its fold, and the only way to do that was to abandon some of the Jewish practices of Mosaic Law. Practices which the Anglo-Roman people would find hardest to accept. As these viewpoints won over, Judaic belief was slowly squeezed out, giving rise to the first-ever independent Abrahamic Religion free of Jewish influence.

However, without adaptation of Mosaic Teachings (the Law of the Torah), the foundations of the new faith were very shaky, not to mention that Egyptians and Abyssinians were also beginning to fabricate their own versions of belief. Aroused by confusion, and of course Iblīs, so began the greatest issue ever debated in Christianity— the nature of Yeshua himself (Isa is the Arabic name, 'Jesus' being the Latin translation from Greek, *Iesous*).

Was he man? Was he god? What was his relationship to god? If he was god, how could he have died? If he was the 'son of god', how could God let him die? If he did not die, what happened to him? What of his miraculous birth? What of the holy spirit? Was it a 'spirit' or 'ghost'? What of his resurrection? If he was god, how could he resurrect himself? These, and so many other questions and speculations created rifts and segregations scattered all across the Roman Empire, east, west, north, and south.

Picture now an era of utmost corruption, oppression, tyranny, and persecution. Nations divided by faith, faith divided by nations. Speculations giving rise to doubt, the doubtless and faithful subjected to torture, and what was meant to be a beautiful, glorious and pious way of life, belief, and spirituality, was steadily becoming a playground of opinionated doctrines, corrupted and distorted by those who *heard* the message, *understood* the message, but *chose*, with arrogance, to defy and *disbelieve*.

All things considered, the Roman empire was now being

threatened by a faith which laid waste to their pagan beliefs. At the turn of the 3rd century, there rose a Roman Emperor by the name of Trajanus Decius Augustus, also known as Trajan Decius, or Daqnayus (Aramaic). He ruled between 249AD to his death in 251AD at the battle of Abritus. According to Roman Historian D. S. Potter, Decius is said to have issued one of the most remarkable and terrible of all Roman Imperial Edicts, stating;

All the inhabitants of the Empire were required to sacrifice before the magistrates of their communities 'For the safety of the Empire' by a certain day. When they sacrificed, they would receive a 'certificate', a libelous, recording the fact that they had complied with the order. The certificate would testify the sacrificant's loyalty to the ancestral pagan gods and to the consumption of sacrificed food and drink, as well as the names of the officials who were overseeing the sacrifice.

This edict sparked a terrible crisis of authority as various Christian sects protested against the orders. Countermeasures were taken in more deceptive forms, as the bishops and their followers were told that their sacrifice was 'on *behalf* of the emperor', and not *'to* the emperor', since the emperor was a man and therefore could not be divine. It was basically a vile attempt at hoodwinking the faithful into committing an act of *shirk* by sacrificing to other than Allāh.

However, anyone who did not comply, including the bishops and his followers, and refused to sacrifice for emperor and empire, were tortured, crucified, and executed. This led to Decius forever being dubbed as a fierce tyrant. Sadly, however, his edicts were continuously renewed by future emperors.

This was the tyranny of Decius, and to better understand his wickedness, let us take a look at how he died.

In June of 251AD, Decius rode into the Battle of Abritus (north-eastern Bulgaria) alongside his son, Herennius Etruscus, and General Trebonianus Gallus, who succeeded Decius.

Herennius was shot down by an arrow early in the battle, and this is how his father, Decius, in the wickedness and greed for the power he so revered, had to say;

In the midst of battle, he proclaimed, *'Let no one mourn; the death of one soldier is not a great loss to the republic!'*

Allāh Most Powerful gave him his taste of death when he too was killed in similar fashion on the same battlefield, and as per his own declaration, no one mourned for him either.

While all this conflict was taking place between the various sects of Christianity, a small group of believers still maintained their faith that God was the One and Only, and Isa was His Messenger just as Zakariya and Yahya were His Messengers.

From among these believers, a group of young men, hanging by the delicate strands between the brutality and tyranny of the

Romans, and the corruption and persecution of the Israelites, decided to part themselves from society as a whole, in order to preserve their faith. Allāh Almighty guided their hearts, and they isolated themselves to a cave.

While they 'slept', the Religion of Nabi Isa, hence the Religion of Nabi Ibrahim, underwent a transformation unlike ever before, and the foundations of modern western civilization, culture, and tradition, were put in place.

THE
BIRTH OF
CHRISTIANITY

As miraculous and wondrous as the tale of the Companions is, it is imperative to regard it not only as a marvel, but as an actuality. Truly, a defining moment in history.

Historians agree that no one moment in time can be exclusively defining to the entirety of the human race. Individually, life is a collection of defining moments, compiled memories and experiences as a result of decisive outcomes. Similarly, humanity as a whole is also a collection of defining moments, compiled as historical events, occurrences, and manifestations. In retrospect, a moment here and now also has a relative moment, or several relative moments, elsewhere. Individually, an event occurring here defines an independent outcome, but holistically, a series of parallel events are required to define collective outcomes, entwined, interlinked and funneled to a conclusion.

Within the context of our study, we are attempting to unveil the End Times of our existence, the decisive advent of a holistic conclusion, which begins with the Dajjāl, which, in and of itself, is entwined with the event of the Companions. However, individually, it is impossible to define the advent of the Dajjāl by a single incident such as the event of the Companions. We must turn our attention to parallel moments in history which collectively defined our present state of existence.

In essence, pebbles in the past lead to landslides in the future. Ripples in the past lead to waves.

The pebbles and ripples of the 2nd, 3rd and 4th centuries

after the birth of Nabi Isa, and during the time the youth isolated themselves, have reshaped our world today in the most mysterious of ways that elude most scholarly minds. In its entirety, the subject may be complex and multi-layered, but not difficult or beyond comprehension.

Essentially, our own history cannot be beyond our understanding, and the key to deciphering the code lies within the pages of the Holy Qur'ān. History penetrated only from informative sources (archeology and science) cannot fully explain the manifestation of Divine advents, especially events that cannot be rationalized by science. Such events can only come from the authentic sources of Knowledge; The Scriptures.

The Divine Word of Allāh remains unchanged for fourteen-hundred years as the Holy Qur'ān, and although Muslims hold a belief in previous scriptures, we fail to acquire authentic knowledge from them due to numerous alterations in history and our inability to sift through the falsifications.

The Holy Qur'ān highlights two core principles uniting the Companions of the Cave; Belief and Scripture. Expanding these principles reveals belief as it had been preached by Nabi Isa and the Injīl, Zabūr, and Tawrāt.

Here arises a major problem for the rest of humanity in later centuries, and in the modern age. How do we recognize Nabi Isa's true teachings? How do we recognize the true teachings of previous prophets? Because *all* those teachings are vital in filling in the gaps of history.

As such, it is imperative to investigate how and when the change occurred. What was the holistic, decisive moment in history, parallel to the event of the Companions, that reshaped humanity to what it is today?

Etymologically, the word 'Church' is derived from Old-English *'Circe'* (Anglo-Saxon language, 5th to 11th century), further derived from Greek *'Kyriakon'* which simply means 'House of the Lord'. The purpose of a House of God as 'a place of worship' originates with the construction of the Ka'abah by Nabi Ibrahim, which was also regarded as such by the Israelites (refer to the historical accounts of Ibn Ishaq, 8th-century). The construction of monotheistic 'temples' came from early Judaism in both definition and structure, a hall of congregation and an altar for preaching, as well as an inner sanctum regarded as the 'Holy of Holies' (Hebrew, *Qodes Ha-Qodasim*. Arabic, *Quds-il Aqdas*). The same constructional layout can be found in modern churches, as well as in Mosques (*Mimbar* and *Mihraab*). In Hebrew, 'House of God' is translated from *'Beit EL'* (Bethel) and similarly in Arabic *'Bayt-ul-llah'*, the House of God.

Even though Islām and Christianity bear some similarity,

120

there is an even greater historical similarity between Christianity and Judaism. In contrast, Islām is directly descended from the Religion of Nabi Ibrahim, through his son Nabi Ismā'īl, who is regarded as the Father of the Arabs. Hence the revelation of the Holy Qur'ān in the Arabic language, and the reverence of Arabic literature both in knowledge (*'Ilm*) and practice (*Dīn*). In essence, Christianity should exist as a 'Isaaic' religion, because Nabi Isa (peace be upon him) is an Israelite by descent. Yet, Catholic Christianity as it has come to be, seems solely a Greco-Roman-European religion, with every word, terminology, description, rite and ritual, derived from Celtic, Latin and Greek tradition and dialect.

History has documented, with evidence, that Christianity did not exist as 'Christianity' for the first three centuries of its infancy. Certain occurrences and ideologies influenced its transformation, which in and of itself was brutal and crude.

Roman rule was, by and large, tyrannical and oppressive. The affluent survived while the impoverished suffered. By constantly adapting varied beliefs of every land and nation conquered, paganism was beyond control.

Following the Schism of Judaism, the various sects of the followers of the Gospel were scattered with their own confined innovations (*Bid'ah*), and the Children of Israel were torn between rebelling against Rome and facing crucifixion, or following Nabi Isa and risk being outlawed by Rabbinic rule.

The 3rd century came to a close with the might of the Roman Empire steadily failing at the brink of collapse, and a large portion of its populous fell into poverty and illness. The various 'churches' stepped in as saviors of the people. Following the reformed doctrines of Paul, converts from all walks of life, but especially the impoverished, began to join the faith in their respective regional sectarian churches.

So sad and miserable were these times, that it felt like the End of Days, very like the divine reckoning of humanity's sins, as Jesus had preached.

Upon the turn of the 4th century, order was once again restored by the Empire, and with this re-stabilization came some of the harshest crackdowns on the faithful. As much as this tightening rule pleased the ruling class and elite of Rome, the scale of the pagans against the faithful was tipping to a point where the empire was doomed to be ripped apart once again.

This is when something miraculous, or rather highly calculated and well executed, happened.

In 312AD a civil war erupted between the faithful and the pagans, shaking the empire to its foundations. At the deciding battle, the battle of the Milvian Bridge, one of the Roman Legion's

Generals by the name of Constantine, had a supposed 'vision', in which he claimed to have been 'told by a divine source' to paint the letters 'CHI' and 'RHO' on the shields of his soldiers, and that if this was done, he would conquer. So it was done, and so he conquered. He won the battle and the day, and became the master of the Roman Empire.

Now as Emperor, he began to repeal all former laws banning the faithful of Jesus, calling for a unification of all the various sects. Before this support from the Emperor, the faithful collectively comprised of only about a tenth of the populous, but within a very short while, they took up half the Roman population, spanning from Anglo-Roman shores to the Eastern Roman Empire. This vast increment of a disunited faith may have raised their numbers, but also magnified their various disputes over the composition of the faith.

The most crucial and mind-boggling conflicts were the issues of the Duality and the Trinity, originating with force from the port of Alexandria and the greater Nile Delta, as well as Abyssinia, Abraha, and Byzantine.

The varied concepts of the Trinity were, in fact, a derivative of the Duality of Existence from the Greek Hellenistic belief in a radical ideology of dualism between spirit and matter, and the belief of 'Christ as a divine Savior' is based on this particular concept. Even though this notion gained immense support by pagan Egyptians converting to Christianity, it was heavily opposed by those who struggled to hold on to true faith, because it made no rational sense with the true teachings of Nabi Isa, that salvation came through moral, ethical and righteous doings.

In essence, Duality and Trinity do not conform to *any* rational belief system, because the existence of God is unlike anything in human comprehension. He does not have an analogy, nor does His Throne, because such Divinity does not exist in a world with left and right and up and down. It is beyond human comprehension and cannot be defined in any analogical or allegorical manner, Duality or Trinity or Otherwise.

In opposition of Nabi Isa's humanity, an Alexandrian priest known as Athanasius the Apostolic, preached that 'if Christ was not completely God, he could not be a Savior', and hence the duality was somehow justified as true of God within man and man within God, transcendental between the spirit and material world.

Due to this dualistic thought, the followers of Athanasius, and the followers of others like him, refused to believe in the Resurrection. They believed that 'Salvation through Christ Crucified was eternal liberation from this human body and human world', and any indication of a 'return' would contradict the 'mission of Christ'. This lead to the belief that Christ's crucification, on behalf of all humanity, was the liberation from his human body, as a god, to the spiritual heaven of 'gods', and only through him can humanity gain passage into his kingdom of heaven. In truth, passage into the Divine Kingdom comes through *following the teachings of Christ,* not through his embodiment.

The event of the Companions of the Cave, hence, was clear and undeniable proof that Resurrection was as real as reality itself, albeit that its concept eludes human rationalization. Further evidence to this can be found in the Apocrypha of the Apostles in which every one of Nabi Isa's apostles, (excluding Paul, the Father of the Catholic Church, who was neither an apostle nor a disciple of Jesus) state clearly that Christ was a Man, he was not crucified, nor did he die, but it was all made to appear so by God as a Divine test of Faith.

This irrefutably complies with the Holy Qur'ān's description that Nabi Isa *was not crucified,* he did *not die,* rather his *Ru'h* and *Nafs* were raised unto Allāh Almighty in a manner similar to the Companions of the Cave, and he will return at his designated time in the near future.

The Holy Qur'ān says;

وَقَوْلِهِمْ إِنَّا قَتَلْنَا ٱلْمَسِيحَ عِيسَى ٱبْنَ مَرْيَمَ رَسُولَ ٱللَّهِ وَمَا قَتَلُوهُ

وَمَا صَلَبُوهُ وَلَكِن شُبِّهَ لَهُمْ ۚ وَإِنَّ ٱلَّذِينَ ٱخْتَلَفُوا فِيهِ لَفِى شَكٍّ

مِّنْهُ ۚ مَا لَهُم بِهِ مِنْ عِلْمٍ إِلَّا ٱتِّبَاعَ ٱلظَّنِّ ۚ وَمَا قَتَلُوهُ يَقِينًا

بَل رَّفَعَهُ ٱللَّهُ إِلَيْهِ ۚ وَكَانَ ٱللَّهُ عَزِيزًا حَكِيمًا

And as for their (the Jews) saying (boasting with sarcasm) 'we killed the Messiah Isa son of Maryam, the Messenger of Allāh', and in no way did they kill him, and in no way did they crucify him, but it was made to appear that way (to them), and those who disagree are full of doubt about it. They have no knowledge of it, except speculation. And they did not kill him, for certain.
Nay, but Allah raised him unto Himself. And ever is Allah Exalted in Might and Wise

[Sūrah an-Nisā 4:157-158]

Yet the speculations endured and multiplied to an extent of ripping apart the hearts of the faithful.

Another major conflict was whether or not to allow those

who had turned away from faith, whether or not to provide a way to redemption for those who had resorted to pagan beliefs when times were difficult and were only returning now that it was convenient.

While these issues tore the empire west from east, Africa from Asia-minor, Europa-Rome itself was under internal siege by those who still clung to paganism and polytheism derived from ancient Nordic and Celtic ways of life.

Out of pure desperation and a dire need to keep his Empire whole, in 325AD, Constantine issued an Imperial Edict summoning *all* of the Empire's sectarian religious leaders, priests, sages, and bishops, pagan and Christian alike, to the coastal Anatolian town of Nicaea, modern-day Iznik in Turkey.

The gathering was arrayed in great splendor, fully paid in Roman coin, by the Roman Empire's treasury (taxpayer money). A total of three hundred and eighteen priests, sages, and bishops, along with their aides, servants, slaves, and concubines, were all treated as esteemed guests with lavish accommodations, exotic foods, and luxurious amenities, all catered at imperial expense, in other words, paid for with taxpayers' monies.

Constantine himself was in attendance. In an elaborate show and display of humility, a masterful ploy of deception, he walked into the Council Chambers, not escorted by personal guards, but by his friends, to advocate a peaceful message that this was not a battle, but a time to come together in unity. The proceedings of this Council, known as the First Council of Nicaea, gathered all the issues of faith from all the different sects, giving each one a center stage to argue its validity with respect to both religion and state. Strangely so, Constantine himself was never Christian, nor did he ever practice Christianity. He was baptized on his deathbed, by Eusebius of Nicomedia, the Bishop of Berytus (modern Beirut), so that he could be 'forgiven in the afterlife'.

In a rigorous political debate lasting weeks at hand, the Council of Nicaea argued, debated, voted and eventually decided on everything, *everything,* from the date of Christmas and how to celebrate it, to the date of Easter and how to commemorate it, which of the Gospels to keep and which to discard, which apostles of Jesus to revere and which to condemn, how to forgive those who turned away, how to administer the communion, how to deliver the sermons, how to set up the hierarchy of every church, how to collect and manage alms, and most importantly, how to integrate the concept of the Trinity with the pagan and polytheistic beliefs of ancient Rome, Greek, Egypt, and Babylon, as well as Mithraic, Celtic, and Nordic practices.

The 25th of December was decided as the date for the birth of Christ (falsely so) because it also celebrated the birth of the Sun

124

God, an ancient belief conforming with the above-mentioned civilizations. Only miracles which complied with the reincarnations of previous deities were allowed in the newly reformed bible. Texts were further altered from 'God' to 'Father', 'Messenger' to 'Son', 'Man' to 'Lord'. Following several more subsequent Church Councils, the Star in the East, the Three Kings, Christmas Eve, Easter, all fabrications upon fabrications, leading to centuries of alterations and additions such as the celebrations of Valentines, Halloween, Advent, Pentecost, Good Friday, Maundy Thursday, Palm Sunday, Lent, Saint 'This Day' and Saint 'That Day', *all* fabrications.

The list is endless, but thus was born a blasphemous and corrupted version of the true faith of Jesus Christ, Nabi Isa (may peace and blessings descend upon him).

His true teachings forgotten.

The authentic Gospel corrupted.

Roman Catholic Christianity born to dominate the modern western world.

The Nicene Creed, still upheld by the Christian Church, states the following;

*We believe in one **God, the Father,** the Almighty, Maker of all that is, seen and unseen.*

*We believe in one **Lord, Jesus Christ,** the only **Son of God,** eternally **begotten of the Father,** God from God, Light from Light, true God from true God, **begotten, not made,** consubstantial of **one Being with the Father.***

*Through him all things were made. For us men and for our salvation **he came down from heaven,** and by the Holy Spirit **was incarnate of the Virgin Mary,** and became man.*

*For our sake **he was crucified** under Pontius Pilate; **he suffered death and was buried.** On the third day he rose again in accordance with the Scriptures; he ascended into heaven and is seated at the right hand of the Father. He will come again in glory to **judge the living and the dead,** and his kingdom will have no end.*

*We believe in **the Holy Spirit, the Lord, the giver of life,** who **proceeds from the Father and the Son.** With the Father and the Son **he is worshipped and glorified.** He has spoken through the Prophets.*

*We believe in one **holy catholic and apostolic Church.***

We acknowledge one baptism for the forgiveness of sins.

We look for the resurrection of the dead, and the life of the world to come.

Amen.

An expanse of studies and scrutinies have been made over this particular chapter in history, by Christianic, Judaic, and even Islāmic scholars. Many of these scholars have condemned the Nicene Creed for altering the true Faith of Jesus, but have also uplifted certain elements of the Creed, such as the prohibition of Usury (*Riba*), adultery, and intoxication. Yet the modern Christian and Judaic world, and by a large extension, the Secular World, has arisen to justify Usury and Interest in every aspect of life, committing adultery without consequence, intoxicating themselves with wine and swine without remorse or guilt of committing acts of *Kufr*.

While the subject, in and of itself, is immensely controversial to its core, we urge the reader and the researcher to handle the matter with care.

Christians and Jews are not our enemies, but among them there are those who can be nothing else but. It is upon the intellectual and knowledgeable believer to tread with care when coming to any kind of conclusion, judgment, or even accusation. It is no man's right to judge another's faith, but every man's right to correct his brother and sister when they have erred. We must enjoin each other in righteousness, truthfulness, and faith, not in mindless debates and speculative conflicts.

To our Christian and Jewish brothers and sisters, we urge you to crack open the spines of your own scriptures, to study every āyah, every word, and seek guidance from your Lord God. We urge you not to blindly follow doctrine and tradition merely because they have been sanctioned by the Church or the Sanhedrin.

THE
JEWISH
INQUISITION

Al-Masī'h, as understood and defined by a majority of scholars, is 'one who is touched by divinity', and the Qur'ān describes it as 'Strengthened by the Holy Spirit'.

Because of this divine elevation, *Al-Masī'h* has the potent ability to do what no normal human being can do, abilities granted unto him from Allāh's Power, such as speaking in the cradle, breathing life into a bird, and bringing the dead back to life.

In history, various Prophets of Allāh were given unique miracles which they performed specifically for their people in accordance with Allāh's will.

Historically, between Nabi Ibrahim and Nabi Muhammad (peace and blessings be upon them), most Prophets were sent to the Israelites, but from among them, Nabi Isa's miracles were, by far, the most exceptional.

Ponder over the wonders of Allāh's predestination and Divine Decree.

The divergence of Nabi Isa's advent was very specific, an advent that was foretold in scriptures prior to his birth. Consider the passage below from Judaic scriptures (our comments are in brackets).

Micah Chapter 5, verse 1 reads;

And you, O Bethlehem of Ephrath (there were two Bethlehems, one in Judah and one in Nazareth, Israel), *least among the clans of Judah* (the lineage of Judah, Jacob's fourth son, bears the lineage of David, Solomon, and

127

Jesus), *From you one shall come forth to rule Israel for Me* (in fulfillment of God's covenant with Abraham), *one whose origin is from old, from ancient times* (a lineage that can be traced back along prophetic lines to Noah).

To clarify a point in the above verse, Jesus was born in Bethlehem of Ephrath in Judah, but prior to his Prophethood, he lived in Nazarath Israel, hence his title as Jesus of Nazareth.

Verse 2 reads;

Truly, He (God) *will leave them* (the people) *helpless* (the Jews were under Roman occupation at the time) *until She* (the Virgin Mary) *who is to bear* (a child through divine miracle) *has borne* (given birth to the Messiah), *then the rest of his countrymen* (all those who follow him) *shall return with the Children of Israel* (the land was not promised only to the Israelites, but to all who followed their rightful leader, Jesus, and so they shall return to Israel together).

Like the Qur'ān, all other revelation from Allāh Almighty comes in two forms.

To quickly summarize, *Ayāt Muhkamaat* are Ayāt which are *Hukm* (law). They are direct and concise, and require only explanation (*Tafsīr*) to be understood. *Ayāt Mutashabihaat* are Ayāt which require interpretation (*Ta'weel*), and interpretation is always subjective to individual understanding and knowledge, to which Allāh Almighty states that only *He* knows their true meanings; (*āl-Imrān 3:7*). It is for this purpose that every scholarly interpretor must always acknowledge that *only* Allāh Almighty can validate the interpretation as authentic and absolute. Hence, in Islāmic Scholarship, interpretations of the Holy Qur'ān and Prophetic Hadīth are always regarded as Intellectual Views of the scholars, to be accepted if, *and only if,* they are convincingly absolute with substantial evidential weight to support them.

In similar pattern, other previous scriptures were also revealed with *Hukm*, and with *Mutashabih*. While Rabbinic scholars refrained, for the most part, from directly and distorting Ayāt which were *Hukm*, Ayāt and passages, like the ones above, were subjected to heavy alterations in their interpretations, or they would craftily 'slip in' a verse to alter a direct command from Allāh. An example of this can be found in the Talmudic Torah;

You shall not charge interest from loans to your countrymen, whether in money or food or anything else that can be charged as interest. (Deuteronomy 23:20)

And to justify their own lust for Riba, the Rabbis added;

128

But you may charge interest from loans to foreigners. Do not charge interest from loans to your countrymen, so that the Lord your God may bless you in all your undertakings in the land that you are about to enter and possess. (Deuteronomy 23:21)

It is only with the aid of the Holy Qur'ān that we can clarify and investigate what still remains pure of previous scriptures, and what they have changed with their own hands.

The question arises once again— *why* would they do that? Why would they *knowingly*, almost unanimously, dare to interfere with the Word of Allāh? Not just once or twice, but continuously throughout the centuries, even coming to the point of publicly declaring their acceptance or rejection of various scripts (refer to the 1885 Pittsburgh Platform as just one such example), and setting the law for the populous to follow in their own doctrines.

Up until the birth of Nabi Isa, Zionism had always been subtly suppressed under True Judaic faith drawn from Mosaic Foundations (the *authentic* Tawrāt).

It may not have been termed as Zionism then, but in its early pre-historic stage it formed the foundation of the radicalization that has come to manifest in the world today. Jewish axiom, since their Babylonian enslavement, has always been drawn to the once magnificent prosperity of Nabi Sulaymān's Kingdom of Israel. In essence, their urge to return to the Holy Land has, for the large part, been for the desire of wealth and pragmatism over spirituality. The same doctrine has descended generations over generations, documented in various publications (see the *Protocols of the Elders of Zion, Chapter 4 - Materialism to Replace Religion*).

While we may sympathize with the Israelites for Babylonian enslavement and continuous trials and hardships over the centuries, one cannot help but wonder whether the calamities they suffered were not by their own hands. The Holy Qur'ān describes their transformation from 'Ruling Nation' to slaves;

$$وَقَضَيْنَآ إِلَىٰ بَنِىٓ إِسْرَٰٓءِيلَ فِى ٱلْكِتَٰبِ لَتُفْسِدُنَّ فِى ٱلْأَرْضِ مَرَّتَيْنِ وَلَتَعْلُنَّ عُلُوًّا كَبِيرًا$$

And We declared to (for) the Children of Israel in the Scripture (all the Scriptures), 'You will spread corruption on the Land, twice, and you will surely attain (a great degree) of (tyrannical) arrogance.
[Sūrah al-Isrā 17:4]

They cannot deny this warning, because their scriptures say in Micah, Chapter 3, Ayāt 9 to 12 (my comments are in brackets);

Hear this, you rulers of the House of Jacob, You chiefs of the House of Israel (speaking to the twelve tribes of Israel, descended from the sons of Jacob), *Who detest justice And make crooked all that is straight* (spread corruption in the land and distort the Word of God);
Who build Zion with crime, Jerusalem with iniquity;
Her rulers judge for gifts (corrupt leaders), *Her Rabbis give rulings for a fee* (Usury and Riba), *And her Priests divine for pay* (payment to the Sanhedrin with Temple Coin);
Yet they rely upon the Lord, saying, 'The Lord is in our midst; No calamity shall overtake us.' (they speak this in way of mockery and ignorance, assuming that after all they do, the Lord God is still by their side);
Verily (this is the warning upon them), because of you (the corrupt Rabbis, Sages, and Leaders) *Zion shall be plowed as a field* (ransacked and razed), *And Jerusalem shall become heaps of ruins, And the Temple Mount a shrine in the woods* (destroyed and left asunder).

The Holy Qur'ān continues to explain and clarify how their decisiveness prompted what could only be described as an alternate outcome in history.

More so, the Holy Qur'ān defines the exact implications of such corruption, as a lesson to be learned by Jews, Christians, as well as Muslims;

فَإِذَا جَاءَ وَعْدُ أُولَىٰهُمَا بَعَثْنَا عَلَيْكُمْ عِبَادًا لَّنَا أُولِى بَأْسٍ شَدِيدٍ فَجَاسُوا خِلَلَ ٱلدِّيَارِ ۚ وَكَانَ وَعْدًا مَّفْعُولًا

So when came the promise, first of the two, We raised against you servants of ours, of great force, and they entered (ravaging) the innermost part of your homes (tore you from your very livelihood, kin, and liberty). And it was a promise fulfilled.

[Sūrah al-Isrā 17:5]

The first of Almighty Allāh's promise upon them, when they turned to corruption, manifested itself by the march of King Nebuchadnezzar of Babylon upon the lands of Judea, a promise they were forewarned in previous scriptures.

Micah Chapter 4, Ayāt 9-10;

Now why do you utter such cries? Is there no king in you? Have your advisers perished, that you have been seized by writhing like a woman in travail?

Writhe and scream, Fair Zion, like a woman in travail! For now you must leave the city and dwell in the country— And you will reach Babylon. There you shall be saved, There the Lord will redeem you from the hands of your foes.

The forewarning of Babylon has also been explained in detail, in the Bible, Jeremiah 25 (Yirmeyah 25 - Orthodox Jewish Bible). It was here that revelation came to them, foretelling a Prophet (Micah 5, v.1-2 above, and in various other scriptures), the true Messiah who would bring them salvation and return them to the Promised Land and its bounty, as was of Nabi Sulaymān (peace be upon him).

Allāh Almighty gave them redemption and returned them to Zion.

The Holy Qur'ān explains what transpired;

$$ثُمَّ رَدَدْنَا لَكُمُ ٱلْكَرَّةَ عَلَيْهِمْ وَأَمْدَدْنَـٰكُم بِأَمْوَٰلٍ وَبَنِينَ وَجَعَلْنَـٰكُمْ$$

$$أَكْثَرَ نَفِيرًا$$

$$إِنْ أَحْسَنتُمْ أَحْسَنتُمْ لِأَنفُسِكُمْ ۖ وَإِنْ أَسَأْتُمْ فَلَهَا ۚ فَإِذَا جَآءَ$$

$$وَعْدُ ٱلْـَٔاخِرَةِ لِيَسُـُٔوا۟ وُجُوهَكُمْ وَلِيَدْخُلُوا۟ ٱلْمَسْجِدَ كَمَا دَخَلُوهُ$$

$$أَوَّلَ مَرَّةٍ وَلِيُتَبِّرُوا۟ مَا عَلَوْا۟ تَتْبِيرًا$$

Then We gave to you the return victory over them (the Babylonians) and increased you in wealth and sons, and made you numerous (in number and strength).

If you do good, you do good for yourselves, and if you do evil, then it is for (unto yourselves); then when came the final promise (We allowed your enemies) to sadden your faces and enter your temple (the second temple), just as they entered the first time (destruction of the first temple), and to lay waste all they conquered with destruction.

[Sūrah al-Isrā 17:6-7]

The second major siege on Israel and Judah, came by the hands of the Romans, *after* they failed the test of faith. In Micah 5 v.2, the statement 'He will leave them helpless', means that God had forestalled the hand of the Romans, until Jesus was born, that is until the test was upon the Israelites. The test of the Promised Messiah came not in the form of riches and wealth, as they had assumed, but by the hands and words of a poor carpenter from Bethlehem, Nazareth. At the time, the arrogant rule of Judea in the south, where the Sanhedrin was established, looked down upon the impoverished Israel to the north.

Following the atrocities of the Pharisic Rabbis, Allāh's verdict descended upon them, as harsh as the first time, perhaps even harsher, for after the Roman's laid siege, the Jews were expelled permanently from the Holy Land, and the Qur'ān enforces this ban;

وَحَرَامٌ عَلَىٰ قَرْيَةٍ أَهْلَكْنَٰهَآ أَنَّهُمْ لَا يَرْجِعُونَ

And it is forbidden (there is a ban) upon a city (Jerusalem) which We have destroyed (the Roman siege on Jerusalem) to which they (the Jews) will never return (to reclaim as their own in prosperity).

[*Sūrah al-Anbiyāh 21:95*]

The interpretation of this particular āyah extends to the one immediately following it (āyah 96), and a deeper analysis has been made in the final chapter of this book, because it relates to *Ya'jūj* and *Ma'jūj*. In order to remain within the current context, we will restrain ourselves to the transpiring events relating to the Second Rabbinic question and the Companions of the Cave.

The ban from Jerusalem was only one side of the coin. To add insult to injury, the Holy Land had not only fallen to the Romans, but in time to come, it fell into the custody of the Christians. The followers of Christ. The followers of he whom the Israelites had rejected.

If we align the events correctly, with respect to time, several incidences and turning points coincide with each other almost in perfect harmony. The following historically documented events occurred in the wake of Nabi Isa's supposed 'crucification';

26–36 AD
Trial and persecution of Jesus instigated by the political deception of the Pharisic Rabbis and the Sanhedrin, and executed by the Romans.

30-70 AD
The Schism, or separation, of the Followers of Jesus from mainstream Judaism, began with them developing their own texts and ideologies branching off Judaism (Gospels according to the various apostles). To the east was the formation of Hellenistic Judaism (by the followers of Jesus) of Alexandria, Aegipta (Egypt), and Antioch (Turkey). During this time, the First Jewish-Roman war erupted and ended with the impactful destruction of the Second Temple and millions of Jews dead, hundreds of thousands enslaved by the Romans. The Sanhedrin (Jewish Tribunal of Rabbis) was moved from Jerusalem to Jamnia (termed the Council of Jamnia in Yavneh, Israel) and so began the period documented as the age of the *Tannaim*; Rabbis who 'organized' and 'elucidated' the Oral Torah (spoken law, not written - akin to AHadīth in Islām).

115-117 AD
Second Jewish-Roman war erupts in Cyprus, Cyrene (Libya), Aegipta and Mesopotamia (Syria and Iraq). Hundreds of thousands of Jews died resulting in the extermination of Jews in Cyprus and Cyrene by Roman Emperor Hadrian.

131-136 AD
Among several edicts passed, Hadrian renamed Jerusalem to 'Aelia Capitolina' and prohibited circumcision (based on the doctrines of Paul). Simon Bar Kokhba, who at the time was assumed to be the Jewish Messiah by the Rabbis, led the Bar Kokhba revolution in response to Hadrian's edicts, resulting in the death of nearly six-hundred-thousand Jews. In the aftermath, Hadrian renamed Judea to 'Syria Palaestina' in an attempt to root out Judaism.

200-500 AD
Began with the Documented Redaction (editing) of the *Mishnah,* which served as Judaic Law (not the Torah as it had been Decreed) since then to the present day. This also marked the Period of *Amoraim*, who were the Jewish Rabbis compiling the *Mishnah* and its commentary (*Gemara*) into the Talmud. It was around this period that the Companions of the Cave were said to have exiled themselves into isolation during the rule of Roman Emperor Decius.

During this Period, the enactments of Emperor Constantine finalized the formation of Christianity as the official state religion, and Christians were forbidden from converting to Judaism. Eventually, *all* Judaic laws were disbarred from the new religion of Christ. Jews were, however, allowed to enter Jerusalem, not as settlers, but as visitors on the anniversary of the Second Temple's Destruction. Between 360 and 361, Emperor Julian called for a review of Constantine's laws and allowed the Jews to return as settlers and rebuild the Temple, but he was assassinated shortly after and all former laws were reinstated.

In 450, the Talmud underwent another series of redactions, and by 550 it underwent yet another series of redactions, with lesser modifications continuing for 200 years.

If the Timeline permits accuracy, and Allāh Almighty truly knows best how these events occurred, *Ar-Raqim* as mentioned in the Qur'ān would have been the only authentic scriptures abiding the laws of the Tawrāt, the Zabūr and the Injīl, preserved with the Companions of the Cave over an age which not only saw the fabrication of an entirely new religion (formed by the laws of man, *not* by Divine Decree), but also a series of well documented alterations and compilations of the Torah and the Zabūr by the hands of the Rabbis.

All of the above events are also documented in Jewish History, yet somehow the event of the Companions of the Cave appears nowhere in record. Again, if the Timeline permits accuracy, the period between the awakening of the Companions and the Jews asking their question would only have been eighty to a hundred years. In essence, the tale would have been, to a certain degree, widespread and well-known with awe.

Suspicions continue to arise. Argumentatively, with what evidence did the Rabbis proclaim that *only* a Prophet could answer the question? In truth, *only* Divine Revelation can give an absolutely accurate account of the event, regardless of which, the Rabbis rejected the Holy Qur'ān's narrative, to which one would then ask, on what basis did the rejection manifest? There was no objective counterargument, no alternative hypothesis nor account provided, only an outright rejection.

The advent of the Companions is highlighted by two key characteristics, both of which are honored in the Qur'ān.

The Companions are described as *Mu'min* (al-Kahf 18:13). While many scholars have conclusively classified them as *Muslims*, historically, they were Israelites who *heard* the Message of Nabi Isa, *understood* the Message, and *believed* in the message. This means that they were not influenced by the Pre-Christianic doctrines arising out of sources such as those of Paul.

The second, and more vital characteristic, is *Ar-Raqim,*

described by the Qur'ān as an inscription, which by interpretation can be understood as something that was pure, authentic and void of any alterations made to previous Scriptures.

By both accounts, the event of the Companions held no place in Rabbinic Judaism, which then conclusively points to the fact that they did not expect a clarification from Nabi Muhammad (peace and blessings be upon him), rather they sought something else entirely.

There are three possible deductions to be drawn from the reasons behind asking the question, and all three bear equal evidential weight.

It is likely that they expected the Holy Prophet to *condemn* the Companions and behold them not as pious, but misguided youths. The implications of this would have upset the balance of Christianity and Islām by its foundations. It would have provided the Rabbis with substantial evidence to justify six-hundred years of atrocity, justified their *disbelief* (note how the āyah explicitly classifies the Companions as *believers*) in Nabi Isa, *and* justified their numerous alterations and redactions of the Holy Scriptures (*Ar-Raqim* preserved as authentic in the eyes of the Holy Qur'ān).

Secondly, Nabi Muhammad (peace and blessings be upon him) linked the event of the Companions to the advent of the Dajjāl in the first ten Ayāt (as protection against the Dajjāl) which also describe and address Christians who follow the father-son doctrine, and Jews who altered the Word of Allāh. It is possible that the Jewish Rabbis hoped to *trick* the Messenger of Allāh into revealing details about the Dajjāl, who to the Jews is their *Moshiach*. The manner in which the event was narrated, in contrast to responding the other two questions, Allāh Almighty deliberately refrained from repeating the question, in addition to which the Dajjāl is not mentioned anywhere in the Holy Qur'ān. Their rejecting the Holy Qur'ān's account may have arisen from the despair that their hidden agenda, behind asking the question, was *not* addressed. At least not to *their* expectations.

Lastly, the miraculous event of the Companions has everything to do with the *Nafs* and the *Rū'h*, their interdimensional existence, and resurrection, all described in great detail in the Holy Qur'ān. Yet, strangely enough, this was not a satisfactory response to their question, because here arises a haughtiness akin to their reaction to the response of the first question. The Rabbinic belief of being the 'chosen people' not only elevates them to an audacity to claim that the Jewish soul is superior, but also elevates them to think that only *they* have Divine Knowledge. They regarded the Companions to be outcasts of Judaism, souls which had condemned themselves to inferiority, and so did not merit such a miraculous advent.

By rejecting their version, the Holy Qur'ān clarifies, without a shadow of a doubt, that no soul is superior to another. Allāh Almighty chose the Companions for a specific reason, which implies that He can choose whomsoever He Wills, Jewish or Gentile. Furthermore, the Qur'ānic description of the Companions' existence, inter-dimensionaly, outrightly refutes the Jewish falsification of the *Rū'h*, which ironically also refutes modern secular scientific explanations of the human soul, spirit, and inter-dimensionality.

It goes without saying, that even in our Modern Age of Information and Technology, the Holy Qur'ān alone holds absolute knowledge of all matters, scientific and spiritual, within its Divine Pages. In the Hearts of the Believers, only the Holy Qur'ān can explain all things.

PART THREE

THE GREAT TRAVELER

POWER
AND
FAITH

وَيَسْـَٔلُونَكَ عَن ذِى ٱلْقَرْنَيْنِ

And they ask thee about the great traveler...

Almost as if it were a psychological trigger, attention is drawn towards the questioner than the responder, and even less to all else in between. Oftentimes, the observer, or listener, fails to notice a crucial point, an unspoken implication, not to be found in the question or the response, but rather in the responder and the tone of response.

Thus far, with regards to the first two questions and their expected responses, we have identified a common trend among the Israelites, particularly among the ruling classes, the Rabbis and Sages.

The question about the *Rūh* was in anticipation of a response conforming to their predominant beliefs. However, the response was in adversity, disclosing to the world the false doctrines they had relentlessly preached. It holds thereof, that the core agenda behind the first question was to uphold Jewish superiority over mankind, a debate that continued to unfold in a greater portion of the Holy Qur'ān, and has continued to unfold over the centuries, laying the framework of the modern age.

The second question was in anticipation of a response conforming to a predominant outlook of the Companions, their belief in Allāh Almighty and their belief in the teachings of Nabi Isa. The complexity by which the event surrounds the True Messiah and the Impostor, and its immense similarity with the modern age, cannot be ignored. It holds, therefore, that the core agenda behind asking this question was to uphold an alternate Messiah (one who would be more appealing to Rabbinic doctrine) over the True Messiah, Isa son of Maryam, and this is also a debate that has continued to unfold over the centuries, embedding itself into, and governing the modern age.

The third question, however, draws an even greater suspicion. The Holy Qur'ān reveals the great traveler by the title of Dhū'l-Qarnayn, and very like the event of the Companions, his journey has not been mentioned in the Books of Judaism. The closest mention of one such individual in their scripts (in the books of Ezra, Isaiah, and Daniel) is a historical figure known as King Cyrus of Persia. His name has only been mentioned as the liberator of the Israelites from Babylon, with details provided as to how Cyrus aided the Jews in returning to the Holy Land and reconstructing their Temple (which became the Second Temple). No mention of two journeys to either bounds of the land has been made.

Historically, Cyrus was a Persian conqueror, who did indeed travel to two ends of the land. The land in context is the far reaches of the Median Empire and the Lydian Empire. His journey, however, is contradictory to the journey of Dhū'l-Qarnayn, as we will see from the Qur'ānic account. Cyrus first conquered Media (east), then Lydia (west), then ventured south to Babylonia. His conquest spanned an entirety of thirty-odd years, and it was during the final phase that he conquered Babylonia and liberated the Israelites. Hence his reverence by the Jewish people. The Holy Qur'ān, however, does not revere Cyrus, nor does it mention him by name. By faith, Cyrus was a Zoroastrian, the ancient Persian worship of a deity called *'Ahura Mazda'*. In old Persian, *'Ahura'* literally means 'Lord', and *'Mazda'* literally means 'Wisdom'. Zoroastrianism, in its ancient form, not in its modern depiction nor its historic Mithraic variation, was the religion of a Persian Prophet by the name of Zoroaster (*Zarathustra* - Persian). This is in accordance to ancient Persian text, and is not mentioned in the Qur'ān, nor is the Persian Prophet.

Notable scholars such as At-Tabari and Ibn Juzay Al-Kalbi have derived some relation to the foundations of Zoroastrianism bearing similarities to Islām with regards to the teachings of Zoroaster. Historically, he was a spiritual and ethical philosopher who preached Spiritual Self-Realization and the Realization of the Divine. Islām advocates both these principles under the foundations of *Imān* and *Ihsān*, however, theologically, little else can attest to any correlation between ancient Zoroastrianism and

Islām.

It may suffice to say that Cyrus may have been a devout believer in One God, but only Allāh Almighty can endorse its actuality, and only Allāh Almighty can validate any truthfulness in Zoroastrianism. The purpose of discussing this matter in our study is not to theologically analyze Zoroastrianism and Cyrus, but to remove any speculations of attaching Cyrus to Dhū'l-Qarnayn. We have no evidence to uphold any of these theories, including the widespread allegations of also considering Alexander the Great or King Hamurabi as Dhū'l-Qarnayn.

As a necessary precaution, we advise the reader and the eventual researcher not to become tangled in the web of determining the reality of Dhū'l-Qarnayn, nor in any way connecting him to any historical figure without absolute and irrefutable evidence. There is a strong deposition to suggest that the Rabbis of Yathrib may have been trying to trick the Messenger of Allāh into conforming Dhū'l-Qarnayn with Cyrus, by way of which no āyah in the Holy Qur'ān conforms this belief.

To remain within the context of the study, we will focus more of our efforts on the occurrences and events mentioned in the Holy Qur'ān, and less on the actuality and origin of Dhū'l-Qarnayn.

The third question was even more craftily concealed. The Rabbis specifically asked about *a* journey to *two* ends of the land, which can be understood as *two* specific journeys. In response to their question, Allāh Almighty describes *both* journeys to *two* ends of the land in either extremity, but further reveals a *third* journey. Were they misinformed? Or were they hiding something?

It is important to note that *Ya'jūj* and *Ma'jūj* are only mentioned *twice* in the Holy Qur'ān. Sūrah al-Anbiyāh, Ayāt 95-96 were revealed in Makkah, *before* the Prophet's migration to Madīnah, and *before* the revelation of the tale of Dhū'l-Qarnayn.

وَحَرَٰمٌ عَلَىٰ قَرْيَةٍ أَهْلَكْنَٰهَآ أَنَّهُمْ لَا يَرْجِعُونَ

حَتَّىٰٓ إِذَا فُتِحَتْ يَأْجُوجُ وَمَأْجُوجُ وَهُم مِّن كُلِّ حَدَبٍ يَنسِلُونَ

And it is forbidden (there is a ban) on a town (Jerusalem), which We destroyed, that its people (the Israelites) shall not return.
Until they have been set loose (allowed to venture forth), Ya'jūj and Ma'jūj, and they descend (emerge and proceed) from every elevation (every direction, high and low).

[Sūrah al-Anbiyāh 21:95-96]

There is limited information concerning the exact chronology of revelation, but the evidence becomes more and more apparent, the deeper we study and investigate. In their undying quest to return to the Holy Land, it is very possible that the Rabbis were prompted by the above two Ayāt to learn more about *Ya'jūj* and *Ma'jūj*, providing them with the necessity to ask the third question, under the misunderstood assumption that *Ya'jūj* and *Ma'jūj* may be their torch-bearers to the Promised Land. This is a strong theory which we will explore further on.

The tale of Dhū'l-Qarnayn was revealed to Nabi Muhammad *after* he had migrated to Madīnah and was narrated to the Jews in their presence. Unlike the rash reaction to the response about the *Rū'h,* they did not pose a reaction to the event of the Companions nor the event of Dhū'l-Qarnayn. At least, there is no record of any response from them, not in Islāmic *AHadīth* and *Seerah*, nor in their own history.

Before we progress further, certain aspects must be clarified in order to follow a proper methodology and arrive at sound conclusions.

When studying the Ayāt of the Holy Qur'ān, every precaution must be taken to abide by accuracy and authenticity. In addition, any interpretation must be acknowledged as a humane study. At the core of all knowledge is the Holy Qur'ān, and we must abide by the underlining principle that only Allāh Almighty knows the true and deepening interpretations and meanings of the Ayāt he has revealed.

As far as methodology goes, we advice the reader and the researcher to also revisit the Heavenly Ayāt from an emotional and dialogical perspective. Meaning, we must recognize the fact the our Lord, our Creator, while bestowing knowledge upon us, is also *speaking* to us through these Ayāt. The tone and emotion behind each āyah is vital, not from an informative angle, but a knowledgeable outreach. It is through emotion that the Holy Qur'ān touches the Heart of the Believer, but it also sheds Light on the *why* and *how* Allāh Almighty formulates his responses, especially to the Israelites. Many a times, the affection or sorrow with which Allāh Almighty reaches out to his slaves is overlooked when reciting or studying the Holy Qur'ān, resulting in a lack of proper understanding.

Now we proceed with our analysis.

Note the response to the question of the *Rū'h*— *And they ask thee about the Rū'h, say 'The Rū'h is from the Command of my Lord...* (al-Isrā 17:85). Clear and concise, preventing the Jews from formulating any more speculations over the matter, as they had done before.

Note then, in response to the question of the Companions,

Allāh Almighty does not repeat the question, but along with the first ten Ayāt of Sūrah al-Kahf, their tale plays a key role in revealing the identity of the Dajjāl and offering protection against him. The mystery behind which Allāh Almighty deliberately keeps the Jews guessing until the Impostor will avail himself, is truly mesmerizing.

Note, however, in response to the third question, Allāh Almighty responds by again repeating the question, but marking the beginning of the response as a clarification against any predominant and assumptive belief surrounding the event of Dhū'l-Qarnayn.

$$\text{وَيَسْـَٔلُونَكَ عَن ذِى ٱلْقَرْنَيْنِ ۖ قُلْ سَأَتْلُواْ عَلَيْكُم مِّنْهُ ذِكْرًا}$$

And they ask thee of Dhū'l-Qarnayn, say, 'I will relate to you something of him, a remembrance (something forgotten).'

[Sūrah al-Kahf 18:83]

They did not *ask* about *Dhū'l-Qarnayn*. They did not provide *any* identifiable marker, title, or name, as to whom they were asking about. They did not say 'king', 'ruler', 'leader', 'saint' or 'prophet'. They asked about *'the great traveler who journeyed to two ends of the land'*, and they kept the name deliberately hidden, but Allāh Almighty exposes their intent from the very beginning. The statement *'I will relate to you something of him in remembrance'*, strongly cites an imposition to negate any predominant information regarding this traveler. It implies that what the Jews had formerly assumed and propagated of the traveler was either a misinterpretation from previous revelations, a deliberate fabrication, a complete lack of knowledge about him, or... Allāh Almighty had finally decided that his promise (*al-Isrā 17:8* and *al-Kahf 18:98*) would now be fulfilled, and Allāh Almighty knows best why he has responded in this particular manner. The response also implies that herein, in the life of Dhū'l-Qarnayn, something had occurred, something that humanity had long forgotten. Something crucial and vital. The revelation of the following events in great detail, would hence come to change the outcome of history in its entirety.

The clarification about Dhū'l-Qarnayn follows with his establishment on Earth as a Just Ruler, representing a Khilāfah; as one who was chosen by Allāh to represent his sovereignty over the people.

$$\text{إِنَّا مَكَّنَّا لَهُ فِى ٱلْأَرْضِ وَءَاتَيْنَٰهُ مِن كُلِّ شَىْءٍ سَبَبًا}$$

Surely we established him in the earth, and We brought him means to (accomplish) everything.

[Sūrah al-Kahf 18:84]

The title Dhū'l-Qarnayn has two possible meanings. One such meaning is 'he of two horns' or 'possessor of two horns', with *Qarn* meaning horn. Going by this definition, gives some evidence to Dhū'l-Qarnayn having possibly been Cyrus, who was known to wear a crown depicting two horns. By this account, he would have been Persian, the King of the Medes and Lydia. His timeline, therefore, would have been between 500 and 400 B.C. There is, however, no historical record of Cyrus building the famous barrier. His only affiliation to the Jews is their liberation from Babylon, and his only connection to Dhū'l-Qarnayn is his Two-Horned crown. Therefore, the 'two-horned' definition is weak, and bears no significant value of adhering Dhū'l-Qarnayn to King Cyrus.

The second meaning, and one which is more suiting to the individual and his characteristic is 'He of Two Ages' or 'Possessor of Two Ages', with *Qarn* meaning 'age' or 'epoch'.

The reason why many scholars, and Allāh truly knows best, have agreed that the latter is more fitting is because 'two horns' holds no significant meaning or value. The two-horned concept has always been revered by the Jews, and is the most attributed symbol in Kabbalism, Zionism, Luciferianism, Black Magic, and Sorcery (see *Of Jinn and Man*). It is highly unlikely that a Zoroastrian King of the same 'two-horned' title would be given such a high status as Dhū'l-Qarnayn in the Holy Qur'ān.

Combining the tone and response of both the first and second āyah of this story, it is doubtless the Jews have had the wrong notion of Dhū'l-Qarnayn, and they did exactly what our own are doing today, by affiliating Cyrus or Alexander to Dhū'l-Qarnayn without properly studying the subject. The bottom line remains— *If* Allāh Almighty wanted us to know Dhū'l-Qarnayn's true identity...

The hidden wisdom and knowledge behind using the title Dhū'l-Qarnayn, comes from a proper methodological understanding of its meaning. The word *Qarn* appears in the Holy Qur'ān about twenty-three times, and in every single context, the word has been used to describe an 'Age', an 'Era', or an 'Epoch'. Not a horn. Not once in the Holy Qur'ān is the word *Qarn* used to describe a horn.

Additional derivatives of the word in the Holy Qur'ān are *Qarinan*, meaning 'Companion', and *Muqarranina*, meaning 'bound together'. Because the title Dhū'l-Qarnayn has been used to signify someone and his achievements, its interpretation also becomes symbolic. Combining the word *Qarn* with the word *Nayn* gives it a 'duplicity'. *Qarn-Nayn,* therefore signifies two epochs or ages with similar symbolical advents. This gives evidence that in the instance of Dhū'l-Qarnayn, the title is depicting 'one who has had an impact on two ages' linked together by a common bond.

'He of Two-Ages' or 'Possessor of Two Ages', Dhū'l-Qarnayn had indeed done, or achieved something, by which Allāh Almighty has clearly stated that he had been 'established on the earth with the means to all ends'.

We explored earlier, that information is not knowledge. Information can result in corruptive power, whereas knowledge only brings Profound Power. The 'establishment' of Dhū'l-Qarnayn implies a rule by which his power is resting on a foundation of Faith and Knowledge. This power was not *acquired* by Dhū'l-Qarnayn. It was *bestowed* upon him by Allāh Almighty, and it is imperative to make this distinction, especially when relating the event of Dhū'l-Qarnayn to the modern age.

Modern secular society imposes that Religion and Politics must be kept separate. They use the word 'politics', because the foundations of Modern Democracy thrives on nothing else but politics. In truth, the occult agenda here is to separate Religion and Power, so that power can be boundless without any religious anchors. *'Practice your faith on your own time, leave the affairs of leadership to democracy'.* By doing so, power bestowed by Allāh Almighty is taken away from the foundations of Faith and Knowledge, and given instead to an artificialized system of governance. This is how the term 'Modern Secular State' comes to being. Secularization, by definition, is the emancipation of Sacred Rule, so that mankind can be 'liberated' from the holds of Religious bond.

Sovereignty, true Sovereignty combines both in harmony. Faith in Allāh and Power from Allāh. We who believe, do nothing of life or faith without first abiding by the same governing laws of life and faith from the same Lord. This is what submission to Allāh means. Surrendering life and faith to His governance. The deconstruction of this school of thought to the formation of the modern age, has been at relentless play for centuries, first begun, if history permits accuracy, by the rise of the British Empire.

Power, when resting on a foundation of Faith, bears great responsibility, because Faith must rest on a foundation of Knowledge, and Knowledge is from the guiding Light of Allāh Almighty. Not only is the lay of the land to be governed by Divine Doctrine, but so is the way of life. Such power can only be earned through spiritual means. Such power is befitting of *Khilafat* rule.

Allāh Almighty tells us specifically, and very categorically, that He had established Dhū'l-Qarnayn on earth, as a ruler, as a king, as a leader. A righteous leader. Whether his faith followed the teachings of the Prophets mentioned in the Holy Qur'ān, or those not mentioned, we do not know. Only that he did indeed serve the One true God.

In a similar manner, Allāh Almighty had also established Nabi Daud and Nabi Sulaymān (peace be upon them) with a status of Sovereign governance in the name of Allāh Almighty, and as we have witnessed from their lives and their style of governance, their wisdom and judgment have descended through the generations with awe and reverence. Such is the status and respect of a righteous leader.

Of the final age, the rule of Khilāfah was entrusted to Nabi Muhammad and his successors, Abu Bakr As-Siddiq, Umar Ibn Khattab, Uthman Ibn Affan, and Ali Bin AbiTalib (may Allāh be pleased with them) and many more who succeeded them, raising Islām to the Golden Age of Knowledge and Enlightenment. Their power and governance did not come from a source of democratic politics, but from a foundation of Faith, and their governance succeeded the Muslim *Ummah* across the plains of Arabia, Turkey, Persia, Khorasan, and all the way to the Straits of Gibraltar.

Their names are called out in every *Khutbah* on every *Jumu'ah* with peace and blessings upon them, just as Dhū'l-Qarnayn has been praised in the Holy Qur'ān for a count of fourteen hundred years and beyond.

The questions then posed, are these;

What did Dhū'l-Qarnayn do, or achieve, for him to receive such a high status?

Why was his Faith tested in such unconventional manners, and How did he find fruition?

This study is vital in understanding how he came to impact upon two ages, in a manner that has not been known of any other ruler in history, for he was not a Prophet, He was not an Angel. He was a man whom Allāh Almighty had chosen for His Divine Decree.

Researching through all related Ayāt in the Holy Qur'ān and the Hadīth of the Messenger (peace and blessings be upon him), we have found no compelling evidence to question his personality or ethnicity. Rather, all information regarding Dhū'l-Qarnayn directs our attention to his conduct, exercise of power, and authority. Herein do we find the profound substance of the Divine Knowledge and Guidance conveyed to us.

THE
FIRST
JOURNEY

To truly understand this section, you the dear reader must first understand, as an axiom, that what transpires in this world is less of paramount importance than *how* and *why* it transpires.

You must face the truth that your mind has been addled by modernity's "profound" ideology that the product is all that matters. What manifests is of the only concern. The means do matter, because per their ideology, the ends always justify the means, and on that account, when we attempt to understand the Divine Speech of our Lord, we overlook the most crucial aspect of His deliverance to us. It is not about what happened. It is about *how* it happened. And *why!*

The following account being of the 'Great Traveler,' you must ask, and be able to answer the question yourself... Which one bears significance? The destination? Or the Journey?

Allāh Almighty declares that he did not only establish Dhū'l-Qarnayn as a rightful ruler on earth, but he also gave him a means to accomplishing everything.

These 'means', or solutions, could have been in the form of handling the affairs of his nation, passing judgment on disputes among his people, establishing a state of governance for them, but also the ability to journey with a mighty and loyal force on the march to bring other civilizations into the fold of true faith, or the fold of Islām as it had been decreed at that time.

It follows that the 'Means to Every Accomplishment' would have only arisen as a rewarding experience. Individually, every

147

human has been defined with micro-purposes within the overall purpose of life. With every problem comes a solution. *With every hardship comes ease (Ash-Sharh 94:5-6).* The implication being that every hardship, perceived as an obstacle to the despairer, and a test to the believer, is put in place by Allāh Almighty. Success thereof proves our capabilities in receiving greater trials for the sole purpose of strengthening ourselves from within and without. To define it in simpler terms, only when we have successfully completed the initial or previous test, do we find a means to advance to the next stage.

In context, each of Dhū'l-Qarnayn's 'means to everything' would have arisen from the successful accomplishment of his previous test.

$$فَأَتْبَعَ سَبَبًا$$

So he followed a means.

[*Sūrah al-Kahf 18:85*]

Thus began one such journey, or in the context of the event, the First Journey. Allāh Almighty does not waste words. In every instance of the Holy Qur'ān, every āyah, every phrase, every word, has its place and purpose. It is imperative to note that not only do entire Qur'ānic events bear immense purpose, so too do internal recounts within every narrative. If this journey has been accounted in the Holy Qur'ān, not only does it serve as a response to the original question, it also irrefutably serves a greater Divine Purpose.

Our task is to determine that purpose. Why is this journey important? What is its relevance?

$$حَتَّىٰ إِذَا بَلَغَ مَغْرِبَ ٱلشَّمْسِ وَجَدَهَا تَغْرُبُ فِى عَيْنٍ حَمِئَةٍ وَوَجَدَ عِندَهَا قَوْمًا ۗ قُلْنَا يَٰذَا ٱلْقَرْنَيْنِ إِمَّا أَن تُعَذِّبَ وَإِمَّا أَن تَتَّخِذَ فِيهِمْ حُسْنًا$$

Until he reached the setting of the sun and found it setting in a sea of murky water, and he found near it a people (community). We said, 'O Dhul Qarnayn, either you punish them (conquer with force), or take them (conquer) in kindness.

[*Sūrah al-Kahf 18:86*]

A Mighty King, marching to a destination, guided by the Light of Allāh, with an army on his back, was on a path to *conquer* and nothing else.

Many have stated that this was his ambition, marching from place to place with the sole purpose of doing *Da'awah*. There is little evidence to back these claims, regardless of which it requires a brief analysis.

Foremost;

Da'awah is the call to the Oneness of Allāh, or the Oneness of God (Tawhīd). Da'awah is not done by the sword and an army!

Dhū'l-Qarnayn was on a path to conquer, with the might of his army and the power of Allāh Almighty. Knowing that his power rested on a foundation of Faith, the duty of spreading the Oneness of God is a given ambition, without which he would have been stripped of his power. This should be understood *within* the *context* of the Qur'ānic account, that an ambition of *Da'awah* may have been *one of his driving forces in life,* but not necessarily the driving force behind these particular journeys, nor the sole purpose of his establishment as a king, ruler, or leader.

Perhaps he was spreading the word of *Tawhīd.*

Perhaps he was on a mission to eradicate wrongdoers.

Whatever his ambition was is a matter of speculation, and because it has not been specified in the Holy Qur'ān it is irrelevant to our study. What we can be absolutely certain of, is that, if he had been established by Allāh Almighty, then he was on a path of righteousness, and therefore all three journeys as 'means to ends' would have added to his piety and righteousness as a Ruler who not only conquered godless civilizations, but in doing so, he also brought about the Worship of One God. This, we feel, is a safer and less speculative understanding of Dhū'l-Qarnayn, and Allāh Almighty truly knows best.

Allāh Almighty guided his path until he came upon a community, a civilization, a kingdom, a people living by the edge of a body of water which was, and still is *murky* in nature.

The āyah does not state that he was *headed* 'in the *direction* of the setting sun' which would mean he was headed westward, but he *'came to the setting of the sun'*, meaning he *arrived*, on his journey, at a *Time* when the sun was setting. Here he found it setting in *murky* waters. Note the elements of *Time* (evening - setting of the sun) and *Space* (location - the sea of murky water). Glory be to Allāh Almighty, for here lies one of the numerous miracles of the Holy Qur'ān. The āyah is providing us with *geographical coordinates* by highlighting the vectors of *Time* and *Space*.

There is some evidence to suggest that he was traveling either from the south, southwest, or southeastern direction, heading north from the direction of Southern Sham or northwest from the direction of Babylonia. This is attested by the origin of his name, or title, which is of a Semitic tongue. However, the actual origin of his journey matters little with regards to the actual destination.

The geographical location of his journey can be plotted with near absolute accuracy using the information provided in the Ayāt. The Semitic origin of his title indicates that he was in a region surrounding the Anatolian, Assyrian and Babylonian lands, perhaps well before the rise of either of these empires.

The only body of water closest in resemblance to 'murky' appearances in the region is, therefore, the Black Sea. The murkiness of its waters has been documented for centuries to date, with generations of sea voyagers describing the depth of the waters to be too dark below a few feet, so much so that navigation prior to technological seafare was an immense challenge and life-threateningly dangerous. The ancient Persians named it *Axsa'ina* (Dark Colored) and the ancient Greeks named it *Pontus Axeinos* (the Hostile Sea).

We cannot pinpoint the exact civilization around those shores without an exact timeline, but their origins are of little relevance here, although many have blatantly stated that they may have been a barbaric and violent people.

The falsity with which modern civilization regards the ancient world as primitive, crude, violent, and barbaric, should be condemned to its core. Without much deliberation, it can just as easily be stated with more than enough evidence, that modern civilizations are far more barbaric and violent than the entirety of humanity.

It is crucial to note that an ancient people do not necessarily have to be barbaric and violent, and even if that were the case, it does not necessarily relate to the entirety of the population. Historical and archaeological evaluations have shown that many such civilizations displayed oppressive and tyrannical characteristics from among the ruling and military class of the people. The much larger populations of peasants, farmers, servants, and slaves were far from barbaric natures due to their oppressed states of existence. Evidence to these evaluations can even be deduced from the manner in which so many ancient civilizations behaved and reacted when the Message of Allāh came to them. Just as the people of Nūh, Lut, Saleh, Ibrahim, and every other Prophet before and after them (may Allāh be pleased with them all). Those among higher societies of all these civilizations were known to be oppressors whereby many among those of the lower classes did accept the Message and were ever oppressed and persecuted. By default, a godless civilization will always be an oppressive civilization, ancient or modern.

This deduction is relevant in understanding how Dhū'l-Qarnayn related with the people he encountered, because herein lies one such test from his Creator. To better understand this first journey and destination, we must place ourselves, however so briefly, in the shoes of Dhū'l-Qarnayn.

A king with an army on his back, on the march to conquer, comes upon a people ripe for the taking. He is a king with faith in God Almighty.

He is a king with intellect and profound authority. He is not a barbarian. He is not a tyrant. He is not a dictator.

What does he do?

This wise king will first send out his scouts. His spies. Gather information on these people. *Let us discern their strengths and weaknesses before we amass an attack if necessary.*

Based on the information acquired, Allāh Almighty now asks him a direct question. *You have been given power. How will you use this power? Will you conquer by might, force, and brutality? Or will you advance with peace and diplomacy?*

Peace and diplomacy do not conquer nations!

Isn't that what *every* other secular state over the last two thousand years has proven? Peace is preached and propagated, but never advocated and implemented. Every opposition is seen as a threat, and so every declaration of peace comes from a defensive standpoint, not for the sake of humanity, but for the sake of personal protection. In essence, secular diplomacy does not advocate peace, it uses 'peace' as an excuse.

Yet here comes the response of a king who first makes the effort to gain accurate knowledge and base his decision from wisdom. He learns that not *all* these people are oppressive and wicked. There are among them those who are pious and righteous. There could be among them those who would turn to righteous faith. Fairness and justice must be offered to every creation before judgment can be passed. Indeed, such is the way of the *Khilāfah*.

And so he responds;

قَالَ أَمَّا مَن ظَلَمَ فَسَوْفَ نُعَذِّبُهُ ثُمَّ يُرَدُّ إِلَىٰ رَبِّهِ فَيُعَذِّبُهُ عَذَابًا نُّكْرًا

He (Dhū'l-Qarnayn) said, 'Whosoever does wrong, him we shall punish, then shall he be sent back to his Lord, and He will punish him with a punishment so terrible.'

[Sūrah al-Kahf 18:87]

وَأَمَّا مَنْ ءَامَنَ وَعَمِلَ صَٰلِحًا فَلَهُ جَزَآءً ٱلْحُسْنَىٰ ۖ وَسَنَقُولُ لَهُۥ مِنْ أَمْرِنَا يُسْرًا

'But as for one who Believes and does good, then for him is a goodly reward, and to him we will speak from our command with ease.'

[Sūrah al-Kahf 18:88]

When Power rests on the foundation of Faith, Faith rests on a foundation of Knowledge, Knowledge is the Light of Wisdom, and so Power is tested with grave responsibility. Had Dhū'l-Qarnayn wished, with the power he held, he would have laid waste to such a people. Conquered them without mercy, and subjected them to his rule. However, by carefully identifying the righteous from the oppressor, he creates a foundation of Truth and Justice, attributed to the Sovereignty of Khilāfah. He exemplifies the fact that Islām is not spread by the sword, a fact that most Muslims tend to forget.

In our desperation to revive the Khilāfah of Islām, we forget that Khalīfah is not Shariah Law, for there is no such thing as Shariah Law. *Shariah* is *Law,* meaning it is a Divine legislation enacted by God Almighty Himself. Shariah is only one portion of Khilāfah. It does not only connote the punishment of crime, rather it attributes every aspect of governance, and is not one that can be implemented by weak hearts and weak minds. The Power of Islāmic Khilāfah must rest on a foundation of *Imān* (Faith), *Ihsān* (Spirituality), *'Ilm* (Knowledge), *Rahmah* (Kindness and Affection), and *Hiqmah* (Wisdom).

It is not a Khilāfah, if it is lacking in righteous justice, lacking in a balance of wealth, lacking in the uplifting of knowledge over economic gain, lacking in the uplifting of humanity over land and resource. It is just another kingdom or empire. Khilāfah is not a political tool of governance. It is a pious and righteous legislation of life, enforced by pious and righteous individuals, and the resultant of Khilāfah is a way of life on foundations of peace without having even a momentary need to draw swords.

The secular mindset *cannot* fathom these notions. It simply cannot bear an adherence to peaceful foundations, regardless of how sound and profound the message is relayed. History has shown and proven, time and again, with the advance of the Egyptian Empire, the Roman Empire, the Persian Empire, the Mongolian Empire, the Huns, the Vikings, the Scythians, Anatolians, Assyrians, and every 'great' civilization that ever existed. Sure their holds were piled with gold, their granaries teeming with resources, their armories stockpiled to the brim, but their armies marched with one intent and one intent only, kill, conquer, raid, pillage, enslave, and eventually impose their own way of life over others.

In our modern world, the same patterns repeat endlessly, magnified in proportion, if anything. The British Empire landing on the shores of the Americas, building an empire founded on pure bloodshed, nearly annihilating the Native Americans. Across the Pacific, they did the same on the indigenous populations of Australia. Ruthless killings and land grabbings of a people who had every right to defend themselves and their property, when the Empire approached with greed and tyranny. The Belgians upon Central Africa. The Dutch upon Southern Africa. The Spanish and Portuguese upon South America. The Italians upon Northern Africa.

India, China, Japan, Russia, the entirety of Africa, not

one modern nation in the world can attest to have been built on a foundation other than bloodshed and tyranny. The implementation of borders, the deliberate renaming of countries, the formation of secular governments.

None of it by accident.

They were designed, crafted and sinisterly executed.

These massive campaigns of dominance and colonialism have only propagated tragedy with tragedy, suffering upon suffering for generations and generations, bringing countless peoples to the near brink of extinction.

THE SECOND JOURNEY

Arithmetically, the shortest distance between two points, regardless of how far apart they are, is a straight line.

Spiritually, the shortest distance is but a thought away.

Reality, on the other hand, is far more complex. The distance may be a straight line, but the journey never is. The path wavers and zigzags, twisting and turning, riddled with obstacles and trials.

Yet the journeyman presses forward.

What gives him the need to push on? What is he anticipating ahead? Why should he keep moving?

Life is ever coercing forward, because Time, for humans, carries everything perpetually forward, like the river carries the water onward. As the sands of life trickle on, so too must the traveler of life move on. Every step forward is a journey into the future, and every step forward reveals a new horizon, yet nothing of the future can be seen. The unknown is a void to the observer, a frontier for the pioneer, and an embrace for the believer.

So why should the traveler move on? What is he anticipating at his destination? What is the need to abandon the cocoon of comfort only to face the perils of the unknown?

As we explored in Dhul-Qarnyan's first journey, his destination revealed something of a marvel for him. Arriving at a horizon whence the sun sank into murky waters, and there by its shores, a people.

Before his feet lay a trial, a point in his life with a decisive outcome. A point in his life, that had he chosen otherwise, he would perhaps have not taken another path. *Fate* was preordained, but *destiny* was his to sculpt and shape. The question is, did he carve it in a manner pleasing to his Creator? Was his decision selfish, or humane?

Here we examine the words used in the Holy Qur'ān, and *why* those words were used. Why Allāh Almighty would deliberate by saying *'So followed a means (18:85)'*.

Why would he follow *those* particular means? Why not any other? Why would he not head south into Egypt instead? Why not venture into lands other than towards the murky waters of the Black Sea?

At its core, the reasoning has everything to do with man and his relationship with Allāh Almighty. The secular mind says 'to sin is in man's nature'. That 'evil is a natural incline'. That 'there is no right or wrong, nothing has absoluteness, because there is nothing absolute to enforce it'.

What of humanity then? Is purity a choice? What makes human, *human?*

Humanity is not an attribute of man. It is not an evolutionary trait. It is the essence of Allāh's Creation. This is why humanity bears a strong affinity to righteousness. A natural inclination towards purity. A child is not evil in nature. A child is pure and innocent, because a child's *Nafs* and *Rū'h* have only just emerged from a state of purity and neutrality. A child's natural incline is towards righteousness and innocence, hence the warm and benign nature of a child, the allure and affection a child draws towards it. As the child grows, develops, and learns the rules of life, adapting to the ability of choice, just as the mature man chooses between abiding by righteousness or abiding by sin. Sin, therefore, is *not* man's nature. Sin is a choice between good and bad, a choice between righteousness and wickedness.

Within this choice, within this frozen moment, is where the guiding Light, the *Nūr* of Allāh Almighty enters the Heart, and triggers an unknown emotion to make a choice, despite what the logic and rationality of the brain might say. This light is *earned*, not acquired. It is a gift, not a right.

Despite what the traveler might be thinking and deliberating, his footsteps are guided upon a path Decreed by the Creator, but only if the traveler has proven his worthiness.

We wonder at the marvels of Dhū'l-Qarnayn's final destination, but seldom do we stop to consider how he arrived there. Was it his own decision to map out his course, towards a destination in the future he could neither see nor comprehend? Or was it the *Nūr* of Allāh that led him there?

The distinction is vital, because one attests to Dhū'l-Qarnayn's personal ambition, while the other affirms his faith.

We are inclined toward the latter, which is why we believe there is a Divine purpose and reasoning behind why Allāh Almighty would deliberately reveal the following āyah *thrice* in this tale.

$$\text{ثُمَّ أَتْبَعَ سَبَبًا}$$

Thereafter he followed another way.

[Sūrah al-Kahf 18:89]

It should also be understood that even though the guiding Light may have inspired the second journey, it was still Dhū'l-Qarnayn's decision to accept or reject the inspiration, just as it is with every other human being. The choice is always before us, in every single instance, a choice between 'The path of those whom Allāh has favored', and 'not of those who have earned His wrath, nor of those who go astray' (*Fātihah 1:7*)

Dhū'l-Qarnayn *chose* his path, carving his destiny along the second journey.

$$\text{حَتَّىٰٓ إِذَا بَلَغَ مَطْلِعَ ٱلشَّمْسِ وَجَدَهَا تَطْلُعُ عَلَىٰ قَوْمٍ لَّمْ نَجْعَل}$$

$$\text{لَّهُم مِّن دُونِهَا سِتْرًا}$$

Until he reached the rising of the sun and he found it rising upon a people for whom We had provided no shelter from it.

[Sūrah al-Kahf 18:90]

So it was the second journey, and from its point of origin, west, he traveled eastward, given by the fact that he was facing the sunrise upon his arrival. Since he has been classified as 'the great traveler who journeyed to two ends of the land', and he reached a body of water (at one end of the land), the implication is that on the other end of the land, he would have arrived at *another* body of water.

'...*reached the rising of the sun*' could mean that he arrived at this destination at daybreak, indicating that he had either made a nightly journey (unlikely as his army would have had to rest the night, unless there was a circumstantial sense of urgency), or that he completed the final phase of the journey in the early hours of the day. Regardless of the time of arrival, the āyah draws our attention to the fact that if he was traveling east from the

Black Sea, he was headed in the direction of the Caspian Sea. The evidence pointing to the Caspian Sea is given by the origin of the question 'two ends of the land', which means from one shore to another. Even though the Holy Qur'ān does not explicitly mention another body of water in this āyah, it still gives us a moderate guideline by which we can geographically map the first two of Dhū'l-Qarnayn's journeys.

The details of his destination are very finite, and these two Ayāt (90 and 91) are particularly difficult in interpreting because of the limited vocabulary in them, but many scholars have agreed that the people he encountered would have been very primitive in lifestyle, or had a very simple and tribal way of life, in other words, uncivilized by the standards of that generational period of time.

'...we have provided no shelter from it', in reference to the sun rising on them, further implies that either their clothing was at the bare minimum, or their infrastructure, housing and shelter, was minimal or lacking. It could also indicate that they were a people living on the bare minimum or subsistence level, meaning that they would be alike with the birds who know not how and where tomorrow's meal may come from. Regardless, it does not necessarily mean that such a life would have been unsatisfactory for them. Contentment is a test on man, as many Prophets, such as Nabi Yahya (peace be upon him), have shown to have lived a life of bare necessity.

This interpretation bears weight and evidence to the two ends of the land that he traveled, denoted by two extremities in civilization and lifestyle. At one end, a civilized society with oppressors and righteous, and at another, an uncivilized populous with a modest way of life.

The Ayāt may have very limited vocabulary by which to understand the details of what transpired, but even in their simplicity do we find the element of a test upon Dhū'l-Qarnayn. Wisdom and Justice is not only tested on an affluent and influential level, but also on a moderate, and oftentimes, a wrongfully perceived insignificant level, for justice, as per the Sovereignty of Allāh Almighty, must be fair and equal for all walks of life.

كَذَٰلِكَ وَقَدْ أَحَطْنَا بِمَا لَدَيْهِ خُبْرًا

Thus (it was). And We knew all concerning him.

[Sūrah al-Kahf 18:91]

'...*thus it was*', can be expanded to mean '...*thus did he find them and thus did he leave them...*' meaning that he left them as they were, not interfering in their lives, allowing them the natural opportunity to grow themselves, rather than conquer and impose his own ideology. This is true to a population or a people who are not advanced in speech and intellect, as compared to those near the Black Sea who were well advanced in both to have built a nation for themselves. The second part of the same āyah conforms with the first, that he had fully grasped and understood the situation of these people, and he exercised his knowledge and wisdom in accordance with Allāh's Sovereignty.

Secular nations, governments, kingdoms, and empires have never cared for indigenous or primitive people. The conquests of the 'great' empires of the ancient worlds have always imposed their authoritarian and ideological rule on every one they could reach. The British Empire was one such example among its familiars, the Germans, Dutch, French, Spanish, Portuguese, and Italians, to follow this barbaric example. It is how the modern world, tinged with secularism, has come to be. It is how, for the last few decades, the western world has brought the rest of humanity to its knees with its Capitalist and Democratic ideologies, proclaiming

'Liberation of the People from their Oppressors'.

The truth of the matter is that in no way have they liberated anything, but to bring power to a Tyrannical State bent on ushering in the harbinger of all evil.

Dhū'l-Qarnayn did precisely what the Modern World has endlessly failed to do. He recognized human rights to be far superior than land and resource, and left them be to their birthright. The same profound approach must not only be followed by those on a path to conquer, but also by those living side by side with a people whose ideologies differ from ours. Nabi Muhammad (peace and blessings be upon him) lived by no different a principle when he allowed the Christians and Jews of Madīnah to abide by their respected faiths should they choose not to accept Islām. He did not shy away from delivering the Message of Islām to them, but neither did he coerce them into accepting it. Similar approaches were also made when sending delegations to Syria, Persia, Egypt, and all other nations.

The same approach was taken by his successors, and one very profound example is that of Umar ibn Khattab when he journeyed to Jerusalem with his aide. Not only did he enter the city barefoot with his aide riding his camel instead of himself, but he also did not march in with an army, nor did he impose anything on the Christians who held custody of Jerusalem. He further paid respect to their places of worship and dealt with them in such humility that Jerusalem was surrendered to Muslim custody by will.

In contrast to such an approach, the ruthless crusades and the barbaric marches of the Papal and Monarchistic European Kingdoms displayed a divergent and opposite manner of engagement. Their conquest was nothing short of oppressive and dominating, all under the falsified banners of 'liberation and peace'.

From a rightfully grounded Khilāfah, we recognize how Islām made its approach. Upon liberation of the Holy Land by Salaah-ud-din, the Christians and Jews were allowed to follow their faith without hindrance by the Muslims. This had been the norm until the Zionist State returned with a brutality, if not similar, even worse than the Crusades.

The repetition of history is revealed by patterns and traits, and a people whose power rested on foundations of faith always prevailed in spreading peace, while a people whose power rested on corruption were left proclaiming peace while spreading bloodshed.

The contemporary argument is that there can be no peace without war. This is true to some degree, in that peace, like war, is relative, both being relative to the other. But in light of whether one must exist for the other to also exist, very much like whether the egg must exist for the chicken to exist, we would argue that peace can exist and prevail without there ever being a war. This is insofar as the political landscape is concerned.

In truth, the Material World, meaning the Physical and Observable Universe, by its nature is not a peaceful realm, or rather there is no absolute peace in this realm. It is a realm of turbulence, of causality, in which damage and carnage is as much a part of its quality as its fruition and endurance. But that is the nature of the realm, which is not a realm of active intelligence. On the other hand, the human being is a being capable of active intelligence. Which is to say that it is well within the being's means to avoid conflict, and by his intelligence he can understand that the result of conflict cannot be tranquility. Once a thing is damaged it is no longer that same thing, even if it is repaired to seem like it once was.

Reality avails that peace is attainable when war, which is avoidable, is indeed avoided. We eliminate conflict when we befriend our enemies. Anything other than that simply compounds and escalates the carnage.

War only begets war.

Vengeance only brings vengeance.

This second journey of Dhū'l-Qarnayn outrightly disproves every secular ideology. He did not preach war. He did not advance in greed. He left them be. There was no battle. No bloodshed. The people lived their lives peacefully.

Here, Allāh Almighty declares what was observed and what was expected of Dhū'l-Qarnayn.

$$كَذَٰلِكَ وَقَدْ أَحَطْنَا بِمَا لَدَيْهِ خُبْرًا$$

Thus (it was). And We knew all concerning him.

[Sūrah al-Kahf 18:91]

It is necessary for us to repeat the āyah, because contained within it are two elements of the same nature.

'(Kadhalika) Thus it was...' denotes what transpired during the event, as what Dhū'l-Qarnayn did at this extremity of the second journey, or second test.

'(Wa Qad Ahatna Bima) And We knew...' denotes the conclusion of the test that was upon him, based on the event as it was presented and the decision taken, culminating a particular outcome.

The results of the test, denoted by *'We knew...'* paired with *'all concerning him'* concludes the test with its appropriate reward, meaning that Allāh Almighty had affirmed that Dhū'l-Qarnayn, the righteous leader, the pious ruler, whom He had chosen, had proven his worth for the next ordained venture.

Allāh Almighty thereafter inspired Dhū'l-Qarnayn to take on yet another path, a more difficult path, one which would engrave his legacy in a manner worthy of remembrance till the end of mankind on earth.

OF IRON
AND COPPER

So far the Rabbinic question was answered in its entirety, whether or not it was pleasing and adhering to their personally opinionated doctrines. The great traveler journeyed to two ends of the land, and both journeys were explained. However, the Jews were arrogant and conniving in their approach, sending the Qur'aysh to do their bidding, and disguising their true intent.

It should be noted that as far as their query is concerned, the tale serves its purpose. We now begin to ponder over *why* Allāh Almighty decided on revealing more. There is wisdom here, not just by spoken words, but also by unspoken words. 'Revelation' comes from the word 'Reveal', and so Almighty Allāh is *revealing* something to us.

Knowledge and Wisdom.

Knowledge of the Unseen and Unknown, a hint and clue of what is ordained to pass. Something within these texts unveils a path which mankind is destined to follow for its ultimate end to manifest by his Will.

Within these texts there is also Wisdom. How to accept, how to understand, and how to act in accordance to what He has ordained.

There are two sides to everything, two scales to the balance. Good and Evil. Righteous and Wicked. Light and Darkness. Both sides have a role to play. While the evil ones will 'do as they will' (satanic doctrine), the righteous will follow the ordained script. To them their way of life, to us, ours (*Al-Kāfirūn 109:6*).

163

We will now be able to see both sides of the field, both extremities. In revealing the following Ayāt, Allāh Almighty is guiding our *Nafs* towards the role of the righteous, and cautioning us against the intent of the vile.

It begins with the tone, emotion, and choice of words by which Allāh Almighty began answering their question, and so He proceeded in disclosing a *third* journey, revealing one of the greatest contributors to the climactic conclusion of humanity on earth.

We now journey back to āyah 83 of Sūrah al-Kahf, the first āyah beginning the tale of the great traveler.

The āyah states *'And they ask thee (O Muhammad) about Dhū'l-Qarnayn...'* exposing a hidden agenda concealed in the hearts of questioners, by revealing the true title of the great traveler with an imposing remark.

'Tell them...' meaning *inform* them with complete confidence, that *this* recount in the Holy Qur'ān is the purest, most authentic, and most absolute of any you will ever hear.

'I will relate to you something of him...' revealing 'something' you did not know before, something you were unaware of, or were otherwise incorrectly informed.

'...in remembrance' recalling an aspect, a moment, a defining occurrence of that *something* which had been forgotten in history. In this Holy Qur'ān will that something be revealed and preserved until the Last Hour.

This is that 'something' that *you*, the Rabbis of Yathrib, were truly after.

Here it is.

Allāh Almighty reveals;

ثُمَّ أَتْبَعَ سَبَبًا

حَتَّىٰٓ إِذَا بَلَغَ بَيْنَ ٱلسَّدَّيْنِ وَجَدَ مِن دُونِهِمَا قَوْمًا لَّا يَكَادُونَ يَفْقَهُونَ قَوْلًا

Then he followed another way.
Until he reached (a pass) between two mountains, and he found therein a people who could not understand his speech.

[Sūrah al-Kahf 18:92-93]

This third journey, granted to him by Allāh Almighty when he had displayed utmost faith, righteousness, and justice in the previous two journeys, now takes him through a path enclosed by mountains on either side, wherein he finds a people whose dialect is unlike his.

Being of Semitic origin, most of the languages in the region had some commonality in both vocal chord and movement of the tongue which allowed anyone of that descent to easily establish a mode of communication. However, here he encountered a people whose language was very different and difficult to grasp.

To understand this variance in language and origin, let us step back for a moment to the great flood, or the immediate aftermath of the flood. When Nabi Nūh's arch settled on land, we know he had three sons. Each of his sons took a different path whose descendants later populated their respective lands.

The Holy Qur'ān says;

$$وَنَجَّيْنَـٰهُ وَأَهْلَهُ مِنَ ٱلْكَرْبِ ٱلْعَظِيمِ$$

$$وَجَعَلْنَا ذُرِّيَّتَهُ هُمُ ٱلْبَاقِينَ$$

We delivered him (Nūh) and his family from the great distress (the flood).
And We made his progeny (his sons) among the survivors.

[Sūrah Sāffāt 37:76-77]

In a Hadīth At-Tirmidhi, Nabi Muhammad (peace and blessings be upon him) said, '*Ham, Sham, and Yafith*', and in another Hadīth, he elaborated by saying, '*Sham was the forefather of the Arabs* (Semites), *Ham was the forefather of the Abyssinians* (Africans, or Hamites), *and Yafith was the forefather of the Romans* (Europeans, or Yaphites, or Japhetites).'

The descendants of Ham populated the North African continent. They were, and are, known as the *Hamites*, or Hemetic people. It is from this descent that we get the Cush (Cushite, originating from Abyssinian regions), Mizraim (Misr, originating from upper Egypt), Phut (originating from Libyan regions) and Canaan (from the Canaanite regions of Phoenicia and Sidonia, not be confused with Nūh's fourth son who was also called Canaan, who had refused to board the Ark and was consumed by the flood).

The descendants of Sham populated what is now the Middle-East, Persia, and Arabia. They were, and are, the *Shamites*, or Semitic people. From this descent do we get the Arameans (of Mesopotamia), Anatolians (through Lud and Lydia), Assyrians (through Asshur), Persians (through Elam) and the Hebrew and Arab people, tracing their origins through Nabi Ismā'īl and Nabi Is'haaq respectively, through their father Nabi Ibrahim (through his forefather, Arphacsad), with the prophetic bloodline tracing further back to Nabi Nūh (peace and blessings be upon them).

The largest in number of descents come from Nabi Nūh's third son Yafith, or Japhet, from whom we get the Japhetites, populating most of eastern and central Asia, as well as Russia, Central Europe and Northern Europe as far north as Scandinavia. We will explore this lineage in the following chapters.

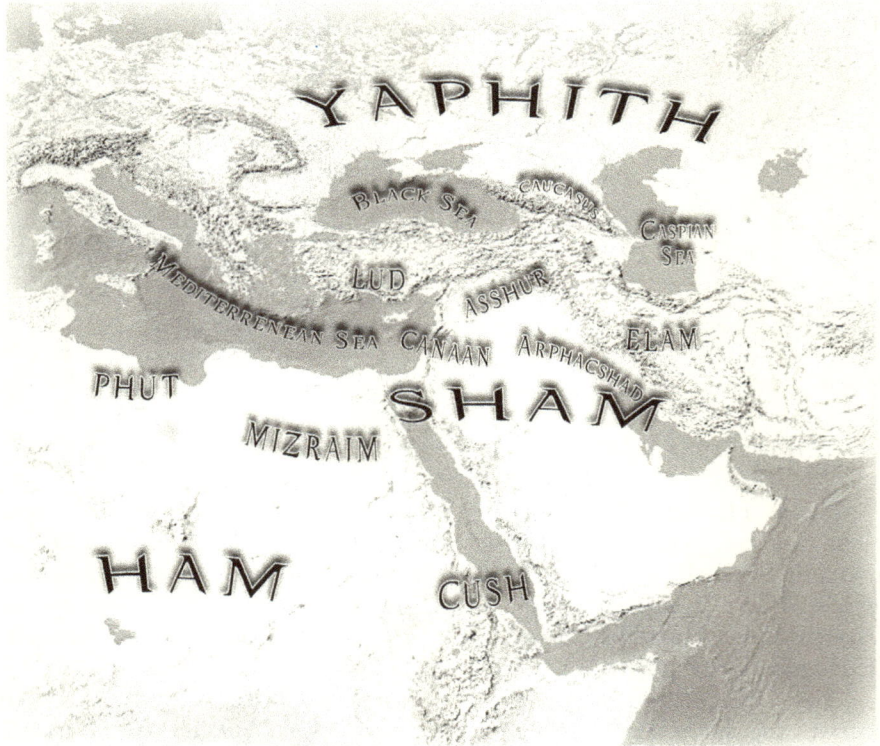

This expanse of regional descent would explain why Dhū'l-Qarnayn encountered a people whose dialect, attributed to vocal cords and tongue movements, was not easily discernible. However, we further see that some communication was eventually established, which also indicates a much longer duration of stay.

By geographically plotting the Black Sea and the Caspian sea, it is possible now, to practically plot the third journey between two mountain ranges as a journey through the Caucasus range of mountains.

166

Drawing an impassable terrain from the shores of the Black Sea to the Caspian Sea, there exists only one such passage linking the north to the south of the mountain range, known as the Darial Gorge.

Ruins of ancient towns as well as fortifications and some evidence of an ancient barrier have indeed been uncovered through archaeological expeditions in the Darial Gorge. One of these ancient ruins may have once been home to the people Dhū'l-Qarnayn encountered on this final journey.

Here, now, we begin to unravel in much greater detail than the recounts of the first two journeys, the essence of Dhū'l-Qarnayn's legacy.

قَالُوا يَـٰذَا ٱلْقَرْنَيْنِ إِنَّ يَأْجُوجَ وَمَأْجُوجَ مُفْسِدُونَ فِى ٱلْأَرْضِ

فَهَلْ نَجْعَلُ لَكَ خَرْجًا عَلَىٰٓ أَن تَجْعَلَ بَيْنَنَا وَبَيْنَهُمْ سَدًّا ٩٤

They said (pleaded with him), 'O Dhul Qarnayn! Verily! Gog and Magog are spreading corruption in the land. May we pay a tribute that you may build between us, and between them, a Wall?'

[Sūrah al-Kahf 18:94]

167

Now we arrive at the crux of the matter, the *real* reason why the Jewish Rabbis of Yathrib posed this particular question.

In so far as the first two journeys were concerned, neither revealed anything substantial to their profit. While a true believer in Islām would draw immense benefit from the first two journeys, so much so that numerous volumes and treatises have been written on them by Islāmic Scholars, he who bethinks himself superior of soul and birthright will hardly see the knowledge and wisdom of Dhū'l-Qarnayn. He will only see material benefit, and so will only seek material benefit, as did the Rabbis.

How they so slyly disguised their true motives. Whyever would they wish to know of *Ya'jūj* and *Ma'jūj?* Perhaps that is not so. Perhaps they only hoped that Nabi Muhammad would sanctify their beloved Cyrus, which did not happen. Did they not openly declare that they who had the Torah held all the knowledge in the world? Why then did they not consult the Torah for the great traveler? Refer back to āyah 83, and the answer to this question reveals itself.

It seems perhaps they really were pursuing a sinister agenda, of one which they had no knowledge whatsoever, and given their historical reputation, the suspision is almost tangible.

We will unravel this mystery further on. Let us explore how Dhū'l-Qarnayn responded to the request of building a wall.

قَالَ مَا مَكَّنِّى فِيهِ رَبِّى خَيْرٌ فَأَعِينُونِى بِقُوَّةٍ أَجْعَلْ بَيْنَكُمْ وَبَيْنَهُمْ رَدْمًا

He (Dhul Qarnayn) said, 'All what my Lord has established for me (bestowed upon me) is better (and in plenty), but assist me with your strength (manpower), I will build between you and them a Barrier'

[Sūrah al-Kahf 18:95]

In yet another test from Allāh Almighty, Dhū'l-Qarnayn once again displays a level of humility and kindness not witnessed of any other leader, then or now. He is satisfied with what his Lord has given him, stating clearly that he does not desire their wealth. However, he is prepared to shed his armor and his crown in humility, to perform an act of charity for a people who are not even of his descent, who do not speak his language, do not share his culture, his views, ideologies or beliefs. Whom he owes nothing.

He does not see race, ethnicity or even faith as a reason to enact charity. He sees humanity, a Creation of his Lord, much like himself. He does what is necessary for the sake of his Creator (*Fi-Sabilillah;* For the sake of my Lord).

For such a task as erecting a structure so monolithic as to bar a passage between two mountain ranges, he is in need of more manpower, atop his own army, which he requests of these people, again displaying an attribute of humility rather than arrogance.

There is another interesting point to note here. Even though Allāh Almighty had given him such power and such a large army, Dhū'l-Qarnayn must have observed something of *Ya'jūj* and *Ma'jūj*, in that his own force would not be able to defeat them. The Messenger of Allāh said in an extensive Hadīth pertaining the End of Times, *'... Almighty Allāh will reveal to Isa, 'I have created (Ya'jūj and Ma'jūj) creatures of Mine, so powerful that none but I can fight and destroy them...'* (Bukhārī and Muslim)

This exemplifies the titanic power of *Ya'jūj* and *Ma'jūj*, capable of utter destruction on earth, that even Dhū'l-Qarnayn's mighty force could not contend with them. Their unique description of *spreading Fassaad* (al-Kahf 18:94) is not just to *Corrupt*, but to *Corrupt and Annihilate*, meaning to completely demolish and reduce to dust, and thereafter reconstruct *everything* in complete contradiction to Allāh's Decree of Creation. In other words, they seek to undo the *Khalq* of Allāh Almighty, the elegance, beauty, and purpose of Allāh's Creations, including humans, and *rebuild* everything in accordance to *their* ideology, doctrine, and decree.

Before such a people, Dhū'l-Qarnayn resorts to taking a defensive, rather than offensive stance. Furthermore, he builds not a *wall,* as the people had requested, but decides to build something stronger and more efficient. A Barrier.

In both linguistic and practical terms, a Wall (*'Sadd'* in āyah 94) only acts as a 'divider' or a 'partition', such as the Great Wall of China, however 'great' it may be, is not impervious to scaling over or digging under.

However, a Barrier (*'Radm'* in āyah 95), acts as an 'obstruction', a 'limiter', an 'obstacle', a 'hindrance', a 'hurdle' or 'impediment', something that would continue in its task of preventing someone or something from achieving their goal or objective of overcoming it and venturing forth effortlessly (until they are set loose).

As we will see, this 'barrier' was not only meant to act and serve its part in *that* epoch of time, but also in *our* epoch of time as well, both *physically* and *symbolically,* attested by Dhū'l-Qarnayn's title of 'he who impacts on two ages'.

So how did he build this barrier?

169

ءَاتُونِى زُبَرَ ٱلْحَدِيدِ ۖ حَتَّىٰٓ إِذَا سَاوَىٰ بَيْنَ ٱلصَّدَفَيْنِ قَالَ ٱنفُخُوا۟ ۖ حَتَّىٰٓ إِذَا جَعَلَهُۥ نَارًا قَالَ ءَاتُونِىٓ أُفْرِغْ عَلَيْهِ قِطْرًا

فَمَا ٱسْطَـٰعُوٓا۟ أَن يَظْهَرُوهُ وَمَا ٱسْتَطَـٰعُوا۟ لَهُۥ نَقْبًا

'Bring me sheets of Iron.' Until he had leveled (filled) between the two cliffs (mountainsides) he said 'Blow!' (with your bellows) until he had made it fiery hot, he said 'Bring me molten copper to pour over it.'
So they (Ya'jūj and Ma'jūj) were unable to scale it and unable to penetrate it.

[Sūrah al-Kahf 18:96-97]

These processes of building the barrier are very unique, requiring an industrial and technological intellect and advancement surpassing the likes of the modern age. Indeed there has not been such an undertaking of construction in the modern age, or even recorded or found in history.

Some who have analyzed the event to great detail have proposed that an Iron and Copper alloy would prevent rust. Similarly, others have stated that it is not a process of creating an alloy, but a process of plating the Iron with Copper with the same objective of preventing rust.

However, both these theories defy the actual processes described in the āyah.

Chemically, creating an alloy would require pre-mixing molten copper with molten iron, along with a *third* element, like Zinc, in order to create an alloy, since Copper and Iron cannot mix without a catalyst. As we can see from the description, neither of the metals were pre-mixed. They were layered. The barrier could not have been copper plated either as that would require an acidic catalyst and a good measure of electricity (considering the size of the barrier) to induce a chemical reaction of copper plating.

We may propose a third theory, but only as a theory for educative purposes, and we affirm that only Allāh Almighty knows best as to the true composition of the barrier.

The Caucasus range does possess a very high concentration of graphite, which is a natural piezoelectric crystal, which when subjected to immense pressure (as would be, considering the size and mass of the barrier) would be capable of generating immensely large currents of electricity.

Given their elemental properties, Iron is a strong metal with extensive magnetic properties, and copper is a very good conductor of electricity. By forming an iron core inside a copper wrapping grounded to a graphite-concentrated earth, Dhū'l-Qarnayn may have remarkably built a barrier capable of creating a *magnetic field* strong enough to *repel,* thus preventing anyone from climbing over, penetrating through, digging under or around the barrier.

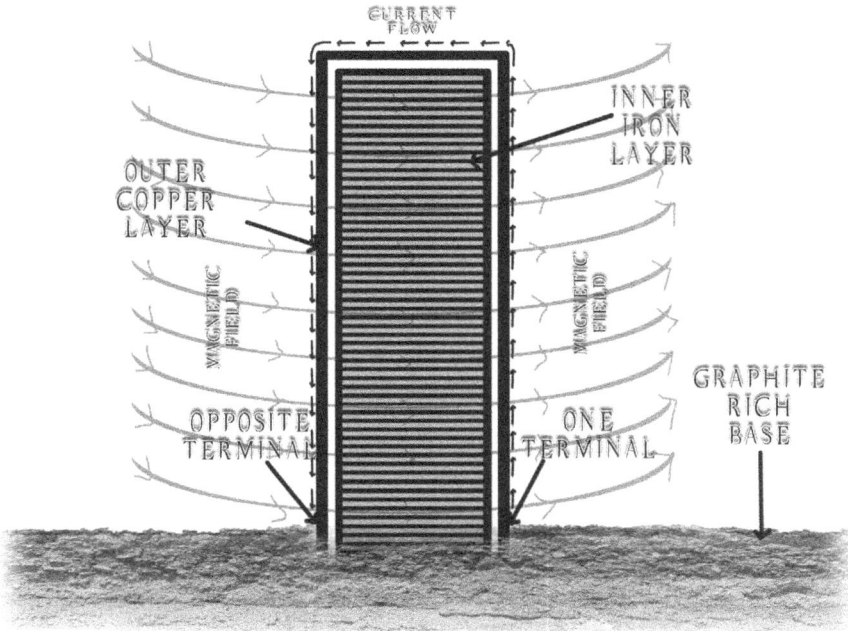

These are all, however, among so many other *theories* surrounding the barrier's construction, and Allāh Almighty truly knows best its composition and capabilities in warding off the tribes of *Ya'jūj* and *Ma'jūj*. They should never be taken as absolute facts or definitive conclusions, and should only be adhered to for educational purposes. For this reason, we bequeath any who venture into a detailed study, to do so with care, and a grounded understanding that unless there is substantial evidential weight, theories will remain theories. Not fact.

Scientifically, we can propose numerous hypotheses and theories to the barrier's physical construction, because it was, as described in the Ayāt, *physically* built with the use of *physical* materials, but it becomes largely speculative if we delve too deep. The Divine knowledge revealed in the Ayāt is purely for the objective of understanding its purpose by way of understanding its construct as a *Radm* (barrier), instead of a *Sadd* (wall).

The reason behind understanding the difference is given by the fact that the people asked for a Wall, but Dhū'l-Qarnayn proposed a Barrier instead, indicating or implying that its construct was of superior design, and would serve its purpose both *physically* (in one age) and *symbolically* (in another age) until the Promise of Allāh Almighty (next chapter) would come true, and *Yaʾjūj* and *Maʾjūj,* or their *descendants and allies* would be held back by nothing save for Allāh's intervention as the only One Who can fight and destroy them.

By its definition of a 'barrier', and the materials used, 'iron' and 'copper', we can formulate an understanding that the barrier's properties are akin to something that would 'prevent' or 'ward off' any approaching force from above, below, or around.

Again, by understanding the precise definitions and properties of the materials used, they would also have been subject to the decay of Time.

Iron rusts and copper corrodes.

Neither is everlasting in nature.

However, even after its physical collapse (see the following chapters) its definitive properties as a barrier should still hold true as a *symbolic obstacle* to the full and final assault of *Yaʾjūj* and *Maʾjūj.*

Therefore, there should also be a *symbolic* attribute to the barrier as an obstacle to any *ideological* attempts of penetration as well.

What we can ascertain with absoluteness is that the barrier served its purpose *then,* has symbolically served its purpose through the ages, and will serve a final purpose in the End Times.

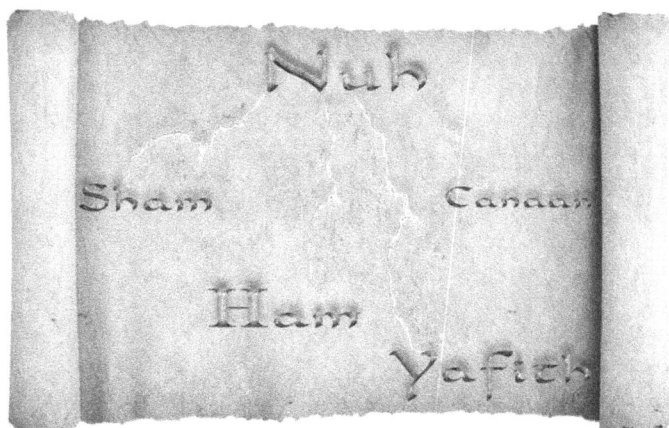

THE THIRD SON

Knowledge pertaining the End Times, such as the event of Dhū'l-Qarnayn *cannot, and should not,* be studied with a streamlined, institutionalized, and narrow-minded perspective. It cannot be analyzed in *literal* senses by deriving *literal* translations and explanations from the Holy Qur'ān and Hadīth. Such a study requires an open mind and an open heart, requires more than earthly scientific and rational knowledge. It requires one to analyze every possibility within reach, and to validate every theory and hypothesis with the Qur'ān.

It also requires one to bear a capability strong enough to distinguish between speculative analysis, and absolute analysis, and one example of speculation is attempting to determine the name, exact age, and origin of Dhū'l-Qarnayn without following a proper methodology of study.

Only Allāh Almighty truly knows best when Dhū'l-Qarnayn lived, how long he lived, how long all three journeys were, and how long he remained at each destination. Numerous speculations have arisen over the past, some bearing moderate weight, many others demeaning and contradictory to what the Holy Qur'ān says.

Regardless, it is also an important part of our history, because the modern age we live in today appears to have no physical barriers containing *Ya'jūj* and *Ma'jūj*, anywhere on Allāh's Earth. Which then signifies, that their existence has transcended and evolved over thousands of years, and in order to accurately identify them, we must trace back their origins.

The importance of this study pertains to the End of Times, and while many have dismissed it to be irrelevant, or still too distant in the future, we have reason to believe it has *everything* to do with our current lives. Most scholarly studies have availed, with a substantial level of inaccuracy, that the emergence of *Ya'jūj* and *Ma'jūj* will *only* occur *after* the arrival of Nabi Isa (peace be upon him), and therefore it does not call for concern as yet. However, we believe this conclusion to have arisen out of an incorrect methodology, as we trace back the footprints and discover the unique link between *Ya'jūj* and *Ma'jūj*, and the ruling class of the Jewish doctrine.

The visual evidence is irrefutable, whether examined politically or philosophically. Albeit a conspiracy, it is no mere 'theory' to state that the permeating webs of reformed Judaic doctrines have so finely been embedded into the numerous occult organizations responsible for architecting the modern world in what they envision as a perfect utopia far removed from the ordinance of God.

Gog and Magog are of the kind of people whose prime ideology is secular, and their language projects a world-view in which man is most powerful being in the world, on which account, man can alter the reality of the world however he so deems. The resultant of this is corruption... *Fasād*. Because the fundamental axiom of reality is that none can change creation but the Creator Himself, and what He has ordained as a design cannot be altered by other than Himself. Any attempt to alter and doctor reality in a manner other than His ordainment results in ruination.

Not only do such people prove themselves less intelligent, if we define intelligence as realizing God's supremacy and sovereignty in the world, by way of altering reality they stand in obstinate defiance against His Divine Authority. To challenge God, by challenging His Law, is the very definition of *Fasād*. Because to challenge the Law is to attempt to change, and being that one cannot change that which is unchangeable, one only succeeds in corrupting it. This is what is meant by Him stating to the Jews (al-Isrā 17:4) that they would cause corruption, *Fasād*, twice in the Holy Land.

In and of itself, this proves to be a complex and difficult endeavor. However, the Holy Qur'ān highlights a few indicators that allow us to penetrate some, if not all, origins of *Ya'jūj* and *Ma'jūj*.

Within this study, we will attempt to analyze certain key elements derived from the Ayāt of the Holy Qur'ān and authentic Hadīth of the Holy Prophet (peace and blessings be upon him), beginning with Dhū'l-Qarnayn's third journey.

Here, we implement the element of Time by understanding the practicality of every event as an occurrence with respect to a Passage of Time. A surface study of the entire tale creates an impression lacking in details, but the reality of its occurrences objectively reveals more to the whole venture than meets the eye.

In reality, a journey across the Semitic lands and to the lower parts of the Caucasus mountains, with an entire army, would inevitably take a very long time, months, if not years, to complete. On horseback, a journey of about fifteen-hundred to two-thousand miles (from a hypothesized region of ancient Babylonia, ancient Arabia, or ancient Judea, to the Anatolian shores of the Black Sea) would have taken about a month or so for a single rider. However, with an entire army hauling supplies, accommodations, weapons, armaments, and gears of war, it could take several months to complete the journey.

Even if we triple that number (to account for all three journeys), it would have taken Dhū'l-Qarnayn, between resolving the conquest at the Black Sea, his journey to the people in the east, and venturing further north through mountainous terrain (further slowing down the journey), his arrival to the people south of the Caucasus would have endured a measurable length of time.

Thereafter, settling down and laying a foundation of communication (due to the language barrier between him and the people), construction on the barrier would have begun with stockpiling immense loads of materials, mining and forging, building the required infrastructure to begin construction, all the while fending off possible skirmishes from the north in between construction.

The barrier itself would have spanned a calculable average of two kilometers across the peaks of the Darial Gorge, and an immense, average height of at least a thousand meters at par with the peaks of the escarpments (this is an estimate of the possible dimensions of the barrier). The time taken to erect such an enormous structure, along with the process of mining, forging, building the foundations, laying the iron base as well as melting the outer copper layer, would have taken years complete.

It can be understood then, that either the numbers of the two tribes north of the Caucasus were few in number (in the beginning), growing steadily with time, or Dhū'l-Qarnayn's force had at least managed to maintain their defensive position long enough to complete the barrier.

In the very least, and Allāh Almighty knows best, this visualization enables us to appreciate how colossal the entire event would have been. It further sheds light on the nature of

Ya'jūj and *Ma'jūj,* that given Dhū'l-Qarnayn's established power over the lands, he still chose to embark on the difficult task of building a *temporary* barrier (āyah 98 below), rather than face and eradicate them, thus solving the problem permanently. Bear in mind that the element of Time passing throughout the entire event would have added to the psychological evolution as well as the physical aging of everyone involved, Dhū'l-Qarnayn, his army, and the native people.

Given this background visual representation, we can now take the study to the next level.

It is not possible, without any *absolute* Qur'ānic evidence, to precisely pinpoint the Timeline of Dhū'l-Qarnayn, but we can estimate that he may have reigned between the ages of Nabi Nūh and Nabi Ibrahim (peace and blessings be upon them) based on the Qur'ānic descriptions of the four civilizations he encountered. Nabi Ibrahim (peace be upon him) is estimated to have lived around the 2nd-millenium BC (given by the age of the Ka'abah).

Allāh Almighty knows best the accuracy of these estimations, because these are not facts but educated theories with a moderate amount of evidence to support them.

Archaeological findings have uncovered the remains of ancient structures as well as shipwrecks at the bottom of the Black Sea, meaning that there may have been human dwellings around the Black Sea prior to the Great Flood (estimated around the 8th-millenium BC based on Radiocarbon Dating). Archeology has also found that the Black Sea and the Caspian Sea were at one point in time united, meaning the entire region would have been submerged due to the Flood. This indicates that Dhū'l-Qarnayn's first journey to *'the setting of the sun in murky waters'* would have taken place well after the epoch of the Great Flood.

The earliest known civilization in the region of the Caspian is Sumeria (estimated around the 4th-millenium BC, based on the Radiocarbon Dating of archaeological findings), closer to the Gulf of Persia. This would place an uncivilized people (āyah 90 *'...a people for whom We had provided no shelter from it')* around the shores of the Caspian Sea at an age much earlier than the 4th-millenium BC.

South of the Caucasus range, pre-historic Georgia is known to be the earliest civilization in the Chalcolithic Age (also known as the Eneolithic Age) placed around the 5th-millennium BC. Linguistically, the Georgian dialect has not only proven to be difficult, or variant to any Semitic tongue, but is also thought to have been unchanged in its roots prior to 19th-century BC.

The most compelling evidence is in the names of the tribes north of the Caucasus.

The designated titles, *Ya'jūj* and *Ma'jūj*, have been widely accepted as the names of both these tribes, but one must recognize that over thousands of years, these names would have changed considerably with regards to their descendants and their respective regions of migration. In other words, *Ya'jūj* and *Ma'jūj* are, in reality, the names of these tribes in their earliest known forms of existence, which would be within the 8th-millennium and 4th-millennium BC, or closer to the aftermath of the Great Flood. Evidence of this is given by studying the lineages of Nabi Nūh (peace be upon him) and his sons.

First we need to establish the fact that;

Ya'jūj is an Ummah of Banu Adam, *and,*
Ma'jūj is an Ummah of Banu Adam.

The Holy Prophet (peace and blessings be upon him) clarified this fact when he said, *'Allāh will say unto Adam, 'Bring out the people of the fire.' Adam will say, 'O Allāh! How many are the people of the Hellfire?' Allāh will reply, 'From every one-thousand, take out nine-hundred-and ninety-nine...'* to which he further explained that, *'nine-hundred and ninety-nine will be Ya'jūj and Ma'jūj...'* (Bukhārī)

This Hadīth should not be misunderstood to assume that the ratio of human to *Ya'jūj* and *Ma'jūj*, or the ratio of Muslim to *Ya'jūj* and *Ma'jūj* will be will be 1:999. Rather it means that *Ya'jūj* and *Ma'jūj* are descendants of Adam (peace be upon him), and the ratio is that of those who believe and abide by the Ordinance of God against those who oppose and deny, whether consiously or ignorantly. It also means that one can just as easily become one of them by following their ideology even if they are unaware of it (al-al-Mā'idah 5:51). Muslims are equally likely to join them in the masses.

Therefore, they are human beings. Living on earth in nations and civilizations, and not some strange creatures, confined to an underground dwelling, breeding uncontrollably and cut off from the rest of mankind. They are very much a part of our world, and are living among us. Their chief characteristic is committing *Fassaad,* and looking around, it takes very little to identify them. Among them are the defilers and corrupters of Knowledge and Faith, and the driving force responsible for the secularization of the world today.

It is also very possible to trace their lineages and origins to a point in time when the earth was repopulated anew.

Of Ham, we have North African Hamites.

Of Sham, we have Middle-Eastern Semites.

Of Yafith, the third son of Nabi Nūh, and the only one to have more sons than his brothers, we have a greater populous, spanning the entire northern hemisphere.

From his son Tiras, we see the descendants of the Thracians and Macedonians.

From his sons Meshech and Tubal, we see the people of Armenia and Georgia, among many smaller tribes in the surrounding regions. It is possible that Dhū'l-Qarnayn may have encountered the descendants of Meshech and Tubal on his First and Third journeys respectively.

Another of Yafith's son, Madai, some sources claim, had married a daughter of Sham, and preferred to live among Sham's descendants, rather than dwell in Yafith's allotted inheritance beyond the Black Sea. In accordance with his brothers-in-law, Elam, Asshur and Arphacsad, he received from them the land that was named after him, Media. Media is mentioned in the Holy Qur'ān as Madyan (*Al-A'araf 7:85*) to whom the Prophet Shu'aib (peace be upon him) was sent.

Javan, another of Yafith's son, is said to be the forefather of the people of ancient Greece and Cyprus, also linked to the Macedonians perhaps through inter-tribal marriage.

Of Yafith's two eldest sons, Gomer and Magog, do we now have the largest of his descendants, who after intermarriage with their cousin tribes, give us the Celts, the Vikings, the Gauls, Galatians, Rus, and Gothic people, as well as later descendants, through more inter-tribal relations with their other cousin-tribes, giving us the Aryans, Hinds, Mongols, Huns, and Buddhists.

It is from this lineage of Yafith's eldest sons that we can now trace the origins of *Ya'juj* and *Ma'juj*. Note, however, that not *all* of these descendants form the umbrella of the aboriginal *Ya'juj* and *Ma'juj*. Many of these tribes were nomads and cousins of each other, and inter-tribal marriages between them further gave birth to various different nations as they have come to be. We are only interested in identifying two specific groups of people from the same descents who have adhered to key characteristics through the generations, and who also bear a genetic code so unique, they cannot be compared to any other race on the planet.

Gomer had three sons, namely Ashkenaz, Riphath, and Togarmah. Assyrian records have identified the descendants of Ashkenaz with their Greek description of the Scythians. Ancient Armenian and Georgian chronicles place the ancestry of Togarmah in the mountainous regions of the Caucasus. Much is unknown of Gomer's second son, Riphath, but some genealogy and archeology scholars have placed him as the ancestor of the Celts, Vikings, and Nords.

Similarly, scholars have associated the Hunnic, Gothic, and Russian races to be descended from Yafith's second son, Magog.

Intermarriage between the Ashkenaz descent and the Magog descent is evident in their genealogy as a people who eventually made the immediate northern Caucasus as their native homeland, unlike the constant migration of their sister and cousin tribes.

Of these natives, two particular descents stand out.

First, the Scythians (Ashkenazi).

History has acknowledged them to be a barbaric, ruthless, merciless people who relied on raiding and warfare to build their military and economic might. Their might spread across the entire Eurasian Steppe, spanning a period between the 9th-century BC to around the 4th-century AD. They are said to have perfected and mastered the art of Mounted Warfare. They did not have a monarchistic system of governance, and instead were the only kind of people to be ruled by a wealthy class known as the Royal Scyths. They later disintegrated into a conglomerate of nomadic tribes living north of the Caucasus and were widely known for being ruthlessly brutal, exclusively belligerent and skillfully talented at flattery, chicanery, and treachery.

The disintegration of the Scythians gave rise to the Hunnic Empire, still bearing the same bloodlines, and while most of the Huns made their advance into Mongolia and China, the few scattered Hunnic tribes who remained, slowly regrouped in the late 6th-Century AD with remnants of the Scythians (Ashkenazis - Scythian is the Greek name) to form what became known as the Khazarian Empire.

Second, the Khazarians.

By the early 7th-century, the Khazarian Empire was capable of withstanding a Byzantine advance from the west while simultaneously holding off a Muslim advance from the eastern Persian Empire, and a Viking advance from the north, thus displaying an unmatched and unrivaled military power worthy of their genealogy. According to both At-Tabari and Ibn Kathir, around the same time period, there was an expedition made by the Muslims, under the directive of Umar Ibn Khattab (may Allāh be pleased with him) to the Caucasus mountains to locate the Barrier of Dhū'l-Qarnayn, which was reported back as lying in ruin.

Indeed, up until that period in history, neither the Scythians, nor the Huns, nor the Khazarian had been able to cross the Caucasus range. All their advancements were either made around the western side of the Black Sea and into Anatolia, or around the eastern side of the Caspian Sea and into Persia.

So what had happened to have brought down the physical barrier?

Well, to begin with Dhū'l-Qarnayn, having impacted in the first age, he had warned the people that the barrier would eventually come down in the next age;

قَالَ هَـٰذَا رَحْمَةٌ مِّن رَّبِّى ۖ فَإِذَا جَاءَ وَعْدُ رَبِّى جَعَلَهُ دَكَّاءَ ۖ وَكَانَ وَعْدُ رَبِّى حَقًّا

He said. 'This is from the Mercy of my Lord. Then when the promise of my Lord comes, He will make it level (with the ground), and my Lord's promise is ever true'
[Sūrah al-Kahf 18:98]

Based on this revelation, there was a Divinely Specified Time for how long the physical barrier would hold or remain. Whether through the decay of Time itself (rust and corrosion), or the triumph of *Ya'jūj* and *Ma'jūj* over the barrier (both are likely), it would come down in a designated epoch of time.

Bear in mind, we are currently only referring to the 'physical' barrier here. As Dhū'l-Qarnayn impacted on two ages, one age begins with the building of the *physical* barrier in this *physical* dimension of Space and Time, and ends with the leveling of this *physical* barrier. The second age hence begins with another kind of barrier, or a series of barriers which are *symbolic* (as symbolic is the title of *Dhū'l-Qarnayn*) and Divinely regulated, one after another, which the descendants of the aboriginal *Ya'jūj* and *Ma'jūj* are endlessly and sequentially 'digging' through, until the final barrier comes down and nothing will hold back their corruption.

Whether we refer to them as barriers in scientific breakthroughs, sociological breakthroughs, trade and economic barriers, technological barriers, or medical barriers, at the front of every one of these barriers is a secular and godless mindset, ever digging, ever pushing through. We will explore these phenomena further along.

So what could have prompted the removal of this first physical barrier?

Simply put, it was the question asked by the Rabbis, following the manifestation of their rejecting Nabi Muhammad (peace and blessings be upon him) and the Message of Islām. It was the final promise of Allāh upon them.

Having faced two major catastrophes in their history, Babylonian enslavement and Roman conquest, the Israelites had been forewarned. Were they to return with their corruption, Allāh would return with his punishment. Following the manifestation of their rejection, certain key occurrences led to the barrier being leveled as the Promise of Allāh Almighty coming true.

This forewarning was also recorded in the Jewish Tanakh and the Babylonian Talmud, in the Book of Ezekiel;

And you, O mortal, prophesy against Gog and say: Thus said the Lord God: I am going to deal with you, O Gog, chief prince of Meshech and Tubal!
(Ezekiel 39:1)

Nabi Muhammad (peace and blessings be upon him) said, *'... Almighty Allāh will reveal to Isa, 'I have created (Ya'jūj and Ma'jūj) creatures of Mine, so powerful that none but I can fight and destroy them...'*
(Bukhārī)

I will turn you around and drive you on, and I will take you from the far north and lead you toward the mountains of Israel.
(Ezekiel 39:2)

Nabi Muhammad (peace and blessings be upon him) said, *'And then Allāh would send Gog and Magog and they would swarm down from every slope. The first of them would pass the lake of Tiberias (Sea of Galilee, Israel) and drink out of it. And when the last of them would pass (on the way to Jerusalem), he would say, There was once water there.'*
(Bukhārī)

These are but a few among mountain-loads of evidence which irrefutably prove that the Rabbi were well aware of what they were asking. They only needed a few more details, and Allāh Almighty deliberately revealed it to them. What they did after, is far greater than we can imagine.

Argumentatively, the release of *Ya'jūj* and *Ma'jūj* is detrimental to all of humanity, but the gravity of their corruption is monumentally inimical to those who would pledge allegiance to them. The cause and effect here, as complex as it may appear, can be simplified into two statements.

Those who would oppose *Ya'jūj* and *Ma'jūj* will face hostility from them in this physical earth, but will earn the bounty of *Ākhira*.

Those who would follow them would receive an indulgence of material benefit in this world, but an eternal imprisonment and punishment in the *Ākhira*.

In order to correctly identify the *Ya'jūj* and *Ma'jūj* of the modern age, as well as their closest allies, we need only look for those who are materially benefiting from creating an oppressive and tyrannical state of the world.

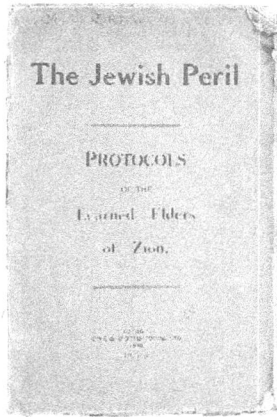

The Jewish Peril

PROTOCOLS
of the
Learned Elders
of Zion.

THE
WAVES

As we pick up the crumbs, track the footprints, and dust for fingerprints, we uncover clues to the greatest obsession influencing the world. From food and drink, medicine, education, geopolitics, and social affairs, to the impending and imposing integration of man and machine, of animate and inanimate.

Our beloved Prophet (peace and blessings be upon him) cautioned us, that *only* a *Believer* will be able to recognize the Impostor, the Deceiver, for who he really is. Only a believer, literate or illiterate, will be able to penetrate the complexity of layers beneath which he lurks, as his vile tendrils reach out and caress our deepest desires, drawing us away from Allāh's Divine Affection to the devil's dank and murky abyss.

And every single footprint leads back to an obsession, a grueling thirst, a burning desire, for the liberation of the Holy Land and its surrender to the Jewish people.

The strangest onset to ever walk the earth, is the actuality of *Ya'jūj* and *Ma'jūj*, amidst all their other attributes, their shared infatuation with the Holy Land, and by extension their strange affiliation with the Israelites (*al-Anbiyāh 21:95-96*). Henceforth, every decisive action ever taken by the Jews has been in desperate accordance with a return, back to the glory days of Israel— The Kingdom of Nabi Sulaymān (peace be upon him).

In order to elaborate how we have arrived at this conclusion, we must recognize the most crucial, most dramatic moment in Judaism and Islām. A moment which led to the manifestation of Allāh Almighty's promise of reducing the physical barrier of Dhū'l-Qarnayn to dust.

Following *Hijra*, when Nabi Muhammad (peace and blessings be upon him) arrived in Madīnah and met the largest and most revered congregation of Semitic Jewish Rabbis, it was one of the most dramaturgic and tense moments in our history. All, in the Heavens and the Earth, were on edge, eagerly awaiting a greatly anticipated unfolding of events.

In their two-thousand year history (before *Hijra*), the Jewish people had received numerous divine prophecies (*Isaiah 42:1-13*) of one who would come, an unlettered Prophet (*Al-A'rāf 7:157*) from the gentiles, one who would be their guiding light towards a path of redemption. The reason they had anchored themselves in Yathrib, awaiting with breathtaking anticipation, the Final Messenger of God, the Seal of all Prophets.

In his profound wisdom, Nabi Muhammad (peace and blessings be upon him) acted in a manner that indicated, without a shadow of doubt, that despite their *Kufr*, *Fitan*, and *Fasād*, despite everything they had done, the door for redemption was still open should the Jews choose to accept his Prophethood.

$$عَسَىٰ رَبُّكُمْ أَن يَرْحَمَكُمْ ۚ وَإِنْ عُدتُّمْ عُدْنَا ۘ وَجَعَلْنَا جَهَنَّمَ لِلْكَافِرِينَ حَصِيرًا$$

It may be that your Lord still has mercy on you, but if you return (with your corruption), We will return (with our punishment), and We have made Hell, for the Disbelievers, a prison-bed.

[*Sūrah al-Isrā 17:8*]

The deliberation of the word 'disbelievers' (*Kafireen*) in the āyah, directly pertains to the act of *'rejecting the Message'* in contrast to the 'believers' (*Mu'mineen*) who accepted the Message. It follows therefore, that the condition to redemption still held true. It had to be earned. *'It may be that your Lord still has mercy on you'*, indicates that a 'chance' is being offered. An opportunity, one last favor to earn redemption.

It must be noted, that the condition still holds for those in the present day. The door to redemption is still open for those who believe and accept Islām, and Allāh Almighty truly knows best.

As the advocate of Allāh Almighty, Nabi Muhammad followed the Divine Decree to offer the rejecting Rabbis an opportunity, and here we see the profound wisdom of our beloved Prophet (peace and blessings be upon him).

First, he prayed in the direction of *Baitul Maqdis* (the Sacred house— the Dome of the Rock). A sacred shrine since the beginning of time. The heart of the mountain upon which Adam prostrated to Allāh Almighty. The *Qibla* that was decreed upon the progeny of Abraham. Facing Jerusalem, Nabi Muhammad (peace and blessings be upon him) prostrated in prayer with the clear intent and sign, that Islām, like Judaism, was also the Religion of Ibrahim (peace be upon him). This was also a test on the Jews, as described in Sūrah al-Baqarah 2:143.

Secondly, he fasted in accordance to the fasting of the Jews (*Hadīth Al-Bukhārī*). The fast of *Ashura*. The 10th of *Muharram* on the Islāmic Calendar (not to be confused with the Shi'ah commemoration of the martyrdom of Imam Hussein, grandson of the Holy Prophet). *Yom Kippur,* the Day of Atonement, dear to the Jewish heart, symbolizes the day of their liberation from the tyranny of Pharaoh Ramses II (*Fir'awn*). When asked by the Jews, why the Prophet was doing so, he responded, '*We are closer to Mūsa than you are.*'

Finally, he reinforced the punishment of adultery in accordance to what was revealed in the Torah (*Hadīth Al-Bukhārī*), a divine law which they themselves had doctored to suit their own evil intents, and were hardly enforcing it. They had rewritten the Divine Ayāt condemning *only women* who commit adultery, claiming that men were exempted from the vile sin (as per their propagation of the divinity of the Jewish soul). We urge the reader and researcher to refer to the Mishnah and Talmud for what they have written, and John c.8 v.3-11 for an account of how Jesus cornered the Rabbis in their own deception.

These were among numerous clear signs that Muhammad, just like Isa (peace and blessings be upon them) could not have been other than the Messengers of God.

Regardless of the Signs, there was major issue facing the Rabbis. It posed a major threat to their way of life. Nabi Muhammad (peace and blessings be upon him) was not a descendant of Banu Israel, and in order to accept him, they would also have had to accept Nabi Ismā'īl, a gentile Prophet and son of Nabi Ibrahim whom they have slandered with such horrendous insult, we are aggrieved to repeat their words. Instead, we urge the reader to see what they have written in the Talmud and Midrash commentaries and interpretations of Genesis chapter 21.

Furthermore, they would also have had to accept Nabi Isa as the true Messiah (thus confessing to their horrendous crime), because the Holy Qur'ān upholds Nabi Ismā'īl, Nabi Is'haq, and Nabi Isa (peace and blessings be upon them) with high regard.

185

They would also have had to confess to the murders of all the Holy Prophets they had killed before Nabi Muhammad (peace and blessings be upon them). Finally, they would have had to step off their high-horses and positions of power, and allow a non-Jewish man of no royal bloodline (according to them) to rule over them. In essence, they displayed the three chief characteristics of Iblīs when he disobeyed in Heaven.

Envy. Defiance. Arrogance.

Upon their utmost rejection, several consecutive things occurred, indicating that the door to redemption was now permanently shut for them. The conclusive and blatantness by which they had made their decision, became apparent, without doubt, by the seventeenth month in Madīnah, when they plotted to assassinate Nabi Muhammad, just as they had plotted to kill Allāh's Messengers before. Their plots were foiled, and Allāh Almighty made clear his judgment on them. Foremost, Allāh Almighty permanently decreed the direction of the *Qibla* for the Muslims, from what was originally *Baitul Maqdis* in Jerusalem, to the Ka'abah in Makkah (*al-Baqarah 2:144-145*). Secondly, He changed the law of fasting to the law abided by Muslims till today, the fast of *Ramadhan*. The Mosaic fast of *Ashura* was no longer obligatory upon the Muslims (*al-Baqarah 2:183*). Thirdly, he overwrote the original punishment for adultery in the Torah, from stoning to lashing, and clarifying that man or woman, whosoever committed the vile deed was just as equally guilty (*Al-A'rāf 7:2*).

By these Divine acts, Allāh Almighty made it crystal clear, whether the Jews understood or not, whether they cared or not, that they were no longer a people promised and beloved by Allāh Almighty unless they took the oath of Islām. No longer will a harmonious integration between Judaism and Islām be favored. Redemption only remains, from thereon to the End of Time, in the acceptance and utter submission to Islām.

The final sign that sealed their fate and indicated that the Last Day (the final age of man on earth) had begun, was the dream of Nabi Muhammad (peace and blessings be upon him);

> *He rose from deep sleep in the house of his wife Zainab (may Allāh be pleased with her), flushed red with terror, 'Woe unto the Arabs,' he proclaimed, 'from a grave danger that has come near! A hole has been made in the barrier of Ya'jūj and Ma'jūj by this much!' He held up his forefinger and thumb in a circle. Zainab asked, 'O Messenger of Allāh, shall we (Muslims) be destroyed even though there are pious among us?' He replied, 'Yes. When Khabath (immorality) prevails.' (Bukhārī)*

186

Many have taken the literal meaning of this Hadīth in the sense that only a tiny hole had thus been made (when the Prophet woke) in the physical barrier, rather than in its symbolical sense, that the barrier had now been brought down, or the process had begun. Allāh Almighty says in the Qur'ān;

$$\text{وَتَرَكْنَا بَعْضَهُمْ يَوْمَئِذٍ يَمُوجُ فِى بَعْضٍ ۖ وَنُفِخَ فِى ٱلصُّورِ}$$

$$\text{فَجَمَعْنَٰهُمْ جَمْعًا}$$

And (on that day) We will leave some of them (Ya'jūj and Ma'jūj) to surge over others (like waves upon waves), and then the trumpet will be blown (signaling the final hour), then We will gather them all together.

[Sūrah al-Kahf 18:99]

There are three implications here.

One, that the Last day, or the final epoch or age of mankind, will begin when *Ya'jūj* and *Ma'jūj* were released. For those under the impression that their release has not yet occurred, it would mean that the Final Age is yet to come. However, following the Hadīth of the Holy Prophet, and connecting the various dots as we have, it would irrefutably appear otherwise. That the Final Age had begun with the arrival of Nabi Muhammad, and the Rabbinic rejection of the message of Islām, and that we are currently living in the End Times.

Two, some of them (the descendants of *Ya'jūj* and *Ma'jūj*) will triumph over others of them, and others of them will triumph over some of them, all hastening toward a common goal like 'waves upon waves'. This allegory of waves, akin to the motion of the seas, staggeringly describes all the major conflicts in the world. It would appear as incomprehensible discords among the descendants of *Ya'jūj* and *Ma'jūj*, chaos erupting as they crash with each other in ideology and doctrine, but they are all wholesomely journeying towards a common goal and ambition. Refer to *Tyrants of the New Age*.

Three, like the chaotic surges of the stormy sea, all these waves will eventually converge into one final wave, headed for shore, and they will continue in this manner until the Trumpet is blown, signaling the Last Hour, whereby they will all be destroyed as one. This also means that their reign will endure through and through, preceding and superseding the reign of the Dajjāl, until the Final Hour.

Sure enough, in wake of the Nabi Muhammad's dream, at the

turn of the 8th century, the *strangest* occurrences in history took place, ostensibly outlining the link between *Ya'jūj* and *Ma'jūj*, and the Jewish Zionist intent. An entire non-Semitic nation accepted Judaism as their official state religion without so much as a hesitation. This was the Khazarian Empire, native to the north of the Caucasus range, crossing over to its might in the 9th century. This was the first major wave, or surge of *Ya'jūj* and *Ma'jūj*, two tribes under one banner.

This first wave ended in the 10th-century following the onslaught of the Rus – an Asiatic tribe from Kiev – who had laid siege on the Khazarian Kingdom. The Khazars were forced to flee, but not destroyed, to Eastern Europe particularly Germany, Austria-Hungary, and Poland.

The second major wave began in Europe when the remnants of the Khazars in Europe reinvented and transformed themselves by adopting their original birthright as the Ashkenazi people. They were now the Ashkenazi Jews. Their influence in Europe gave rise to the European banking system with the introduction of the Sterling Pound, which became vital in funding the crusades for the purpose of liberating the Holy Land from the hands of the Muslims. Their power was put to the ultimate test when they successfully managed to part the western Catholic Church from the Byzantine Orthodox Church (the 1045 Schism of Christianity), preempting the Catholic Pope into approving the crusades. In 1095, following the Schism, Pope Urban II made the most influential speeches of the Middle-Ages, calling all Catholic Christians to wage war against the Muslims *and* the Orthodox Christians to reclaim the Holy cities of Jerusalem and Constantinople. In his speech, he proclaimed 'Deus Vult!' or 'God wills it!' and thus manifested the strange Judeo-Christian alliance, described in the Holy Qur'ān;

$$\text{يَـٰٓأَيُّهَا ٱلَّذِينَ ءَامَنُوا۟ لَا تَتَّخِذُوا۟ ٱلْيَهُودَ وَٱلنَّصَـٰرَىٰٓ أَوْلِيَآءَ}$$

$$\text{بَعْضُهُمْ أَوْلِيَآءُ بَعْضٍ ۚ وَمَن يَتَوَلَّهُم مِّنكُمْ فَإِنَّهُۥ مِنْهُمْ ۗ إِنَّ ٱللَّهَ لَا}$$

$$\text{يَهْدِى ٱلْقَوْمَ ٱلظَّـٰلِمِينَ}$$

O ye who believe, do not take (certain) Jews and (certain) Christians as allies, who are allies of each other (Judeo-Christian alliance). And whoever among you takes them as allies, then he indeed is one of them (no longer in the fold of Islām). Verily Allāh does not guide a wrongdoing people.

[Sūrah al-Mā'idah 5:51]

This surge upon the earth merged the agendas of *Ya'jūj* and *Ma'jūj*, and the Dajjāl for the first time in history, represented by the Order of the Knights Templar (Monks in Armor). Refer to *The Abyss of the New World*

This gave rise to the third major wave, which reached its zenith in the 17th century when an Ashkenazim from the house of Rothschild succeeded in monopolizing the wealth of the world (governed by the Sterling Pound) by means of flattery, chicanery, and treachery via a cabal of his sons and descendants strategically placed throughout Europe and the New World, America in its infancy.

Simultaneously, we see the secular western world arise from the Dark Ages (pre-10th Century), to the Crusades (10th to 13th-Century), to the Renaissance Age (14th to 16th-Century), to the Scientific Age (16th to 17th-Century), with the Industrial Age (18th and 19th Century), and the Age of Information and Technology (21st Century) following the Age of Enlightenment (17th and 18th Century).

The fourth major wave arose nearing the end of the 17th century when the *Fassaad* (corruption) of *Ya'jūj* and *Ma'jūj* intersected yet again with the *Fitan* (tribulation) of the Dajjāl forming the independence of America under George Washington, a 33rd degree Freemason, as well as the birth of the Illuminati Order (Illuminated or Enlightened Ones) by another 33rd degree Freemason, Adam Weishaupt, and the rise of the Luciferian Church under another 33rd degree Freemason, Albert Pike. For those unfamiliar with Freemasonic hierarchy, a 33rd degree Freemason is the highest of its order above which an even more powerful hierarchy rises, known in the modern world as the 'Elite' or the 'Powers Behind the Throne'. Refer to *The Abyss of the New World*

The fifth major wave hence began at the close of the 18th-century with an even stronger allegiance between *Ya'jūj* and *Ma'jūj*, and the Dajjāl, when the financial strength of the Rothschild united with the political muscle of Zionism which was now under the might of western Ashkenazi Jews and Sephardic Jews (from 12th-Century Spain), and at the dawn of the 19th-century, they formed the Zionist movement with the Protocols of the Elders of Zion becoming so formidable that their influence spread like wildfire to every corner of the world. It also led to the establishment of the infant Zionist state of Israel which in both substance and essence bears no spirit to the ancient Khilāfah state of Israel. It has been built on a foundation of *Fitan* (Wickedness of Dajjāl) and *Fassaad* (Corruption of *Ya'jūj* and *Ma'jūj*).

Now we begin to understand the *correct* interpretation of Ayāt 95 and 96 of Sūrah al-Anbiyāh, the town destroyed, the people banned, not to return until (with the aid of) *Ya'jūj* and *Ma'jūj* are released, descending every elevation, wave upon wave.

These Ayāt were very cryptic when they were first revealed in the time of Prophet Muhammad (peace and blessings be upon him), because the actual manifestation did not come to realization until all the events throughout history had occurred with respect to the Passage of Time.

Even before the arrival of Nabi Muhammad (peace and blessings be upon him) on earth, the rejective stances taken by the Rabbis were not unknown, nor were they unheard of, as much as their history has attempted to disguise it. The first 8 Ayāt of Sūrah al-Isrā describe a totality of three, among numerous minor occurrences, whence the Israelites had shown defiance and arrogance against Allāh Almighty and His Messengers.

The promise of the first punishment upon them manifested in the form of Babylonian enslavement. There they were saved and returned to the Holy Land.

The second punishment manifested after their despicable acts of treachery upon Nabi Isa (peace be upon him). Driven out by the Romans, with a Divine ban on their return. Āyah 8 of Sūrah al-Isrā informs them that their Lord may yet have Mercy on them, and the condition was to accept Nabi Muhammad (peace and blessings be upon him) as the final messenger. The Ayāt also come with a warning— should they return with their corruption, Allāh Almighty will return with his punishment.

The Divinity of Allāh's Decree from that point onward is not just a punishment in this world. Incidentally, they no longer seem to be affected, or for that matter, even *bothered,* by earthly punishments, and so Allāh Almighty decrees for them a punishment of eternity.

The series of events explained in the initial Ayāt of Sūrah al-Isrā lay out the basis upon which redemption or condemnation would be Decreed upon the wrongdoers, despite what their ancestors may have done in the past.

In other words, their liberation and reinstatement as God's Chosen, as well as their return to the Holy Land, was *conditional* upon their behavior.

It is important to note this key factor, as it is also mentioned in the Torah;

The Lord appeared to Abraham and said, 'I will assign this land to your offspring.' (Genesis 12:7)

Meaning, the land was to be inherited by *both* his sons and their children. The Holy Land, by *their own scriptures,* does not belong exclusively to the Children of Israel. However, Allāh Almighty did bestow the Holy Land upon a landless people following the Exodus from Misr. The Holy Qur'ān says;

$$يَٰقَوْمِ ٱدْخُلُواْ ٱلْأَرْضَ ٱلْمُقَدَّسَةَ ٱلَّتِى كَتَبَ ٱللَّهُ لَكُمْ وَلَا تَرْتَدُّواْ عَلَىٰٓ أَدْبَارِكُمْ فَتَنقَلِبُواْ خَٰسِرِينَ$$

(Said Mūsa unto the Children of Israel) 'O my people, enter the Holy Land which has been ordained by Allāh to you, and do not turn away, for surely ye will turn back as losers.'

[Sūrah al-Mā'idah 5:21]

The land was certainly given to them as a favor from their Lord. Strangely though, they will never quote this āyah from the Holy Qur'ān when justifying their deliberate and oppressive conquests over the Holy Land, because the Holy Land was not just *given*, it was *loaned*.

They reworded their scriptures to disguise this clear fact. The entirety of this statement made by Nabi Mūsa cannot be found *anywhere* in their texts, removed or revoked by their own hands in order to transfer exclusivity of the Holy Land only unto themselves. If they were to abide by the above āyah from the Holy Qur'ān, it would cause them to admit every wrongdoing they performed in the forty year ban outside the Holy Land, all described in the Holy Qur'ān.

Instead, they abide by the following verse from the Torah;
And the Lord said to him (Moshe), 'This is the land of which I swore to Abraham, to Isaac, and to Jacob. I will give it to your offspring. I have let you see it with your eyes, but you shall not go over there.' (Deuteronomy 34:4)

In the Book of Leviticus, however, the Holy Land is clarified as *not belonging* to the Children of Israel, rather only bestowed upon them 'on lease' for lack of a better word;
...for the Land is Mine (God's); you are but strangers resident and sojourners with Me.
Throughout the Land that you hold, you must provide for the redemption of the Land.
(Leviticus 25: 23-24)

Without much deliberation or interpretation, these, among several other Ayāt, hold that the Holy Land is not of the Children of Israel; the Children of Israel are of the Holy Land, and it holds that the Land of Israel, the Holy Land, was indeed *bestowed* upon the Children of Israel as an *Amaanah*, as a Trust or a Covenant based on Conditions of Righteousness. This covenant was made (according to the Torah) on the outskirts of the Holy Land superseding the Exodus from Misr (eastern Egypt and upper Nile Delta);

(Said Moshe unto the Children of Israel) I make this covenant, with its sanctions, not with you alone,
But both with those who are standing here with us this day before the Lord our God and with those who are not with us here this day (those present in the present, and absent from the present).
(Deuteronomy 29: 13-14)

The question to be asked now, is whether the *inheritance* of the Holy Land, by the descendants of the Israelites, was based on a 'birthright' of inheritance from the progeny of Ibrahim?

If so, abiding by the most rational laws of inheritance, even the descendants of Ismā'īl (peace be upon him), meaning, the Arabs have a right to claim their portion of the Holy Land.

The Holy Qur'ān clarifies;

$$وَإِذِ ٱبْتَلَىٰٓ إِبْرَٰهِـۧمَ رَبُّهُۥ بِكَلِمَـٰتٍ فَأَتَمَّهُنَّ ۖ قَالَ إِنِّى جَاعِلُكَ لِلنَّاسِ إِمَامًا ۖ قَالَ وَمِن ذُرِّيَّتِى ۖ قَالَ لَا يَنَالُ عَهْدِى ٱلظَّـٰلِمِينَ$$

And when his Lord tried Ibrahim with His Word (His Divine Testament), and he (Ibrahim) fulfilled them, He (Allāh) said, 'Verily! I have appointed thee a leader upon mankind', he (Ibrahim) said, 'And from my progeny?', He (Allāh) said, 'My covenant does not extend to the wrongdoers.'

[Sūrah al-Baqarah 2:124]

The Holy Qur'ān further clarifies what was revealed to the Israelites through Nabi Daud (peace be upon him);

$$وَلَقَدْ كَتَبْنَا فِى ٱلزَّبُورِ مِنْ بَعْدِ ٱلذِّكْرِ أَنَّ ٱلْأَرْضَ يَرِثُهَا عِبَادِىَ ٱلصَّـٰلِحُونَ$$

And We have written in the Zabūr (Psalms) which followed (Our declaration in) the Dhikr (remembrance of the Torah) that the Land (Holy Land) shall be inherited by (only) those slaves who are righteous.

[Sūrah al-Anbiyāh 21:105]

Now the inheritance of the Holy Land is clarified. It is not by 'Birthright', as claimed by the Jewish people, modern *and* ancient. It is by virtue and righteousness, meaning, by *any* who follow the true Religion of Ibrahim (peace be upon him), and by extension, the Religion of Muhammad (peace and blessings be upon him).

One begs the question then, if there *is* a condition, and the condition is irrefutably clear— why the rejection?

Because following the Religion of Muhammad requires a colossal sacrifice on their part— to relinquish their old ways. Oppression. Murder. Intoxication. Riba. False indoctrination. Alteration of Divine Script. Imposition of State Law over the Sovereignty of Allāh's Rule. Worship of Money. Witchcraft and Sorcery.

Witness the world today, and we require little clarification that neither of these allegations are false.

Regardless of warnings upon warnings, they still proceeded to justify their inheritance by 'birthright', and the rewriting of certain Ayāt in the Torah have enabled them, even in the modern age, to justify an illicit claim over the Holy Land;

> *It is not because of your virtues and your rectitude (your righteousness) that you will be able to possess the Holy Land; but it is because of their wickedness (the Gentiles) that the Lord your God is dispossessing those nations before you (to bow in servitude to you), and in order to fulfill the oath that the Lord made to your fathers, Abraham, Isaac, and Jacob.* (Deuteronomy 9:5)

Meaning, it is not because of any righteous Israelite that they have a claim over the land, *not at all,* but due to the wickedness of *other* races, the Israelites, who have a 'purer soul' than the rest of mankind, and are the 'Chosen People of God', they alone merit the Land and the 'right' to bring order to earth and humanity.

Here we see the allegiance and direct correlation between the ideologies and doctrines of *Ya'jūj* and *Ma'jūj*, and the treacherous alterations made by Rabbinic Priests to justify those doctrines, all underlined for material dominance and selfish gain.

By justifying the above altered verse, they can now openly justify that they, the Jewish people, are under no divine obligation to fulfill righteous conduct, for by the righteousness of their forefathers, the covenant of righteous inheritance was already fulfilled with Nabi Mūsa following the forty-year ban. That the inheritance of the Holy Land is theirs, *unconditionally,* whether they follow the Religion of Ibrahim or not. Whether they are ighteous, or wicked.

193

Following this argument, one fails to see how this justification can be made in *any* court, religious, state, or even on a humanitarian level. Yet, strangely so, nation upon nation is openly pledging allegiance to the establishment of a Zionist state and home for the Jewish people by any means necessary, even if it requires the ruthless and merciless killing of women and children, a doctrine which has also found its way, by the hands of the Rabbis, into the scriptures. Of these we have quoted some of the lesser explicit Ayāt, for the height of vulgarity in the doctored books is truly repulsive, heinous, and repugnant to even mention.

> *'Extermination of the Christians is a necessary sacrifice.'*
> *(Zohar and Shemoth)*
> *'A heretic Gentile you may kill outright with your own hands.' (Abodah Zara)*
> *'A Jew may violate but not marry a non-Jewish girl.' (Gad Shas)*
> *'Property of gentiles is like the desert; whoever among the Jews arrives first, owns it.' (Baba Bathra)*
> *'Even the best of the Goyim should be killed.' (Soferim)*
> *"Thou shalt not kill' only pertains to a Jew. 'Love thy neighbor' only pertains to a Jew. A Goy should be killed, for a Goy is not a neighbor, it is a wild beast.' (Sanhedrin)*

Savagely, viciously, and demoniacally founded on these wicked falsifications, alterations, and additions to the Divine Scriptures, the Zionist Movement relentlessly pursues the campaign to 'liberate' the Holy Land for the Jews, unconditionally.

With sadness and sorrow, those among the Jewish community who can *see* the treachery for what it really is, are left helpless and forlorn, unable to raise even a finger in opposition. To them do we reach a comforting hand. To them do we extend our friendship. To them do we plea; take the oath of Islām and free yourselves from the ideological tyranny of the oppressors of mankind in this modern age.

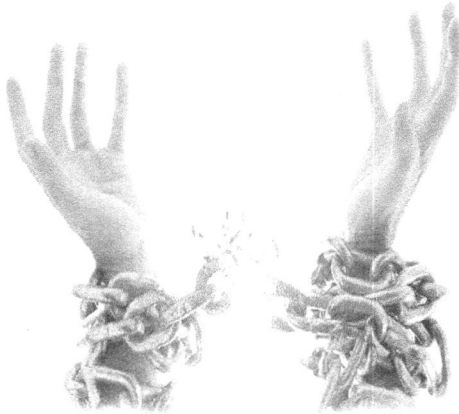

BREAK
FREE

Envy. Arrogance. Defiance.

That which the *Shaytān*, Iblīs, shamelessly enacted in Heaven, against the *Amr* and *Khalq* of Allāh Almighty, eternally dubbed him as a *Kāfir*, the despairer, the deceiver, for the rest of his miserable existence.

Whosoever, Muslim, Christian, or Jewish, does as Iblīs did, even but a morsel of it, so too is he dubbed a *Kāfir*. Where then does the False Rabbinic doctrine stand?

Envy— The superiority of the Jewish Soul.

Defiance— Jesus was a fraud. The *Moshiach* is our savior.

Arrogance— No other has a claim to the Holy Land. None but the Jew.

The most distinctive feature on the forehead of their leader, the Dajjāl, is the word *Kāfir*.

The reason we introduced this book with the subjects of Time and Knowledge, is because merely absorbing information is useless. In this modern age, information has become purely subjective and opinionated, and has been craftily shrouded and presented as 'Knowledge'. The resultant being that a vast majority of us accept whatever is presented, so long as it is well-dressed with rationality and logic, and while a moderate portion of it may contain some truth and authenticity, we fail to realize the actuality of knowledge as a result of intuition, inspiration, thought and contemplation.

We ask 'What?' and accept the given response.

We have stopped asking 'Why?' and 'How?'

The entire incident of the three questions, their responses, the reactions and emotions attached, and the recurring manifestations and decisive outcomes have all been cleverly disguised and deliberately suppressed over history. Eliminated from Jewish and Christian script, and sadly so, not studied even by our own scholarly institutes. The Muslim mind thoughtlessly accepts the moderate 'what happened?' as a satisfactory response, and is left groping in the dark for an explanation of What is happening and *Why* it is happening..

Yet before our eyes, within the Divine Scripts, our Creator warns, cautions, advices and explains everything. Every link. Every trail. Every decisive outcome.

The link between the beginning of humanity, and its climactic conclusion, can almost entirely be condensed in the tale of the Companions of the Cave. Of Time, of Faith, of Life, of Death, and of the Hereafter.

Albeit buried under layers upon layers of the artificially induced complexities of this modern age, we find ourselves in no different a plight. Every man, woman, and child desperately clinging onto their faith is coerced to tyrannical oppression and doctored misguidance. In contrast, those among us who deny any tyranny or deception, those among us who can satisfactorily claim *'nothing is wrong'*, should reexamine the world around them.

Look with external vision, and we will only see what the Dajjāl wants us to see.

Look with internal vision, using Allāh's *Nūr* as a guiding light, and we will penetrate the dark veil over our eyes.

The fact of the matter is, if the state of the Muslim world is not under an authentic and absolute Khilafat governance, then *everything is wrong!*

Almost the entirety of humanity today lives its life confined within a tiny particle the size of a grain of sand on the shores of existence, and this particle perception has been rooted into us from cradle to grave, passed down from parent to child, generation after generation. This multi-layered particle has been programmed to display a moderate range of possibilities, a moderate range of how things are and how they should be, a systematic approach to life as per the deceptional systematic architecture of the Impostor. Denial of this may be an option, but it does not validate any personal opinions. The truth of the matter is that denial only affirms the effectiveness of a deceptive programing.

This programming begins from birth, when the body, the soul, and spirit, emerge in the purity they were created, and our parents take us by our hands and teach us to walk, talk, and behave. They teach us the world as it was taught to them, a perceptual program refined and fine-tuned through generations. They do so, not out of malevolence for their children, but because they too were raised in no different a manner. Inside a perceptual particle designed when the physical Barrier came down. When the Impostor was crowned the eminent leader of the two tribes, upheld as saviors by the rejecting Jews.

Their craftily and prudently programmed doctrines are downloaded into us from birth, and within three or four years, we are at a desk before an authoritative figure advocating the rules of the perceptual particle. A figure who has also been programmed to govern when we have to arrive, when we can leave, when we can speak, when we can eat, and in the entirety of our childhood and young-adulthood, we are continuously downloading the perceptual reality of this particle to follow and obey that authoritative figure and its legislature.

Ironically, we pay for our own programming.

We then exit this stage with an already existing enormous debt and seek an entry into yet another artificial structure, be it sciences, agriculture, academics, industry, or technology, and we take with us that core program of reality, the perceptual particle, where not only do we have to shed off a preexisting overburdening debt, but we are *told* how much our *worth* truly is. We are *told* how much our life, our time on earth is worth by the hour, by the week, by the month, up until retirement.

In an architected quest to acquire all that has been materially destined for us, propagated and programmed to seem like survival is impossible without, we find ourselves drawn away from the essence of our existence. Our youth, whom we push to learn the Holy Qur'ān, forget its value. Whom we enforce to worship God, no longer see any virtue in it. They are enticed by the materialism around us, drawn further and further away from knowledge, and deeper into hollow desires.

Faith becomes an opinion. Religion becomes a choice of lifestyle. Spirituality conforms to fantastical and mythical tales. Integrity is subjected to compromise, and principles are condemned to radicalization. We value tangible transactions, and debase ethereal bonds. Drop by drop, we squeeze out our humanity and replace it with technology.

The advent of *Yaʾjūj* and *Maʾjūj*, and their leader, the Dajjāl, is crafted around one wholesome frontier against the divine purpose of humanity. It is to design the perceptual particle, and confine our minds and hearts within it. The entire architecture of this particle is artificial. Illusory. Layers upon layers of wealth and money. Luxury and technology. The objective is not to impose these layers on a freethinking mind, but to coerce and caress it into lustful desire. To entrap not just the mind, but also the heart.

To the Muslim, to the true believer, is the greatest threat.

Protection, therefore, comes only from inwardly and Divinely guided recognition, rationality and sense, and detachment from the illusory world thereafter. Protection from the Dajjāl comes, as the Holy Prophet (peace and blessings be upon him) prescribed—the Holy Qur'ān.

By studying, understanding, contemplating, and empowering each other with its knowledge, the Holy Qur'ān, and in particular, Sūrah al-Kahf reveals the true identities of the Dajjāl, and *Ya'jūj* and *Ma'jūj*.

Our greatest weapon, therefore, is to step out of our perceptive particles, to shed our opinionated beliefs, to emerge out of the dark and into the Light and Knowledge from Allāh Almighty. The more we know about *Ya'jūj* and *Ma'jūj*, the more we know about the Dajjāl, not just their descriptions and phenomenons, but every single front so craftily and cunningly disguised, the better we are protected from their wickedness and corruption.

Can we break free and struggle towards the light, the *Nūr* of Allāh?

Or should we confine ourselves with comfortable and familiar illusions?

Truth or Habit?

Light or Shadow?

Embrace reality, and the truth will avail itself.

Embrace the truth, and reality will avail itself.

MORE BOOKS BY

ABU BILAAL YAKUB

abubilaal@ironheartpublishing.com

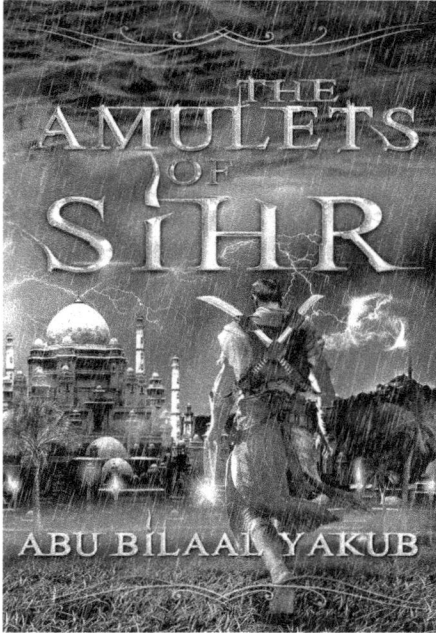

THE AMULETS OF SIHR

Part One of a Four-Part Fantasy Series depicting an Islāmic World with essential morals, virtues, and culture.

Mukhtar is a young blacksmith, facing everyday struggles to support himself and his widowed mother.

Life is brutal and harsh, even harsher while the empire only looks after its own, and the rest of the people are left to fend for themselves. In an impulsive moment Mukhtar frees four slaves from their captors. Little does he know how this would shape his destiny. As the turmoil unfolds, his mother unveils her most guarded secret - an ancient and powerful amulet once belonging to his long-lost father. The Amulet sets Mukhtar on a path to unraveling a grim and dark part of his bloodline.

Now, at the crossroads of good and evil, he must face his life's greatest trials in order to save the empire from annihilation.

Enter the realm of the Unseen...

Prepare to face the evil beyond the veil...

THE EYE OF KIBR

Part Two of the Fictional Series.

Mukhtar's tale continues as he sets out to right the wrongs of his father.

ABUBILAAL YAKUB

As the King lies on his deathbed, the Empire hinges on the whims of his successors while evil forces both from within and without conspire to conquer the world of man.

Mukhtar's brother, Zaki, establishes himself with the Crowned Prince, while Mukhtar, displeased with his brother's bureaucratic approach, takes matters into his own hands to find a resolution to the crises.

Along the lines, those whom they thought were their enemies are discovered to be mere pawns of an ancient order known as the Hidden Ones attempt to restructure civilization to their liking, all the while following the whispers of the Hand of Azazil who is on the cusp of breaking free from his bonds.

THE DIVINITY OF TIME AND COSMOLOGY

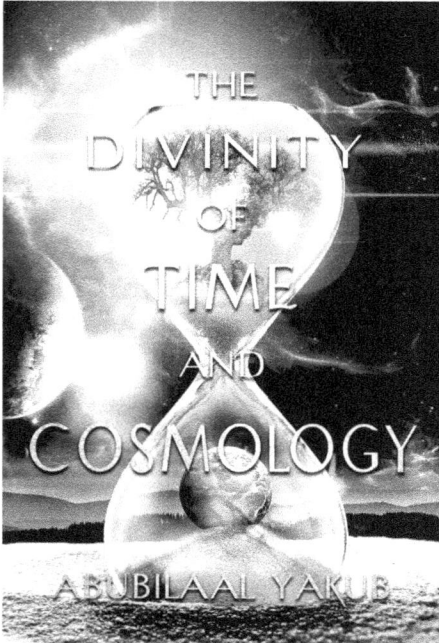

Part One of a series titled *The Impostor and The Two Tribes,* an abridgment of the much larger philosophical work entitled *Time, Light and Being.*

In a devious ploy of secularizing and institutionalizing education and academics, from childhood to adulthood, for generation after generation, the Modern Age has thus far succeeded in the secularization of the Golden Knowledge of Islamic Sciences. It is upon us, the Muslims, the Believers, to revive the Golden Age of Islamic Knowledge and Sciences by revisiting the Knowledge of the Holy Qur'an and Hadīth.

This book begins with the beginning, with the Elements of Creation, Time, Light and the Cosmos, with the hopes of enabling the Believer with the ability to see with his inner eye, and pierce through the Dajjalic veils of the Modern Godless Age.

THE
CRUCIBLE OF
ABSTINENCE

An Inquiry into the Nature of the Heart and the Essence of the Being

Who is this 'Being' that the Lord Almighty has created? What is its excellence? Where lay its origins? Where is he destined to be? Who is he destined to become? What is his Purpose of Being? Modernity argues that the human being is a mere accident of spontaneous causes and effects. A random set of material events. Here to entertain and be entertained. But you must ask yourself, are you what they say you are? Will you pass a fleeting speck of dust. A bemoaner who never rose. Just a collection of flesh and bone. A consuming leech. A reactionary husk. Or will you be what your Creator wants you to be? One who is raised in rank, upon whose shoulders would descend the robe of honor, to become a being of purity in the Divine Presence.

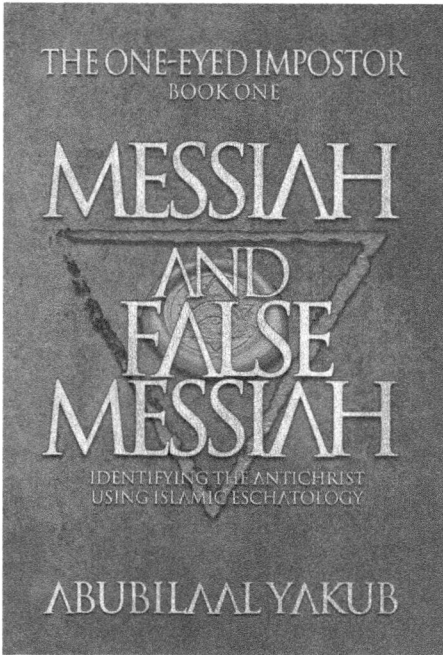

THE ONE-EYED IMPOSTOR
Book One
MESSIAH AND FALSE MESSIAH

An Eschatological work focusing on the subject of the center-most figure in the End Times Eskhatos.

Humanity is no stranger to its finality. Only a fool is oblivious to the ultimate conclusion of man's existence in this world. Our acknowledgement of this as the bedrock of a strange transformation, unprecedented in human history, is that this is a manifest fulfillment of Divine Prophecy.

This book seeks to examine the central figure, described as the One-Eyed Impostor, the Dajjal, the Antichrist, whose prime role is to set the stage for the final act mankind will play before the curtain is drawn on human history.

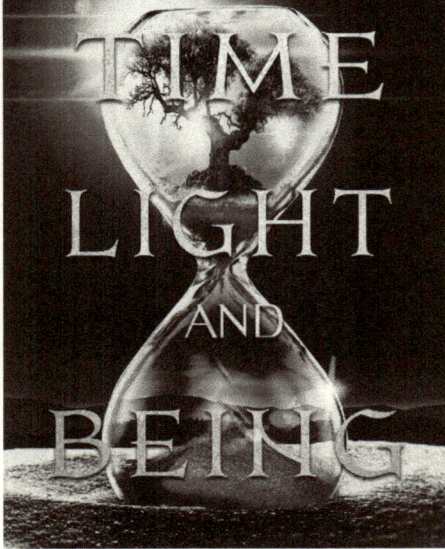

TIME,
LIGHT,
AND BEING

A philosophical work on the prime ontological elements that form the crux of existence for the human being.

Seldom does man think of his being, his purpose of existence, where he came from, where he is, who he is, and where he is destined.

Seldom does man think of his being, and what he is becoming.

Why did God create you?

Why are you here?

What does it mean "to be," and how does one realize the essence of being existent in Time?

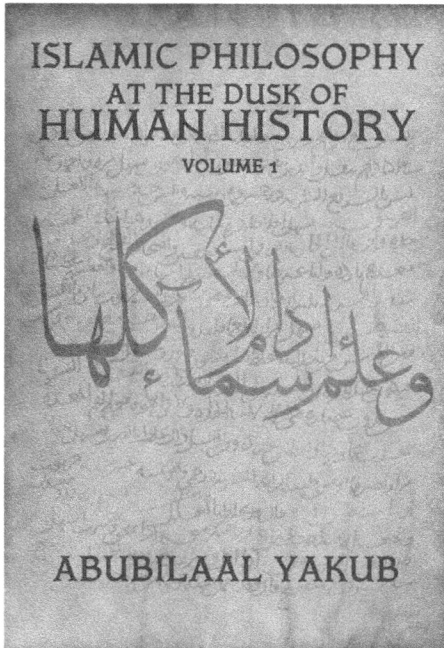

ISLAMIC PHILOSOPHY
AT THE DUSK OF
HUMAN HISTORY
VOLUME 1

ABUBILAAL YAKUB

ISLAMIC PHILOSOPHY AT THE DUSK OF HUMAN HISTORY vol.1

The first volume in a series that seeks to revive the true wisdom of Islamic Thought in an age deprived of it.

Philosophy, in the Muslim World, played an important role in cultivating deep and critical thinking to resolve queries into existential matters. In recent history, driven by certain influences, philosophy has been unjustly classified as *non grata*, deemed as something disapproved by Islamic doctrine.

Yet the world is shaped by philosophies unfounded in religious thought, rendered unchallenged to reign free. This series seeks to revive the critical thinking once beheld by the Muslim Civilization that challenges the ideologies of modernity.

www.ingramcontent.com/pod-product-compliance
Lightning Source LLC
Chambersburg PA
CBHW022006090426
42741CB00007B/914